UNDER THE E

this book is supported by a generous grant from

Jewish Federation of Greater Hartford

'agle

Samuel Holiday, Navajo Code Talker

Samuel Holiday

and

Robert S. McPherson

University of Oklahoma Press : Norman

Library of Congress Cataloging-in-Publication Data

Holiday, Samuel, 1924–
Under the eagle : Samuel Holiday, Navajo code talker / Robert S. McPherson.
pages cm
Includes bibliographical references and index.
ISBN 978-0-8061-4389-7 (hardcover : alkaline paper) 1. Holiday, Samuel, 1924– 2. Navajo code talkers—Biography. 3. Navajo Indians—Utah—Biography. 4. World War, 1939–1945—Cryptography. 5. World War, 1939–1945—Participation, Indian. 6. Marines—United States—Biography. 7. United States. Marine Corps—Biography. 8. Oral history—United States. I. McPherson, Robert S., 1947– II. Title.
D810.C88H65 2013
940.54'8673092—dc23
[B]

2013001303

The paper in this book meets the guidelines for permanence and durability of the Committee on Production Guidelines for Book Longevity of the Council on Library Resources, Inc. ∞

1 2 3 4 5 6 7 8 9 10

To Navajo warriors past, present, and future
who have fought for American freedom

Contents

Illustrations

Acknowledgments

One of the most enjoyable parts of writing a book is to thank people who have helped along the way. This work is no exception. I express appreciation to Samuel Holiday and Helena Begaii, his daughter, for inviting me to participate in this project. There are relatively few Navajo code talkers remaining who are able and willing to share a part of their life that was difficult and frightening. Samuel is one of those who has a clear memory of events and is willing to talk about them. His son, Herman Holiday, recorded part of this story in the early 1990s and willingly shared this information with me, adding some wonderful detail that did not surface in my interviews. That is not to suggest that Priscilla Parrish from Monument Valley and Lucille Hunt from Blanding did not do an excellent job in subsequent interviews, which Lucille transcribed. Both were highly involved and skilled in presenting the nuanced meaning of the Navajo language in English.

Individuals within agencies played a huge role in helping this work come to fruition. Ron Maldonado of the Navajo Nation Historic Preservation Department was instrumental in assisting during the initial stages of the project. He understood that working with a World War II veteran is something that cannot be postponed and so did everything he could to expedite the necessary paperwork for an ethnographic permit. Kent Powell of the Utah State Historical Society and Megan Van Frank with the Utah Humanities Council were just as helpful in providing a grant for translating interviews from Navajo into English. Their timely assistance made it possible for Samuel to share his story in Navajo, the language he is most comfortable with and in which he can be the most accurate. Photographs were another important aspect. Roy Webb, Lorraine Crouse, and Krissy Giacoletto in Special Collections, J. Willard Marriott Library of the University of Utah, and Doug Misener of the Utah State Historical Society Library were very helpful in providing photographs. A special thanks goes to Nancy K. Whitfield at the U.S. Marine Corps University for her dogged determination to provide photographs of combat in the Pacific and Navajo code talkers. She persisted when others would have hung up the phone. At the University of Oklahoma Press, Associate Director Charles E. Rankin and Acquisitions Editor Alessandra Jacobi Tamulevich made the acceptance and production aspects a rewarding experience.

Finally, thanks to family members—especially my wife, Betsy—for their unflagging support of this and other projects. On a wider front, I express appreciation to all Navajo veterans who served when their country called, as have all veterans who understand the individual sacrifice necessary to maintain freedom.

Robert S. McPherson
Utah State University, Blanding Campus

Under the Eagle

INTRODUCTION

Decoding the Past

Origin and Context of Under the Eagle

Samuel Holiday's living room, in many respects, looked like any one of the dozens of Navajo living rooms I have been in both on and off the reservation. The ubiquitous wood burning stove (dormant now), a few pieces of cedar (juniper) stacked neatly beside it, a small galvanized metal pail with lumps of coal, and a four-bladed ceiling fan kept the temperature comfortable. Two well-used couches and an easy chair clustered around a cluttered recreation center with a television screen in the middle. Above the East-facing door hung a traditional bow and arrow with a woven sash announcing "God Bless Our Home." The bow and arrow hanging over the door is in keeping with the Navajo belief that the weapon protects against the entrance of evil and is within reach as one goes forth into the outside world of danger. To the Navajo, the East is a place of protection because no evil came from that direction, only Holy People. Thus, sand paintings have an opening to the East, whereas the other sides may be protected by pictures of rainbows, feathers, yé'iis (gods), and other objects that keep evil at bay.[1]

There was also proof that Samuel had participated in defending against evil. A glass case held a folded American flag, stars out, with five medals—including a Purple Heart—pinned to it. A marine dress sword rested on a rack not far from a Japanese samurai sword, while on a shelf were the carved letters "USMC." A small bronze statuette of a Navajo code talker rested nearby. On the wall hung a painting of Samuel dressed in the official code talker uniform, first designed in 1973. There is nothing subtle about the uniform's bright colors, perhaps an ironic statement to compensate for the twenty-three years the activities of these Navajo servicemen remained closed to public knowledge.

I have been in few Navajo homes that have not had at least one wall dedicated to family pictures. Usually there are school and graduation photos of children and grandchildren, a few young men and women dressed in military uniform with Old Glory in the background, and perhaps some light-faded images of parents and grandparents from years gone by. Throw in a painting or two and a poster and one can tell what is important to that family. Samuel's home was much the same, with one exception—the number of pictures. From the living room to the kitchen and into the entryway there were snapshots, formal portraits, certificates of appreciation, newspaper clippings, and memorabilia that shouted love of family, service to country, and traditional Navajo practices. Appearing in many of the more recent photographs was Samuel dressed in the aforementioned distinctive uniform of the Navajo code talkers that expressed those values. The abalone-colored shoes represent the sacred mountains, light-colored trousers for Mother Earth, gold shirt for corn pollen, turquoise jewelry for the Navajo people—the means by which the Holy People would recognize them—and the red cap for the U.S. Marine Corps. Samuel identified strongly with each of these.

My journey with Samuel had started with a telephone call two weeks before when his daughter, Helena Begaii, contacted me to see if I would be interested in helping her dad with his life history. She had heard of my work with Blessing Way singer John Holiday, a brother to Samuel though they were not raised together; John continues to live in Monument Valley, Utah.[2] Helena explained that her father had been born in the same area but now lived at the valley's southern end in Kayenta, Arizona. During World War II he had served with the marines as a Navajo code talker and now wished to tell his story in a permanent form. Because I lived only a couple of hours away, understood elements of traditional Navajo culture, and was known in the community, she thought I might be willing to assist. I told her I was definitely interested and tentatively arranged for a first meeting. Two well-placed phone calls—one to the Navajo Nation Historic Preservation Office for a Cultural Resources Investigation Permit, which was expedited, and a second to the Utah Humanities Council to seek funding for help with translation in this oral history project—and the process started. Both organizations anxiously agreed. On May 9, 2012, translator Priscilla Holiday and I were knocking at Samuel Holiday's door.

Samuel greeted us when we entered his home, then sat in a recliner anxious to begin. Dressed in black slacks, blue plaid shirt, prominent turquoise belt buckle, and low-cut sneakers, there was nothing out of the ordinary about his dress other than a large medallion, inscribed with the familiar scene of the flag-raising on Iwo Jima, centered on his chest. This iconic picture represented a proud moment for the Marines Corps—one in which Samuel had indirectly participated that day as he sent messages not far from the beach below. His hair was strikingly black for an eighty-seven-year-old man and would have given an appearance of youth, except for the creased brown age-lines at the corner of his eyes and mouth. The tint of his glasses changed according to the light, going from clear to gray as Samuel turned his head to expose his right ear, the one that heard most clearly.

Priscilla and I took our position on the couches, having placed two digital recorders close to Samuel. He had already set some publications about code talker history nearby before launching into his experience. Sharing his story was something he had been doing for a long time—forty-three years to be exact. His daughter Helena suggested that we come prepared with questions because a lot of the time he mentioned only the highlights of his experience in a well-rehearsed explanation. She was right, but as we left the worn path of memory, he opened up with new insight, sharing his past through the eyes of a person raised in a very traditional Navajo culture. While he tried to do his best in English, Priscilla and I soon decided to conduct the interviews totally in Navajo, where his fluency with the language gave a much richer description of events. Words flowed. From them ensued more questions, subsequent interviews, a fuller context, and a discussion of things that he had not thought of for years. His son, Herman H. Holiday, had undertaken a similar project eighteen years before, hoping to capture his dad's experience and eventually get it published. The fifty-page manuscript, which he willingly shared, was a tremendous help in clarifying and adding information about events that otherwise would have been lost. In subsequent interviews with Samuel, he and his family shared other items collected over the years—newspaper clippings, books, pictures, and memorabilia—which added sharper clarity to his life.

Eventually it was time to move Samuel's voice to paper. Because Priscilla lived so far away, did not have access to computers, and was not as familiar with some of their programs as well as part of the more traditional teachings discussed, I enlisted the help of Lucille Hunt, a meticulous translator who

Samuel Holiday displaying the medallion he received for serving in combat with the Fourth Marine Division as a code talker during World War II. This picture was taken in Kentucky (2006) while Samuel was on a speaking tour. (Photograph courtesy of Holiday family)

as a child was raised in a hogan with nine other family members and was knowledgeable about Navajo ways. Conversant with computer programs and Navajo spelling while harboring a true interest in the topic, Lucille set about translating the interviews and asking some questions of her own. Later we visited Samuel for further clarification discussions. Satisfied with both the spirit and technical aspect of what had been recorded, we returned to Blanding and I set about placing his story in narrative form.

That was the process; what resulted needs to be discussed before venturing with Samuel into his life story. The reader has to understand that oral history provides a glimpse into events like nothing else can. The detail, perspective, and personal account are irreplaceable and give immediacy to experience. Good autobiography sweeps readers into the world of the narrator and transports them into the culture and history of the time. Many people like to use it as an internal measure to see how they might act or react in similar circumstances, which is particularly true with topics dealing with war and different cultural occurrences, two prime ingredients found here. Understanding what it was like from a different perspective is an invaluable part for all of us who share this human experience.

Yet people who work with oral history also understand its shortcomings. Interviewing Samuel highlighted that although he had an amazingly good recollection of certain events, there were also things that he had either forgotten or was incorrect about in his recall. Knowing that in his autobiography he talks about people, places, and times from more than eighty years ago and that his war experiences were more than sixty-five years distant adds meaning to the problem of recalling pinpoint-specific information like dates, ages, names, and events. Christopher Chabris and Daniel Simons in *The Invisible Gorilla: And Other Ways Our Intuition Deceives Us* remind the reader of problems with historical memory.[3] The person recalling an event must make sense of what has occurred and fit it into a pattern of familiarity, associating it with what is already known. "What is stored in memory is not an exact replica of reality, but a re-creation of it. We cannot play back our memories like a DVD—each time we recall a memory, we integrate whatever details we do remember with our expectations for what we should remember."[4] Although a person may have a very strong notion of something that happened, there very well might be things missed or added to as it is recalled.

Samuel was no exception. For instance, there were a number of things that he felt happened around the age of eleven or twelve but in reality occurred earlier at different times. Samuel thought that three events—when he saw his first white man, when he moved to Kayenta, and when he hurt his knee swimming—had happened at roughly the same time, although there were more likely months, or even years, between these three events. Fortunately there were other historical markers to help clarify the chronology. Still, Chabris and Simons have pointed out that the context in which an event is established in the mind can also have an adverse effect on accuracy. When the context includes personally relevant information or experience, with heightened emotion, even more inaccuracy can creep in.

> The critical factor driving the illusion seems to be the extent to which a memory triggers a strong recollective experience. In other words, if you recall *how* you experienced and learned something rather than *what* you experienced and learned, you are far more likely to trust the veracity of your memory. Just as the vividness of our visual perception makes us think we are paying attention to more than we are, our experience of fluent, vivid recollection fuels the illusion of memory.[5]

None of this is to suggest that what Samuel experienced is intentionally fabricated or even inaccurate. The main point is to recognize that oral history is fallible, shaped by circumstances, and subject to emotions.

As I interviewed Samuel and later worked with various materials, I realized that there were a number of things to consider in its presentation. Previous works concerning Navajo code talkers, about a half dozen in number, had taken a different approach than what I contemplated. One of the first substantive publications to discuss the topic following its declassification in 1968 was *The Navajo Code Talkers* by Doris A. Paul.[6] The book has brief chapters that take the reader from the program's inception, through training, into combat, then return. The final chapter covers material ranging from the government's release of information about this secret project and the public's knowledge of the Navajos' contribution to the formation of the Navajo Code Talkers Association and national recognition.

Interest skyrocketed, but it was not until 2001 and the publication of *Navajo Weapon: The Navajo Code Talkers* by Sally McClain that a more detailed account of their activities was available for the general reading public.[7] McClain did an excellent job using government documents and a dozen interviews conducted in the early 1990s with code talkers to examine not only the genesis of the project, but all of the Pacific Island battles these men participated in—from Guadalcanal to Okinawa. Maps and photos elucidate how each campaign unfolded while depicting the conditions the code talkers faced. Entire books have been written about each of these battles, which she summarized effectively to give the reader a general account. The epilogue tells the rest of the story, including the Navajos' return to the United States and subsequent events up to 1994. McClain's work in the National Archives and the Marine Corps Historical Center is commendable.

Another excellent book, the first autobiography of a Navajo code talker, arrived ten years later. Judith Schiess Avila and Chester Nez teamed up to write *Code Talker*, which follows Nez's life from the mid-1920s to 2011 when the book came out.[8] Chester, like Samuel, came from a traditional Navajo home and culture. Raised between Gallup and Zuni, New Mexico, in what is known as checkerboard land due to Navajo allotments, Chester lived in a region where the Navajo people were substantially acculturated into the dominant society—in contrast to Samuel's experience in Monument Valley. Yet both men shared a common heritage that proved important in later years during the war. Chester, as one of the original twenty-nine code talkers, saw action on Guadalcanal, Bougainville, Guam, Peleliu, and Angaur. His experience, like Samuel's, had its hair-raising moments as well as the tedium of daily military service. His description of the code's origin and its stringent field-testing before deployment gives an important inside perspective of how Navajo participants felt about its development while they were locked away in a secured area. The entire book is well-written and interesting.

Still there was something missing. Although Chester does talk about life on the reservation, including some cultural practices and a few important events in Navajo history like livestock reduction and the boarding school era, his personal voice is lost. The writing style is similar to a historic novel, using words, thoughts, and emotions that move far beyond a normal narration and recall of a person being interviewed. This is not to criticize Judith Avila for placing words in Chester's mouth. She had conducted seventy-five hours of taped interview that provided a rich source of material. But then again, Chester would not talk like this:

> The smell of Auntie's coffee and the bleat of a lamb awoke me well before sunrise. Opening my eyes to slits, I looked for old Auntie. Was she still angry? Yesterday my older brother Coolidge and I had lagged behind the herd, playing with our slings. We got in trouble with old Auntie.
>
> Ah! There she was, piling juniper branches onto the campfire. Her form etched a black shadow against the dark gray landscape. *Shimá Yázhí* ("auntie" or "little mother") hummed as she worked. She must be in a better mood.
>
> I turned and stared up into the dark. The sky arched above me, decorated by First Man and First Woman with familiar groupings of stars. The rain had stopped. Lying still, I savored the aromas of earth, wet pinyon, and sagebrush. The comforting smell of damp wool and the fragrance of juniper sticks burning in Auntie's fire told me that all was as it should be. I breathed quietly, not wanting Old Auntie to know I was awake. In a few minutes I'd get up and start chores.[9]

While everything described could have happened, the "voice"—though gripping and immediate—is not Chester's from an interview. Stylistically, it is that of a novel. Every writer asks similar questions. How much from an autobiographical interview should be directly used, and how much change should be implemented for a reading audience. In English, there are very different expectations when writing than when speaking. In Samuel's case, I have separated his words from other elements found in each of the chapters. The reader can easily determine which are his thoughts and expressions and which are mine. I have kept his voice separate and with relatively little change from that which has come through the translator. To ensure accuracy in content and expression, I have read all of the manuscript derived from interviews with him and corrected any discrepancies that may have arisen. To the best of our knowledge, what follows in the sections of the chapters in which he speaks is as he wished it communicated.

Another main difference between this autobiography and Chester's, as well as the other books written about the code talker experience, is the cultural aspect. Previous works share limited information about these men being Navajo and make short reference to reservation life and their cultural experience but little more. Most have appendices, one of which is a replication of the code as it existed in 1945. Some may make mention from interviews about praying in a traditional way or the thought that the code and language were weapons, but most center on the familiar wartime narratives of men in combat from a white perspective. Indeed, with a few exceptions many of the books, even within those parts derived from interviews, could be as much about a white marine as a Navajo. In some cases, this perspective is all right, because many of the code talkers were acculturated by the dominant society, believed in Christianity so were unfamiliar with traditional Navajo teachings, and had a minimum of a ninth-grade education. While all were fluent in the Navajo language, the amount of cultural understanding and individual experience varied.

In Samuel's case, as with others brought up in a more traditional setting, the Navajo perception of the experience was far different. Having been raised in a very rural environment where daily life and thought derives from a rich body of teachings passed down from Holy People, Samuel viewed a world framed with spiritual powers and populated with supernatural beings. Whereas white Christian culture relegates worship and interaction with Deity primarily to Sunday, the Navajo day starts, ends, and has many points in between concerned with different aspects of religion. Instead of learning of Holy People from the written pages of the Bible, Navajo people for centuries depended on an oral tradition rich with stories, teachings, and instruction. There are other American Indian tribes that also have an extensive system of beliefs based in sacred stories, but few can compare with the diversity and extent found in Navajo culture.

These stories—often referred to as myths—are defined here as sacred and true to those who believe and practice their teachings. They are the powerhouses that drive traditional Navajo culture. It would be hard to overemphasize their importance not only in a religious but also a daily context. Having had the opportunity to learn from Navajo people for over thirty years, I believe this point is also central to understanding any historical experience, including that of a code talker. Time taught me this lesson. When I first started interviewing Navajo elders, I would approach them with what seemed to me to be a straightforward history question. For instance, "Tell me about your experience during the livestock reduction." Invariably, the man or woman would go back to the time of creation to talk about something that the Holy People had done, the introduction of sheep into the world, how the Navajo obtained them, and some historical bits and pieces along the way before we ever arrived in the 1930s and reduction. It might take a half hour to get there, and by then, my Anglo mind was reeling with what seemed irrelevant details that were a run-around.

Now, my understanding has changed to the point where I know that those "irrelevant details" are the heart of perception. They are the scaffolding that makes sense of a world framed by religious teachings. Maureen Trudelle Schwarz, at the end of her study on Navajo women ceremonial practitioners, said it well: "Thus, stories such as those about the origins of desire, the separation of the sexes, the birth of monsters, or the establishment of gender roles are not simply quaint artifacts of bygone times. They continue to offer guidance to contemporary Navajo people because they compress historical knowledge and human experience into vivid narratives that can illuminate and educate."[10] I would add to her "illuminate and educate" the word "empower," because to the Navajo the understanding and application of these stories in life do just that.

In the Navajo world, everything is either male or female—everything. From trees and rivers to body parts and implements, everything enjoys this sexual division, a point to be discussed later. For now, the reader should realize that this is also true with stories that share teachings for both sexes. Within the Navajo pantheon there are role models for women, the most prominent being Changing Woman (Asdzą́ą́n nádleehé), sometimes referred to as White Shell/Bead Woman. She is a kind, beneficent deity who sets the standards, literally from birth to death, as to how a Navajo woman should act. Her tools such as grinding stones, stirring sticks, the fire poker, and hairbrush are implements of the home and domestic life, collectively called habeedí . The distinctive Navajo cradleboard is a replica of the one that First Man discovered the infant Changing Woman lying in on top of Gobernador Knob (Ch'óol'į́'í), New Mexico. The Navajo puberty ceremony, kinaaldá, is a celebration of a girl's change to womanhood that follows the pattern first established by this female god. And for our purpose, she is the mother of the two Navajo twins, Monster Slayer (Naayéé' neizghání) and Born for Water (Tó bájísh chíní).

For males, the Twins are their role model. In the past, the Navajo held to the teachings of a warrior society based on the exploits of these two brothers. Born in a world of monsters and chaos, at first unaware of their divine parentage with their father Sun Bearer (Jóhonaa'éí), but anxious to learn and do, the boys set off on a journey with supernatural aid that allowed them to successfully destroy surrounding evil and make the earth safe for humans. Their story is fundamental to Navajo culture. Noted anthropologists Clyde Kluckhohn and Dorothea Leighton put it this way: "The Hero Twins—Monster Slayer and Child of the Water—are invoked in almost every Navajo ceremonial. Their adventures establish many of the Navajo ideals for young manhood. They serve especially as models of conduct in war and can almost be called the Navajo war gods."[11]

Their story is told here because it is part of Samuel's story. Early in the interview process, it became evident that how he viewed his early years, boarding school experience, and involvement in World War II came very much from this traditional Navajo background. The symbols, metaphors, and explanations were those of a person raised in a world steeped in traditional teachings. Included in each chapter here is a part of what happened to the Twins as they set out on their odyssey. For readers looking for a straight war narrative there may be disappointment. In some respects this book is as much about religion and worldview as it is about combat. Others may feel that the inclusion of mythology is a literary gimmick to make the book read like something Indian. Nothing is further from the truth.

Here is the framework within which Samuel and other, more traditional, code talkers placed their experience. The reader will find that there are some comparable instances that fit directly into both stories. For instance Samuel's belief of white men as monsters, his preparation for war, the use of language as a weapon, and the black sands of Iwo Jima are comparable to things and events encountered in the myth. Making these comparisons could be viewed as superficially contrived except for the fact that Navajo people familiar with these teachings readily do it. The pattern established at the beginning of time by the Holy People is the means by which experience in this world is interpreted now. In a very real sense, one walks the same path today, on a different scale, as did the Holy People earlier. And all of the physical and supernatural assistance the gods received to help them triumph during their trials is still available now to help a person get through the rigors of life. In Samuel's view, the real "Navajo code" is in these stories, so that if a person understands all that is contained within he will comprehend the real code for a happy life. Whereas white people are fascinated with the language transmitted over the radio by the code talkers, from Samuel's perspective it was the teachings and power of the Holy People that helped one survive. If there is one consistent theme throughout his life, it is this: the Holy People and their teachings are real and effective.

The story of the Twins is central to our understanding, but there are many other stories equally important. At the beginning of most chapters there are compressed versions of these teaching tales that assist in explaining things that Samuel mentions but may not explain. Indeed, in some instances, he may not be aware of why certain things are done, only that it is the Navajo way. As with all people immersed in their own culture, a lot of things are handled in a certain fashion without understanding why or where they came from. As with a fish in water, culture is not analyzed or much of a concern until suddenly we, as fish, are jerked out of the water and given opportunity to think about it. Thus, to better understand the role of corn pollen, what the ocean means in traditional Navajo teachings, and why the rattle stick is decorated as it is for the Enemy Way ceremony, there are origin stories to accompany what Samuel discusses.

Following his narration, there is also a commentary. Rather than interrupt his flow of events, this section provides an interpretation or further explanation of what he has discussed. Take for instance his involvement on four different islands in the Pacific: Kwajalein (Roi-Namur), Saipan, Tinian, and Iwo Jima. Each was different in its own way, had varying strategies and objectives, and obtained distinct results with differing amounts of loss. Samuel, as a radio operator on the ground, was not aware of much of what went on beyond his personal experience—what he knew was what occurred on his part of the battlefield and on the tactical communications net he operated. He says a number of times that he felt he knew more about what was going on in the fight than most other people, but still this was a small piece of the overall action. The commentary sections either fill in information that Samuel was not aware of or provide cultural explanations he did not express.

As mentioned previously, there are a number of books that deal with the origin of, the organization of, and the services rendered by the Navajo code talkers. What follows is a brief summary of key points to give Samuel's experience a broader context. Tracing the concept of American Indians using their native language to communicate tactical information on the battlefield begins in World War I with the Choctaw from Oklahoma. The whole idea came about by chance when an officer heard some Choctaw men speaking their language and decided to put their talent to use. Eventually elements of the 142nd and 143rd Infantry Regiments of the Thirty-sixth Infantry had nineteen such communicators placed in several field company headquarters sending and receiving radio messages that the Germans could not decipher.[12] They even developed their own code for military words not found in their vocabulary so that a platoon of men became "thong," the first battalion was "one grain of corn," a company was a "bow," and a patrol "many scouts."[13] Other Native American groups, including the Cherokee, Cheyenne, Comanche, Osage, and Yankton Sioux, although not as numerous as the Choctaw, also used their language to effect in the Meuse-Argonne offensive in October and November of 1918, just prior to the armistice.

During World War II, a similar practice continued. Although the Navajo program was by far the largest—compare its total number of 420 men to the next two closest groups of the Comanche and the Chippewa-Oneida, each with seventeen communicators—and one can see how actively the Marine Corps recruited for its program.[14] Historian William C. Meadows has studied all twenty-one tribes and their service as code talkers and classified them according to the type of message encoding they used. Type I is based in developing a code within a language, such as that used by the Comanche, Chippewa-Oneida, Meskwaki, Hopi, and Navajo. The first three of these groups were recruited before the Navajo program started, while the Hopi began in 1943.[15] The second kind, Type II, depended on normal use of the language, which for the enemy was confusing enough. Tribes belonging to this category were various bands of Sioux, Cree, Kaw, and Choctaw. Criteria for the selection of a tribal language included the following: "whether or not their language had been recorded; the number of males of appropriate age to serve who were both fluent in their native language and English; overall willingness of tribal men to serve in the U.S. military; and the number of these individuals who could read and write English."[16] The Comanche devised a code with 250 special words and terms, while the Navajo code eventually expanded by the end of the war to over 600.

The Navajo Nation during the 1940s was, as it is today, one of the largest tribes in the continental United States. Demographically there were approximately 50,000 Navajos living on the reservation, 8,000 of whom were males, 75 percent of whom were of military age, 500 to 600 of whom had a high school education.[17] Because of their relative isolation and because they were still reeling from the livestock reduction of the 1930s that changed their way of life, the Navajo sought a means to survive economically while practicing traditional values. As the Civilian Conservation Corps and other New Deal programs faded and the Great Depression became an event of the past, the Navajo cast about for other types of employment. On the reservation, employment opportunities were extremely limited. The wage economy found off the reservation seemed to be part of the solution, yet there was another thing to consider as war clouds loomed on the horizon.

Every tribe has its qualities and personality, one of which for the Navajo is patriotism—fighting for their country, yes, but more specifically for their homeland bounded by the four sacred mountains. That is why during World War II peak employment at the Fort Wingate Ordinance Depot reached 800 workers, with 500 more Navajos employed building the Navajo Ordinance Depot at Bellemont, both of which are in Arizona. Others flowed to defense industries on the West Coast; many more worked as migrant laborers throughout the Southwest and neighboring regions. Another 3,600 chose to wear the uniform of the U.S. Army, Navy, Marine Corps, or Women's Army Corps. In 1945, the Indian Service estimated that as many as 10,000 Navajos were involved in war work.[18] Employment plus patriotism fit well into the Navajo character. These two qualities encouraged many to move off the reservation and into the white man's world.

But it would be the Anglo son of a non-denominational Christian missionary couple, Philip Johnston, who would give birth to the idea of recruiting Navajos as code talkers. He has provided elsewhere a good explanation in a somewhat dramatic fashion about how at the age of four his family moved to the Navajo reservation in 1896, where he remained for approximately twelve years before attending a number of schools then moving to California in 1915.[19] Many of his playmates while growing up were Navajo, providing him with an excellent fluency in the language and personal experience within the culture. A brief stint in the military during World War I and a career as a civil engineer in Los Angeles kept Johnston far from the reservation, but when the Japanese bombed Pearl Harbor and dark days descended upon the United States, he remembered his friends. It happened one day when he read about an armored unit in Louisiana using Native American soldiers to communicate during field exercises. The next day Johnston was on his way to Camp Elliott, seven miles north of San Diego, to visit marine signal officer Colonel James E. Jones and present an idea.

Colonel Jones was open to but not excited about the possibility of using Navajos as communicators, yet Johnston pushed for a test run to

Technical Sergeant Philip Johnston (1944) is credited with starting the code talker program with the U.S. Marines in 1942. In his advisory capacity in recruiting for and supervising this project, Johnston drew on his knowledge of the Navajo language and his boyhood experiences on the reservation. (Photograph courtesy of the U.S. Marine Corps)

prove the scheme's value. He further explained that the plan called for the development of a code, not just the straight use of the language. The civilian spoke a few words of the Navajo language to show the difficulty in pronunciation and interpretation. "If I had lighted a string of firecrackers and laid them on the desk, their effect could not have been more startling. Colonel Jones sat bolt upright in his chair and gazed in frank disbelief. That such sound could possibly issue from any vocal organ was incredible."[20] The men agreed to hold a test-run to check validity of the idea. Johnston returned two weeks later with four educated Navajos he cornered in Los Angeles, had them speak over field phones in separate rooms, and checked the six different transmissions for accuracy. The results were excellent. Major General Clayton B. Vogel was also highly impressed, enthusiastically pursuing development of the program.[21] There was a fair share of nonbelievers who had to be converted to the idea, giving rise to a number of trial runs—right up to the code talkers' first deployment on Guadalcanal in September 1942.[22]

The marines recruited what has since become known as the "Twenty-nine," the first group to devise the code; this will be discussed later. Headquartered initially in Camp Elliott and later thirty miles north at Camp Pendleton, the men involved in this secret project were under stringent rules never to divulge its activities. The marines cast a wide net for recruitment of Navajos both on and off the reservation, insisting inductees had completed a minimum of nine years of formal education, according to Johnston. In reality they accepted others with less; for example, Samuel had only completed the seventh grade. Some were high school graduates, and one held a college degree. The first Navajo marines to develop the code came directly from boot camp and selected their own leaders from amongst them to initiate the process. At the conclusion of their eight weeks of advanced training, two members from a class (and later as many as five from a class) stayed on as instructors before eventually rotating out for combat. The initial code, according to Johnston, began with 211 words, which increased by the end of his enlistment to 411.[23] By 1945, a year after Johnston had been released from service, the word count had risen to over 600. Johnston, who volunteered at the age of fifty to enter into the corps, received the rank of staff sergeant and the assignment of being in charge of the program. He reported that, "Within two years, some 300 Navajos qualified as 'communicators.' The percentage of failure was fantastically low—about five out of each hundred. And only one of that multitude 'went over the hill.'"[24]

Recruitment still had its problems. Because Navajo families were widespread across a 25,000-square-mile reservation comparable in size to West Virginia, the usual practice of sending a recruiter to a central location then having potential enlistees travel there to sign up was ineffective. Problems included making individuals aware of where and when recruitment was taking place, travel difficulties, and cultural practices such as sheep herding, ceremonies, and local events that conflicted with recruitment times. Soon the recruiting effort took a new path where mobile teams of Anglo and Navajo marines, as well as other government officials, traveled to communities. These men placed special emphasis on boarding schools to find young men with sufficient education, but they also visited trading posts, work sites, and social gatherings. This hit-or-miss approach left large holes in the record of who actually joined—one of the reasons that even today there is no really firm number as to how many enlisted, were trained, and qualified as code talkers. Major Frank L. Shannon, who served as marine liaison officer with the Navajos, explained the result:

> Insofar as I know, there is no complete list of Navajos available. I have the list by name and serial number of all those that I have personally procured under the Special Navajo Program. However, a considerable number of Navajos voluntarily enlisted in the United States Marine Corps prior to May 1942; also it is entirely possible that some enlisted in Colorado and in Utah. Those who were inducted in any district except Santa Fe, New Mexico, or Phoenix, Arizona, would not be marked Navajo, since they are carried on Selective Service records as white.[25]

The Navajo Code Talker Association, while still seeking "lost" code talkers, is today challenged to know even what states some of their members were from. To the best that I can determine, there was a small handful of men recruited from southeastern Utah for the program. Samuel and Bud Haycock are officially listed as from the Oljato area in Monument Valley while Jack Jones and Wilmer Belinda hailed from the Aneth region. These men are the only four recognized as code talkers from Utah. Undoubtedly there were others, especially when one considers how places of origin blur with people living near state boundary lines in the Four Corners region. Navajo

Mountain that sits on the border of Utah and Arizona is a good example, with code talkers coming from there being credited with Arizona citizenship.

Following completion of boot camp, those selected as code talkers began their communications training, which is discussed later. An instruction manual for the "Navajo Talkers Course" emphasized that the teacher must have "persistence, patience, and close supervision" over his students. Memorization of the code and its accompanying alphabet were imperative. Marine commanders did not allow code books into those parts of a war zone where they could be captured and compromised. At the same time, transmissions in combat needed to be fast, accurate, and automatic with no room for misinterpretation. Constant repetition and drills were the answer. The more difficult part was for the men to understand technical terms and a growing array of equipment on the battlefield. That is one reason the code kept expanding: more and more specific information needed to be communicated. Training and retraining with new elements introduced into the developing code was a constant concern. Still, the instruction manual was very positive about the students:

> The Navajos' attitude toward schooling is very good. He is anxious to learn and will work for long hours without losing interest or grumbling. Because of his limited education and experience in technical subjects, he does not really grasp the technical terms in the instruction of communication subjects. By placing emphasis on mechanical practices of setting up and operating communication equipment, he will, after practice, become proficient in the operation of telephone and radio equipment.[26]

Indeed, the radio equipment was the code talkers' "bread and butter." Unlike the marine infantryman who earned his pay with a rifle, these radio men saved lives and took lives with their language and a radio.

Surprisingly little is found in the literature concerning code talkers and the equipment they used, although the importance of this topic is unquestionable. It is understandable, however, that talking about antiquated radio systems is not very interesting, but even in interviews with Samuel and other code talkers, not much is said about such systems and the radio's nomenclature is often forgotten. A number of the communication sets were heavy yet fragile because of the glass vacuum tubes within, were difficult to waterproof because of open ports for ventilation, and were subject

Left, Private First Class (PFC) Preston Toledo and *right*, his cousin PFC Frank Toledo, both from New Mexico, demonstrate the use of the TBX radio during training (1943). This eighty-pound radio could transmit voice and Morse code communication, but it required at least two, often four, men to carry it. The TBY series of smaller radios eventually replaced it. (Photograph courtesy of the U.S. Marine Corps)

to moisture from the air and static electricity from storms. The TBX radio, which went through eight modifications, communicated from boat to shore. Powered by both battery and hand-crank generator, it could be transported by two but preferably four men: one carrying the radio, another a battery and accessory box, one the generator, and another the twenty-four-foot collapsible antenna. This low-powered, high-frequency radio was line-of-sight and could transmit voice and Morse code, if unobstructed, for over a hundred miles.[27] An unidentified code talker, serving on Guadalcanal, provided the following account:

> We used several types of radio sets. The TBX unit was the one that we used the most. It weighed about eighty pounds—very heavy to lug around. We had two sets: a transmitter and a receiver connected with junky cable. We tried to set the generator on a bench of some

> kind when we could, so we could straddle the bench and crank the thing. But this didn't work on a location where it was sandy. So the coconut tree came in very handy. We hooked the generator to the trunk, straddled the tree and cranked. It took two men—one to crank the generator and get the juice going into the mike, and the other to transmit the message. We got information off the ship after a landing, and kept those in charge of the operation informed.[28]

While the noise from a hand-cranked generator could give away a friendly position, it was at least a dependable source of power. A far more portable radio, the TBY, also went through eight modifications, weighed thirty-seven pounds, was backpack portable, and was powered by batteries. Its limited battery life forced operators to turn on their radios only during predetermined times then turn them off when not needed. It also was a line-of-sight radio that could transmit up to fifteen miles in the clear but was reduced to less than a mile in the jungle. By 1943 the SCR-300 joined the TBY as a slightly lighter backpack model, easy to use and reliable, while its FM (frequency modulated) capacity allowed it to communicate with moving tanks on the battlefield. Its battery life was from eight to twelve hours, and its range was from ten to twenty miles.[29] Finally, there was the small hand-held SCR-536 "Handie-Talkie" radio. This push-to-talk device had a range of from 100 yards to three miles and was used by company- and platoon-sized elements to maintain contact on land and sea. The effects of terrain, weather, and its limited ability to tie into all of the frequencies of the TBX and TBY and none of the SCR-300's exacerbated some of its shortcomings.[30] Code talkers generally used this radio on an extremely limited basis because their responsibility was to communicate to headquarters on a much higher level.

Although the radios had their share of technical problems, the code talker behind the radio was fast and efficient. Whether during field training exercises or in combat, commanders marveled at how quickly and accurately transmissions were completed, bypassing all of the encoding and decoding necessary when employing mechanical devices. Even with the coding used with mechanical devices, the enemy was able to decipher what was sent by these machines and thus could anticipate tactical plans. Such security breaches did not occur when using code talkers, who simply received a message and spoke it over the radio set to another Navajo radio operator, who wrote it down and passed it along to the commander. Code talker Alex Williams described it this way.

> We would receive it [a transmission] from a division then we would send it out to the regiments, then from there out to the three battalions at one time. We'd call a signal over in English to get the receiver's attention then read it in Navajo. . . . Then they'd answer back. Then we sent them off from the regiment. Then when they finished, whatever name, he'd call in. The other fellow would call in and if he gets it all, he said "roger." "Roger" wasn't in Indian. The same for all three battalions, once they sent their "rogers" in, we knew the whole regiment has got it. So that's how it went.[31]

Practice made transmissions flow automatically while established procedure decreased confusion. There were few, if any, complaints about the effectiveness of the code talkers as an organization.

Indeed there was glowing praise given in a report entitled "The Use of Navajo Indians for Radio Transmission Security Purposes" dated April 15, 1944.[32] By this time approximately 250 Navajos had been trained, and a good number of those had seen combat. While "Marine officers state that the gibberish of the Indians" was unintelligible, they were confident that the code was effective and difficult to compromise. Some of the Navajos were serving as radio operators, others as messengers, who when "on their own in the jungle or wooded area, are much more hardy and self-supporting than the normal white man. . . . [and] have a knack for agile escape and adequate self-protection." Their ability to memorize and retain information was noteworthy, while "the ability of these Indians to receive and transmit under battle conditions and noises is good, if not better, than their English-speaking fellow soldiers." This evaluation of Navajo code talkers remained consistent throughout the remainder of the war.

Samuel, as one of these code talkers, joined the Marine Corps in 1943. Prior to that and where his story starts is in the northern end of Monument Valley, Utah, figuratively beneath the shadow of a stone monolith, Eagle Rock. As the reader progresses with him through the events and practices that shaped his life, other eagles appear in various contexts—with a "living" feather, as messenger, in prayer, and the one atop the Marine Corps globe-and-anchor. Samuel's life "under the eagle" is one of challenge and protection. Spanning both Navajo and Anglo culture, linked between the spiritual and physical world, important in both war and peace, this bird as symbol represents those values important to Samuel: family, country, and religion. There is no separating them, for they are all "under the eagle," as will be apparent as he tells his story.

CHAPTER ONE

Establishing Beliefs

Birth and Early Years

THE TWINS: PREPARING FOR LIFE

In the palm of time following the emergence of the Holy People from the worlds beneath, the gods roamed the earth, making laws and creating things helpful for the future. They formed two women—one from turquoise the other from white shell, Changing Woman (Asdzą́ą́n nádleehé) and White Shell Woman (Yoołgai asdzą́án)—who grew in miraculous ways, one day equaling a year of human life.[1] Before long they were mature females who conceived through the supernatural means of sunlight and water, producing two boys. The newborns were foreordained to "take care of the ruination on the earth and to kill all of the monsters after which peace would be restored."[2] These children, like their mothers, grew rapidly so that in four days they were twelve years old and ready for instruction. Talking God (Haashch'ééłti'i) and Water Sprinkler God (Tó Neinilii) invited them to a long race, but by the time it was half completed the Holy People were running behind the boys, scourging them with mountain mahogany branches, urging them to move faster. Talking God won the race, promising to return in four days to give the boys another opportunity to compete.

The lads were sore, tired, and discouraged, wondering how they could ever triumph against the powers of Talking God and Water Sprinkler. The Holy Wind (Níł'chi), which had been placed on their ear folds, learned of their concern and told them that if they practiced, they could beat the older men, because youth was on their side.[3] For four days the boys trained hard, maturing into strong young competitors. When the race started, the confident runners began passing the two deities so that by the time the race around a mountain was half completed, the roles had reversed and the boys were behind the gods, scourging their backs and encouraging them onward. The oldest of the twins won. The gods were highly pleased at the progress the two boys had made, laughing and clapping their hands in praise of their success.

SAMUEL: ESTABLISHING PATTERNS

My name is Samuel Tom Holiday, and I am of the Tódich'inii (Bitter Water) Clan, born for the Bit'ahnii (Folded Arm) as my paternal clan. My maternal grandparents are Tsi'naajinii (Black Streaked Wood People), and my paternal grandparents are Tłizíłáni (Many Goats Clan). I did not know my paternal grandmother and grandfather very well because they lived in Denehotso, or Reed Valley, at a place called Lók'aa'haagai (White Patch of Reeds). It seemed very far away because we had to walk or ride our horses or travel by wagon. That was the only way we could get there.

I was born around June 2, 1924, an approximate date, since in those days dates were determined by the time of year, the season, or a memorable event. The site is five miles east of present-day Gouldings, Utah, just south of Eagle Rock and Eagle Mesa in Monument Valley.[4] One day my mother, Betsy Yellow, whose Navajo name was 'Asdzáán Tódích'íí'nii (Bitter Water Woman), and I were driving to Blanding when she pointed out my birthplace near Eagle Rock among the juniper trees at a place called 'Adahiilíní (Where the Water Runs Down). Mother pointed to some old logs sticking out of the ground, remnants of the shade house where I was born. My umbilical cord is buried within that area and so my thoughts return to home.

My Navajo name as a child was Awéé' zhóní (Beautiful Baby), and later, when I was about thirteen years old, my older brother Henry gave me the name Samuel. While I have either seven or eight brothers and sisters, I only lived with my mother, sister (Emma Nash) who is about four years older than me, and my little brother, Joe Holiday. I did not really remember my biological father, a medicine man whose name was Billy Holiday, until I met him later in life.

My story is true and starts when I began noticing and remembering things about my daily life and surroundings. I recall my mother praying

Eagle Mesa with Eagle Rock (*separate spire to left*), Monument Valley, Utah. On this sagebrush-covered plain south of the mesa stood the hogan where Samuel Holiday was born. Today nothing remains of the campsite. (Photograph by Kay Shumway)

early in the morning to the dawn where the new, good things of life come from. We prayed to the Holy Ones, who provide all the elements of life like the heat from the sun, the sacred water, and air.[5] The Holy People gave all of this to those who live on the earth. Water is the most sacred and strongest element. The earth was made holy by covering it with water from the ocean. If it had not received this baptism, it would have dried up and died. The earth had been on fire when the Holy People took water from a sacred place and put it on the land so that plants could start growing. The plants grew from their seeds and then animals and insects were made with water and finally people. Water is everything. In the past the Navajos practiced a ceremony called Tó'ee (Of the Water) because water is sacred.[6] Now there are few who know it. God worked with all this and he put a soul or spirit that is holy into it all. When we pray we pray for the spirit and that is why we pray for all things, even the sheep and land. Mother used to say that everything has a soul and is alive because of water.

She would awaken the children before sunrise and give us white cornmeal to offer during our prayers. Then we faced east before the sun came up, pleading for good things to happen, to obtain material blessings, and enjoy safe and productive lives. Other things we prayed for were that the plants would grow, the sheep would be well cared for and increase, that the rain would bring water to drink, and the grazing land would turn green for all our animals. That is how we prayed. I did not like being awakened that early, especially when it was cold, but Mother always said, "You will be healthy and strong if you get up very early in the morning." At first, I just copied her, but later I realized that my prayers for rain and blessings would come true if I was sincere.

Next my older sister did her running. Mother suggested that I also do it and so later I followed my sister but did not travel as far as she did, turning around about half way. When I was older, mother awakened us early in the morning, pulled off my sleeping blanket, and threatened to splash cold water on me if I refused to get up to run. My sister and I were forced to exercise, which I did not like at all, especially in cold weather. In the winter when the first snow fell, mother made us take off our clothes and roll in it. In those days the first snow fall was usually very deep, and as freezing as it was, I had to roll around, tumble, and take a bath in it. It was very, very cold so that by the time this ended, I was shivering. My mother would put a blanket around me and tell me to go inside, but not by the fire, so that I would warm up slowly before I got close to the open flame. She warned us never to run to warmth when freezing because by bathing in the first snow I would become tough and strong to withstand harsh weather. It was a strict practice in Navajo culture to raise children that way, especially in the past, when the People had a lot of enemies who attacked any time of day or night. We were trained to always be prepared for this. Parents also made children run to a lake or pond, break the ice, bathe in the water, then bring a chunk of ice home. This made them alert and able to run for their lives if necessary. Even then, mother told us that we had it easy and children never talked back to their parents—they obeyed, so I did everything she told me to do. Today it is reversed, with children ruling the house and telling their parents what to do.

My earliest memories were of our large flock of sheep, goats, and horses. I do not remember my father at this time because he had married another woman and left us. My mother's older brother, 'Adika'í (Gambler), took most of my mother's livestock, telling her that she did not have a man to take care of them and that he would. If she ever needed some he would let her have whatever she wanted. But that did not happen. Every time mother asked for a sheep he denied her request and soon the livestock no longer belonged to her. I was about four years old by the time my mother had regained her own flock of about 200 sheep but remember my older sister and I herding for the family. While we did that, mother tended to our needs at home and rode a horse or donkey to buy groceries at the Oljato (Moon Water) Trading Post.[7] This store seemed so far away but was the only one in Monument Valley at that time.

My older sister and I herded our livestock every day, sometimes on horseback but most often on foot. There was always work to be done with the herd. One of the biggest jobs came when the ewes were birthing. In the winter we had to take the newborn back to the hogan to get them out of the cold until they were stronger. My sister used to make me carry them back, but they were heavy and sometimes I'd get butted by the mother ewes that followed their young. In the summer we tied our lunch and water to the saddle but did not eat until the herd settled down, usually in the shade of a tree or rock, later in the afternoon. Sometimes we climbed on top of the rocks to pick berries, gathering as many as we could carry for future use.

In the winter we wore blankets when we tended the herd, but when it was hot we wore them like a belt around our waist. It seems like it was not as cold then as it is today. Maybe I was used to it or it was my songs that kept me warm. Mother taught us songs to sing when we got sick and were not feeling well. She also knew songs for when one got lost in cold weather, saying, "When you sing this song you won't freeze to death." I remembered part of it for a long time. Then one day, after my wife and I had children, my daughter Lisa brought me an electric blanket. My prayers and songs had come true. But before that I sang lots of times in the winter when I got cold; these prayers worked because I actually felt warmer when I sang them.

She had learned about these prayers and ceremonies from her father named Tsi'naajinii, (clan name given to individual) who lived at Tsiiłchin Bii'tóhí (Water with Reed). I was too young to understand, even if she had taught them to me. I mostly learned them by myself, selecting what made me happy then practicing while I herded sheep. Mother also instructed us about Navajo medicine men with their ceremonies and prayers that provided safety and well-being. She shared songs for protection so that we could have good, strong, and happy lives. Phrases like "blessings of peace" and "beauty before us and behind us" were part of those prayers. These teachings came from true medicine men as taught by the Holy People. She could also feel a person's ailment by waving her hand over them. She knew how to heal with Navajo herbal medicine as well as through hand movements in accompaniment with crystal gazing. What she did is called "'ak'indilnih" (waving a hand over it [the body]), through which she helped many people.[8] This traditional practice uses key points on the body that give a sense of why a person is in pain and then removes it. For instance if someone had a headache, she would pass her hand over their head and remove the pain, which is different from how hand trembling and crystal gazing are used. People came from miles around traveling by horse or donkey for her assistance.

As children we had other daily chores like hauling water for washing, cooking, and drinking. We obtained it by either digging a hole in the ground then scooping it out from the pool that formed or from a rock basin under waterfalls after it rained, but it always seemed available. I didn't like this job, however, because our usual source was half a mile away and the gallon cans we carried had wire handles that cut into and stung our hands as we hauled the water home. We also had to drive our cows, horses, and sheep to water as well as irrigate our big cornfield where we also planted squash and melons. It used to rain all the time, but when it did not, there was a water fall in the canyon where we could obtain it.

I did not know that there was such a thing as being poor or rich. We always had food, clothes, and a place to stay. Our daily diet was goat's milk, mutton, and cornmeal, which we prepared in different ways. In the summer we had fruit grown by relatives who planted trees in the mountains where there was plenty of water. Peaches, apricots, and apples were a nice change from a steady diet of what we grew supplemented by coffee, flour, sugar and canned goods. My favorite food from the trading post was canned tomatoes. From flour mother made fry bread cooked in mutton tallow. This was very simple fare and there was not very much of it. My mother made all our clothes with cloth she bought at the Oljato trading post. Still, we felt well cared for.

Early one morning my sister excitedly told me that we were going to herd the sheep to Sentinel Butte in order to pick sour berries and herbs for food. My mother went with us to teach us which plants are eaten and which can be sucked on when thirsty. She occasionally would do this, emphasizing that we should not kill animals without a purpose and that destroying plants was wrong because these things belonged to Mother Nature and were holy. Inappropriate killing or disrespect would later cause sickness that only a medicine man could heal.

Each time we herded sheep together, mother taught these kinds of things that applied to my life later on. Birds, wildlife, trees, and plants should be cared for while certain types of herbs are used for medicine, but back then I did not really know about them. She taught me how to find herbs and the proper way to harvest them to help when I had an ailment. People in those days depended on them completely and not on treatment at the hospital. Mother knew which herbs healed headaches, fevers, aches, pains, and other types of sickness. She walked to nearby places where different plants grew, especially by Eagle Mesa. In those days there was a lot of rain, making the land very green with medicine plants which were not hard to find. One of her favorite collecting spots was a place of many juniper trees called Tsin Diłhiłí (Black Forest). Today there is no rain so medicine plants are scarce. They all slowly went away through the years. As mother collected, she would say, "This is how it is used. Here is a plant to help you when you are thirsty, ch'il yilt'o'í or ch'iłt'ó'í (sucking plant). You suck on it and swallow its juice to quench your thirst. Another one is k'aabiizhii (arrow reed)." She taught that some were used for food, such as a plant that makes flour for bread when white flour could not be obtained from the trading post. We also ground a lot of cornmeal, butchered sheep for meat, and got milk from the goats. That is what we ate.

Often my sister and I were left alone to take care of our home and herd while mother went to visit her sisters and brothers living near Lukachukai (White with Reeds) and in Crystal, New Mexico. Her family had originally moved there from the Gallup area. She went every year and would be gone for quite a while, sometimes as long as two months. My oldest sister, her husband, and their first baby lived about half a mile away so they occasionally checked to see how we were doing because mother and little brother, Joe, were gone much of the time. Later mother lived with a man named Ted Yellow and so did not travel as much. By then I knew we had older brothers and sisters but had not seen them. My aunt had mentioned them once in a while, saying that they were living with my grandmother's sister, Asdzáán Bikinii (Woman Who Owns the House). I did not actually meet them until I was about eight or nine years old.

Asdzáán Tódích'íí'nii (Bitter Water Woman), or Betsy Yellow, mother of Samuel Holiday. This photo, taken in her later years, is one of the few still remaining, the rest having been burned in a family house fire. She provided her son with many of the traditional teachings that carried him through life. (Photograph courtesy of Holiday family)

One day mother went to visit a maternal uncle, a medicine man, who lived two miles away, so I asked if I could go with her. After some persuasion, she finally agreed. When we arrived at his hogan, he rode in on a horse with a bundle tied to his saddle. As he dismounted, his children—a little girl and boy—ran out to meet him. He picked them up, hugged them, and brought out from the bundle a small paper bag filled with striped candy canes purchased at the trading post. His children were so happy to see him and called him "Dad, Dad." This pleased him and he immediately gave each a piece of hard candy and then some to me. That was the first time I ever tasted it. As the children were calling him "My Daddy," it made me wonder what it would be like to have a father. He really loved them; then I realized what I had been missing. I will never forget that because my sister and I did not have a father who cared or would hug us like that. I longed for a relationship with a dad I had never known. I thought, "This is what it's like to have a father," and that night cried myself to sleep wishing for one. I admired how my mom's uncle took pride in his children and how he loved them, so later I asked my mother where my father was and she replied that he lived far away and was married to another woman. He had left my mother when I was a baby to marry a person from Oljato, and so it was a long time later before I finally met him. As for my uncle, after that I did not see him again until after the war, although he didn't live very far away. His home was by the road that has since been replaced by the main highway so now there are only traces of where he lived.

Another thing that I grew to understand was about the white man. Mother taught that they were a fierce and mean people so I was very afraid to meet one. She told me frightening stories about them and how my maternal great-grandmother Asdzáán Deedįį'ii and Asdzáán Bikinii, my great-great-grandmother, were living at Tójís'ą́ near Tóniłts'ílí (Crystal, New Mexico) east of Lukachukai. The Mexicans and government soldiers often invaded their camp and forced them to flee to Tsé Biyi' (Canyon De Chelly), where they eventually took up residence to hide. There they grew peaches and large fields of corn and other vegetables. Young Navajo warriors who were always on guard for many years tried to protect the people living in the canyon until the government sent soldiers to fight them. They killed the Navajo warriors and their horses and burned all the cornfields. The men tried to save the people but there was no food, causing some to starve to death while others, mostly the elders and small children, surrendered to the soldiers. The warriors did not return to their families because they were afraid.

One of my other grandmothers, Asdzáán Bighan Shą́ą́'jí' Sinilí (The Woman Who Lives on the Sunny Side), also surrendered to the soldiers and with others was herded out of the canyon. My great-grandmother 'Asdzáán Deedįį'ii was too feeble to walk and soon died. Kit Carson was a mean man who loved to watch the Navajo people suffer, kill them, and throw their bodies in a ditch or off a cliff. His soldiers were the ones who made fun of my great-grandmother Asdzáán Bikinii as she tried to defend her family and especially my great-great-grandmother who died. They threw many people off the cliff, especially those who were already dead and were going to do that to my great-grandmother's body but Asdzáán Bikinii stood up to them so they left her alone. The soldiers placed 'Asdzáán Deedįį'ii's corpse in a wagon until they came to a resting area, where she was given a proper burial. Asdzáán Bikinii eventually died from nightmares and reliving the events she suffered during the Long Walk period. Because of this story and others my mother told me, I became scared of the white man. When I was about four or five years old, living in Monument Valley I wondered what they looked like.

At that time there were only a few white traders who ran the trading posts in Oljato, Monument Valley, and Kayenta. My mother told me that others were moving into the area, which both scared me and made me curious as to how they appeared. Mother told us that a white man and his wife had moved to Tsé Gizh (Gap in Rock), a canyon near present-day Gouldings' trading post, which was later renamed Dibé Nééz (Tall Sheep) after the man, Harry, who was tall and went around purchasing sheep from the People. They were living in a tent and seemed like a happy, kind couple.[9] Even though my mother said they were very friendly, she still did not trust them because they might help the white government agents looking for Navajo children to be taken away to schools far from their homes. Later I learned that the Gouldings were only buying rugs and sheep, but my mother still did not trust them as they visited hogans in the area. They might come and identify her children to be taken away.

One morning, Harry Goulding and his wife, Mike, were traveling about taking pictures of Navajo sheep in Monument Valley. Since they had gotten to know my mother and had quickly learned to speak Navajo, they paid us a visit. Both rode in on packed horses and began pointing at all the rock monuments, saying, "Beéso (money), beéso, beéso, beéso." Mother was puzzled and asked me, "Why is he pointing to the rock monuments and calling it money." Later I realized that he had made a lot of money by taking pictures of the rock monuments and selling them. At this time he was planning for the future when he said "money." To me he became a millionaire by taking lots of home movies and photographs of the rock monuments and selling them.

I was told that this white couple was building a house out of cut stone near Gap in Rock. My brother-in-law Billy Nez (Tall), whose name later changed to Nash because of the English pronunciation, was husband to my oldest sister. They had a couple of children and lived close to us. He and others helped with the construction while Ted Yellow used his wagon and a team of mules to haul stone. Even with all this help, it took three years to finish the project. Once the structure was finished, Mike ran the store and Harry took tourists into Monument Valley on horseback for four- or five-day trips to see all the canyons and rock formations. Most of the mesas and buttes are named after what they look like: Bear and Rabbit, The Rooster, Stage Coach, Eagle Rock, King on the Throne, The Three Sisters, and many more. Later the tourists traveled in jeeps, which only took a day to tour the valley. The Gouldings also brought movie-makers to Monument Valley. Among the films created there that I remember were *Stage Coach* and *She Wore a Yellow Ribbon* with John Wayne starring in them.[10] Later my wife, my sister-in-law, and I had our picture taken with him when he was filming *The Searchers*.

Still it was a long time before I saw my first white man. I had heard that there was one living at the Oljato trading post near my paternal grandmother's home where we lived in the spring and summer while helping with her cornfield and peach orchard. In the winter we moved back to our hogan and resumed our life there. The first day I went to that post with my mother I was shy and frightened. I stood by the store door and saw a white man laughing and talking to Navajos inside. Afraid to enter, I watched and studied this man known to the Navajos as Bilagáana Tso (Big White-man), or in English Reuben Heflin. He was the only trader around Oljato at that time, but he later moved to Shonto (Water on Sunny [South] Side). I must have been about eleven or twelve years old before I stopped being afraid of white men.

Harry Goulding (*right*) and a Navajo customer (*left*) stand outside of Goulding's Trading Post, Monument Valley, Utah, in the 1930s. Navajo labor quarried and laid the stone to build this two-story structure. It was also the site where Samuel's mother met her future husband, Ted Yellow. (Photograph courtesy of Utah State Historical Society)

One evening in the spring when we were putting the sheep in the corral, there was a wagon parked by our hogan with four mules nearby. When we went inside there was a tall Navajo man with a mustache sitting on a sheepskin smoking a Bull Durham cigarette. Mother took my sister and me outside and told us that the man sitting in our home was our new father named Ted Yellow. He worked at Gouldings helping to build the trading post. In Navajo she explained that she was now with him and that they planned to move to Kayenta near his family, about twenty-five miles from where we then lived. I was at first afraid of this man but later grew to appreciate him. We learned that Ted Yellow's wife had died and that he was now working for Harry and Mike Goulding. Mother was the cook for the workers, and that is where she met Ted Yellow, my future stepfather.

Several days after meeting him, we loaded our sheepskins, blankets, pots, and pans on horses while my brother-in-law put the rest of the animals in my mother's corral. I saddled my horse named Nah-yi-zi Bi-cha (Pumpkin Hat) and started the journey. My sister and I herded the sheep to our new home in Kayenta, which took about three days. At the time it seemed very far away from where we used to live. There were no real roads, just wagon trails and very few cars. As we approached I looked across the desert and saw the smoke stack of the power house by the Warner Trading Post. We settled down on the south side of the creek near the dirt road that served as the main route to Shiprock to the east, Window Rock to the south, Tuba City to the west, and Utah to the north.[11] The place my stepfather chose was dense with brush at a time when the whole area between Kayenta and Agathla (Lots-of-wool), a volcanic core now called El Capitan, was thick with vegetation. There was more rain and plants back then and so the area was much greener than today. He cleared a place amidst the brush for our bedding and a cooking area then crossed the creek to chop trees into logs which he brought back to build a hogan. With my in-laws and others, the men completed our home in two weeks.

The Warren Trading Post has since been torn down, but my mother and I used to take sheep pelts there to trade.[12] The first time I went with her I just stood at the doorway and watched. Soon I was coming with the pelts by myself. We used to get seventy-five cents for each pelt. In those days things were not expensive—a twenty-five-pound bag of flour was seventy-five cents, and if one added coffee, sugar, baking powder, and salt it would total one dollar. The storekeeper's name was Tsííłchii, which means Red Hair, but it later changed to Diiłchii', which means the same thing but is pronounced a little differently. He owned the first truck that I ever saw when I was around the age of eleven. He used it to bring food and supplies to his trading post. I thought it was a good idea to have a machine that ran faster than a horse so that one can get to a destination more quickly, but the problem was that it had to move on graded roads and there were not many. One time a truck startled me because it was so close that I ran for the rocks.

Eventually, Navajo people obtained their own. Fred Bradley bought a truck while working for traders shearing sheep. Other vehicles became common to the area, six altogether. Two big trucks belonged to medical doctors who traveled on dirt roads that connected Flagstaff, Gallup, and Kayenta. Another big truck belonged to Lee Bradley, who took the mail from Kayenta to Tuba City once a week on a dirt road that went all the way to Cameron. Drivers had a hard time going from Tuba City to Kayenta during the winter because the roads were muddy, washing out from snow and rain. Most Navajos continued to use horses to visit or travel to ceremonies and trading posts, and not many had wagons. My stepfather did, however, which helped when it came to hauling water. Otherwise we used donkeys for that chore.

After getting established, we planted a cornfield where the highway is now. During the planting time my father and brother-in-law would take a team of mules for plowing or to clean irrigation ditches. One day I went along with them and found many men working with horses and mules to do most of the heavy labor. They plowed in one field then moved the whole group to another, helping each other with digging furrows and planting crops. This happened every year and became part of my life, my main job being to round up the livestock early in the morning. At noon as the men ate lunch, some other boys and I watered and fed the horses and mules. When we finished taking care of the animals we ate leftovers from the worker's lunch. I really liked eating the sweet things like canned fruit and tomatoes. The men would smoke and joke after lunch amidst occasional roars of laughter. Later in the season another difficult task was gathering and laying out the corn to dry, but all of this work made the summers pass quickly.

Once I overheard the men talking about two white traders. One was named Bilagáana Nez (Tall Whiteman) and the other Old John (John Sani), one of the earliest traders in the Kayenta area.[13] John [Wetherill's] wife was Louisa, but her Navajo name was Asdzáán Tsosie (Slim Woman). Both men were here with their wives. The Navajos also talked about another white man, a range rider (Leads His Horse Around) who worked for the government. These men received that name when livestock reduction was taking place because they were always riding around looking for flocks of sheep and goats.[14] The range riders told us we had too many sheep that were ruining the roads and trails, turning them into deep ditches, using up grass and water, ruining the land, and they were useless as livestock. At this time my stepfather's and mother's sheep were together. So to fool the range rider, we divided the flocks and took half to another sheep camp. They counted my mother's herd and gave her a sheep permit for a certain number because they did not know about the other animals. We later put the two herds back together and did not lose any of them. We did a good lie; no wonder we survived the Long Walk.

I grew even more afraid because men like these were also responsible for hunting children, taking them from their parents, and sending them to government boarding school. One of them was now living in Kayenta. I hid from range riders who sometimes had a Navajo interpreter with them. When mother expected someone or received a message saying officials were looking for children, she would send us away, reinforcing our fear of them. With the sound of a vehicle, we looked around not knowing what to expect. It was scary for me, nowadays being similar to fearing the approach of an outer spaceman. When we heard that they were nearby my sister and I made our lunch, took some water, and fled to the mountains, not returning home until we thought it was safe or my mother came to get us. Now that I was living in Kayenta, however, I saw more and more white people at a distance and so was less frightened.

Our fear of being caught went back to our ancestors' Long Walk experience. We did not want to suffer like them when they spent four years at Fort Sumner. Stories were told that the Mexicans and soldiers raped and sold young Navajo girls and captured strong young men to be sold as slaves. Everyone suffered except for those helped by some Mexican women who were nice to the Navajos. They came into camp and showed them how to cook rations like coffee and flour, because the Navajos did not know how to use this type of food. Some became good friends with these Mexican ladies.

In the fall when it began to get cold, we moved to our winter camp about nine miles west of Kayenta near my stepfather's family's area where there was already a hogan and corral. Ted Yellow was even stricter than my mother about getting up before dawn to run. The first week was half a mile, with the distances increasing each time. He had me run as hard as I could and yell to increase my stamina. When the first snow fell, my stepfather and I took our clothes off and ran away from the hogan to roll in the snow. He made sure the snow touched every part of my body. Finally he let me go and I ran as fast as I could for home, thinking I would not make it because of the cold. But once I got inside, my mother again warned me not to get close to the fire, but instead wrap myself in a blanket. She had been easy on me during the previous years because she had rolled me in the snow right next to the hogan.

Again she explained why this was done to the children, saying, "We make you run a race fast at long distances to strengthen your body and build endurance against hardship. You are preparing and protecting yourself."

I then received more information about the old days and fighting. She told me a story about her grandfather Na-bah-hi (Warrior) and how he used to make the boys run to a pond or river, break the ice, and bring a chunk of it home. Na-bah-hi had fought the enemy many times and could outrun their horses. My mother's grandfather told her, "When I was small, we would get thrown in the water because we did not know when the enemy would attack. They might attack at midnight, in the morning, or during cold winters. That is why we were made to roll in the snow and run in the mornings."

In the past, most of my father's family got away from Kit Carson by escaping to the northwest of Kayenta. Hashké neiniih (Giving out Anger) fled to the canyon country and passed these stories down about when Kit Carson had moved into Navajo land.[15] The families fled to the top of Narrow Canyon where there were lots of ravines and canyons. Carson's army gave up trying to get at them because his men could go no farther or would get lost. That was the reason we were thrown in the snow and made to run in the early mornings, so that we would always be ready.

One summer when I was around thirteen years old and after we had moved back to our summer camp near where the bridge is now in Kayenta, a very good looking boy came to our hogan on horseback. He was dressed in store clothes and wearing shoes. My mother and I were at the door, my sister with the sheep. As the boy approached mother went running to meet him saying, "Shiyáázh, shiyáázh, Haasí wodí" (Tough Warrior). Mother hugged him and kept saying "Tough Warrior." It turned out that he was my brother, Henry Holiday, who was about nine or ten years older than me and had come to Kayenta to catch a ride to the Tuba City Boarding School. He had been living with our father in Oljato during the summer then attending school in the winter. He stayed with us for about a week. I kept looking at his clothes, his store-bought shoes, and his haircut. I finally asked him where he got all that. He said that his father bought it for him. My real father had taken Henry with him when my parents separated, so Henry had stayed with him all this time. My brother helped my mother, stepfather, sister, and me by hoeing weeds in the cornfield while I herded sheep.

I could not get over how nice Henry looked dressed in white men's clothes—nice pants and shirt—and how he laughed at my homemade, baggy, oversized trousers. He probably was thinking to himself that this shabby-looking boy is his younger brother, and so he asked me one day if he could cut my hair. I stared at him and saw that his hair was shaved off, and that with his nice clothes and shoes, he looked like a white man. My father had taken really good care of him and now he was going to school and knew English; he even tried to teach me some words by talking to me. The more I thought about it, the better it seemed and so the next day I gave permission to cut my hair. I do not remember how big my hair bun was, but it had not been cut since I was born. Only recently have I come to realize that a person's hair is very sacred and important in Navajo teachings and that it represents the rain.[16] Since he did not have scissors he used sheep shears and once he had cut it, the hair was gone; I do not know what happened to my bun. I was excited to think that with this haircut I truly must look good like a white man now. I felt happy. I thought I was really somebody as I watched my shadow with the short hair.

Henry also gave me my name, Samuel Tom Holiday, that same day. He asked my mother about my birth month, and she told him that it was during the time of Big Planting (June) and that I turned four years old when the Goulding's house was finished. My mother could not remember if it was the first day or the second, so my brother picked the second day. Later I read a magazine about Harry Goulding and compared my birthdate with when the home was finished and that date is about right. We stuck to that for my birthday. After my brother's visit, I started thinking about the white man's school, of how they had changed my brother with his haircut, the way he dressed, and the English he spoke. I wanted to be like him so I wished to go to school. This was also around the time that I lost some of my fear of white men. That summer a woman came to our hogan and spent two or three days with us. She kept calling us her children. Her name was Asdzáán Hasbídí (Mourning Dove). She took my sister with her to help care for her sheep and perform other chores. I never saw my sister again after that because she died when I was in the service.

Every year I herded sheep across from Laguna Creek near where we made our home on the top of the hill. There was no bridge at that time, and the road was very poor. It used to rain a lot, creating a waterfall about eight feet high in one part of the creek where children used to swim. One very hot summer day when I was thirteen years old, I was returning from herding sheep and decided to go swimming. I let the flock go back to the corral on their own after they finished drinking. In those days there was always a lot of water flowing in the creek that filled a deep pool where the stream had gouged out the rocks. I climbed up on the bank to a rock on a

Warren Trading Post, 1920s. Samuel's first extended encounter with white men occurred at the Wetherill post in Oljato, Utah, and this one in Kayenta, Arizona. Stocked shelves with food, dry goods suspended from the ceiling, and a stove in the "bullpen" where customers could congregate were beckoning aspects from the Anglo world. (Photograph from Warren family photos, Northern Arizona University, Cline Library)

high spot over the pool, took off my clothes, and dove in, my knee hitting some stones that I hadn't seen under the water. When I emerged my left leg was bloody, the skin around my knee badly torn, and my knee cap visible. The blood ran into the water and was all over me. I struggled to put my pants on, crawl up the steep bank of the creek then go around the thick brush to get home. I could not really walk so just dragged my leg while becoming increasingly faint. It was a long way to limp with that kind of intense pain. I was almost home and could smell the mutton my mother was cooking when I felt dizzy, fell down, and passed out.

My mother saw me limping then fall. She was more frightened when she ran out to meet me and saw all the blood. Mother had been looking for me earlier and asking people hoeing in a nearby cornfield if they had seen me. Now she quickly ran to these men for help. They spread a blanket on the ground, wrapped me in it, hauled me home and then to the clinic. By the time I awoke the doctor had sewed my knee and the nurses covered it with medicine and bandages. I think they also had to put blood in me. As soon as I opened my eyes I identified the smell of medicine and knew I was in the hospital. The doctor spoke to me in English, which I did not understand, so I just stared at him. My knee really hurt, but I noticed that some Navajo school girls were working there and recognized two of them. They interpreted to me what was being said in English and asked how intense the pain was in my knee so I replied that it felt like a sharp sting. They told me to rest and asked if I wanted food. I accepted and lay in bed in a very strange environment.

While recuperating I at first just played cards for a couple of weeks while I stayed in bed. Then, in a month, I was able to limp about with crutches and later a cane. I started to notice there were children going to school in a small side room, and so they asked me to attend class with them. I began learning the *A*, *B*, *C*'s and enjoyed it. I was at first afraid of white men, but here I was now learning from them. I liked the way they treated me at the hospital school, which was very different than my later experience in boarding school. The doctors and nurses were close by to help me heal. They took out my stitches and monitored my progress. They told me to be careful the way I walked and limped around.

My mother came to visit me and always said that I would be coming home soon, which gave me hope to hurry and heal even though the hospital treated me well. After three months my leg had repaired and I went home. But while I had been in the hospital the doctors had discussed with mother about my continuing to go to school. She did not want me to and tried to tell them that I was the only one to herd sheep for her, but the doctors replied that she had already been taking care of the animals while I was in the hospital and that she could do it some more. As far as I was concerned, I wanted to learn to speak English and had already learned a few basic words like "milk" and "water." Knowing more about the white man's world now seemed appealing.

In three months another boy and I were falling behind in school. The administrators at the hospital told my mother that I was being enrolled at Tuba City. Hugh Burn from the agency told me that school was good and that the government was trying to educate the Navajos so they would not have to herd sheep the rest of their lives and would have cars to drive and

Kayenta Hospital, 1920s. Samuel's positive experience here following his knee injury not only healed the extensive wound but exposed him to his first formal educational experience. Officials from this hospital ensured that he had other opportunities at the Tuba City Boarding School. (Photograph from Warren family photos, Northern Arizona University, Cline Library)

houses with running water so that it would not have to be hauled. I was told that the Navajo religion was no good. Your life will not improve. It keeps you herding sheep and not going anywhere, but by going to school I would learn the white man's way. I would learn many things. In a way they were right. The old Navajo people were not in favor of white education. My mother said when the people from the school came to her to get her approval for me to go, they told her many things. But she told them that even without the white man's education we had everything we needed to survive. We had medicine and the type of medicine we used the white man did not have. It healed and helped us live strong lives. And our prayers were heard by Diyin (gods). She said that was how she argued, but it was in vain. She had to say okay for me to go to school. That is what my mother told me. Willie Weaver was the other boy from the hospital who went with me to Tuba. They told us we had learned a lot here and now we will learn more at Tuba. So they took us to the Tuba City Boarding School.

Commentary: Worldview—Of Mothers and Monsters

The world that Samuel Holiday entered at birth near Eagle Rock was one of accelerating change.[17] Monument Valley astride the Utah-Arizona border was already a destination spot for tourists with money who were willing to rough it. A dirt road covered with wind-blown sand snaked its way between dramatic rock formations, over hills, and through sagebrush bottoms. Officially, the lands lying south of the San Juan River extending all the way to the Arizona border were called the Paiute Strip and managed by the Bureau of Indian Affair's Western Agency in Tuba City, Arizona. While the dramatic rock formations of Monument Valley would later become symbolic of Navajo tribal holdings in general, they would not officially be part of the tribe's land base until 1933, when a sweeping agreement added this area and a section of land in the Aneth region of Utah to the Navajos in exchange for other lands north of the San Juan River. The first white settlers in this area were traders John and Louisa Wetherill, who built the first Oljato trading post in 1906. Four years later they abandoned it for a new post in Kayenta. A second Oljato post, the one Samuel visited, started in 1921, while the Warren post in Kayenta opened a few years later, slightly before the time that Harry and Mike Goulding began their operation in Monument Valley proper in 1925. All of these posts and others provided different types of economic opportunity ranging from sale of wool, blankets, and livestock to employment in different aspects of the tourist trade, cultural exploration, and even mining. They also introduced new products and twentieth-century material culture, triggering what was at first a subtle and later became a pronounced shift in Navajo values.

Yet this was also a time of highly traditional culture, before significant inroads from white society created irreversible change. People still depended heavily on their livestock and agriculture along with what was obtainable from trading posts for sustenance and dry goods. Ceremonial practices shaped the life of the Navajo, and as seen in Samuel's case, framed a worldview centered in religious explanations. From his earliest years to present, he has lived a deeply religious life from which he interprets then explains surrounding events. Singing sacred songs to stay warm, saying daily prayers and giving offerings of pollen, witnessing his mother's healing practices, and learning of the Holy People laid a solid foundation of belief that carried him through the most difficult times. Even when fighting on Pacific islands during World War II, Samuel recalled his mother and her prayers and made comparison to things he learned while under her tutelage in his home.

There are two prominent themes running through this first part of Samuel's narrative. The first is his role in a matrilineal society, and the second is the history of the Long Walk period. Just as Changing Woman, in the beginning of this chapter, raised the Twins without any male assistance, Samuel lived in the world of his mother. Although he always wondered who his father was, it was not until he reached young manhood that he would finally meet him and receive the supernatural assistance that protected him against the evil forces he encountered during World War II. Until that time, his mother trained him in what he needed to know, introduced him to basic survival in an austere desert environment, and tried to prevent him from venturing forth. The love and dedication that son had for mother is obvious.

Traditional Navajo culture, based in matrilineal kinship practices, emphasizes these bonds between mother and child. From the start, when a baby is born, it is said to have been "born in" the mother's clan and "born for" the father's clan, meaning that while each provides certain rights and responsibilities, the most prominent one is that of the mother. Even grown men who are well-established still recognize their responsibility to mother and her relatives as a primary responsibility; likewise, if life turns bad, a son or daughter is always welcomed back to the refuge of their family home. As anthropologist Gary Witherspoon noted, "Mother and child are bound together by the most intense, the most diffuse, and the most enduring solidarity to be found in Navajo culture. . . . The relationship of Changing Woman to her children provides the major conceptual framework for the Navajo cultural definition of motherhood."[18]

Witherspoon also pointed out that motherhood as a living, practiced symbol of relationship is extended to the role of Mother Earth, who provides for the Earth Surface People (humans), as do agricultural fields, corn, and sheep. All are referred to in the Navajo language with a reference to being a mother and provider. Just as Changing Woman was kind to her children, giving them food and plants for medicine, the riches of the earth for their benefit, and protection when necessary, so should a mother in caring for her children today. Indeed the whole pattern for life relationships is framed by the mythic past and her actions. Thus, the ideal mother is "one who gives life through birth to her children, and then sustains the life of her children by giving them both physical and emotional sustenance. The acts of giving birth and sustenance are imbued with meaning from a cultural system and this meaning is described as intense, diffuse, and enduring solidarity."[19]

Thus Samuel's constant reference to the teachings of his mother, his view that he was always well-cared for even though by some standards his family was barely eking out an existence, and the fact that she always referred to him as "Beautiful Baby" even when he returned home as a man speak volumes concerning the relationship. To borrow the title of a book on Navajo views on personhood, Betsy Yellow ('Asdzáán Tódích'íí'nii) was "molded in the image of Changing Woman."[20]

For a woman to be modeled after Changing Woman was truly the ideal, which was reinforced throughout Navajo culture when a young girl reached womanhood through her first menses and had a kinaaldá (puberty) ceremony performed for her. All through this four-day celebration and intense work, the young woman prepared food eaten by a large number of people attending to participate in the blessings she is provided. On the last day, one of the main events is when she was "molded" to become a provider and to bless her future husband, family, and the Navajo people in general. At the end of this ceremony, for a short time, she becomes and holds the powers of Changing Woman, blessing both young and old, before assuming the tasks of an adult woman.[21]

Although men in the traditional society of Samuel's time held primary sway over ceremonial knowledge and performance, political activity, hunting, and, if necessary, war and maintained their own wealth, women also held "ownership of property, their system of tracing lineage through the female line, the prevailing pattern of residence with the wife's people, the fact that more women than men had a ready and continual source of income (through their weaving), all [of which] gave women a strategic advantage. Such situational circumstances were reinforced by mythology and folklore."[22] Thus Samuel's mother was a potent force in her son's life, her role and responsibility permeating every aspect of his childhood years.

Samuel's life also followed a pattern based in mythology and historic events. One cannot miss the major influence he felt concerning war and preparation for it. Like the Twins, he was raised by only his mother, with no strong male influence in the home. He questioned often who his father was and why he was not present, and there is no indication that he actually had a male puberty ceremony (yilzį́į́h) performed for him. Many males did not, but if he had, it would have followed the teachings derived from the Twins' experience. A typical recognition of moving into manhood would include an older man taking the initiate and performing a Blessing Way ceremony for him before entering a sweat lodge. Starting at noon, the two would make footprints with white cornmeal outside the entrance, just as Changing Woman showed Yé'iitsoh when he questioned her about the footprints around her hogan. The young man would start running with people accompanying him, taunting and testing his ability until he ran back to the sweat lodge to be instructed by a half dozen elders. Each time one of the old men finished his teachings, the young man would emerge from the structure and be "molded" with objects associated with manhood and success in life—a horse bridle, a bow, an arrow, and an unblemished buckskin, representing wealth, protection, supernatural power, and ceremonial knowledge. Next he was covered with white cornmeal (male) as the men sang about his being a child of the Holy People. Later older women instructed him about how a good man acts, then gifts were given.[23]

While Samuel missed this introduction to manhood, there is no missing his preparation for other aspects of a tough future. The extended running and rolling in snow to harden the body and inculcate alertness were common Navajo practices to prepare for hardship and provide strength. Fred Yazzie from Monument Valley clearly links winter activities with training as a warrior. After describing his running and shooting with a bow and arrow, he says: "Ice was broken in a pond and we would go into it. There was also snow on a tree shaken on us. It felt like it was cutting when it fell on you. You eventually did not feel it. It was like this with these teachings."[24] Too much sleep, comfort, and laziness could lead to death for a warrior and his people surrounded with monsters.

Just as the Twins trained for those times when the monsters would appear to exact their toll and would have to be destroyed, so did Samuel. There was a wide variety of these creatures, such as the Bird Monster (Tsé nináhálééh), who carried Earth Surface people to its nest on Shiprock to feed its young; Snapping Vagina, who destroyed the unsuspecting traveler; He-who-kicks-off-the-Rock-Rim (Tsé dah hódzííłtáłii), who pushed people to their death below; the One-who-slays-with its-eyes (Bináá' yee aghání), who killed by staring; and many more. Each had its own way of destroying the unwary, all representing some type of snare and entrapment common to man.[25] As Monster Slayer said, "Until each one of them is destroyed, there will be disorder on the surface of the world."

In the view of a young boy raised upon these teachings, the white man very well embodied in physical form the types of evil depicted in the stories. Carrying off children to school, raping young Navajo women, impolitely staring with eyes fixed on a person, and tossing Navajo captives off cliffs were part of the world discussed around the fire at night. At no time were these qualities more evident than in the stories of the Long Walk period when the Navajo people fought the U.S. military and its allies. The fear Samuel felt toward these enemies of the past is abundantly clear in his narrative, by his family's personal encounters with white men during this time. Traditional Navajo thought easily equates the two.

The history of this period of warfare is indelibly ingrained in the tribal memory, giving rise to two schools of thought. The most common one follows Samuel's view and is popular today with many Navajo and non-Navajo people sympathetic to past grievances. There is a body of literature that supports this view.[26] Based in the oral tradition, the common, oft-quoted belief is that the U.S. military became so frustrated with the Navajo, a generally peaceful people, that it began a scorched earth campaign to destroy them, tantamount to genocide. Cruelty and military efficiency characterized the roundup of the people, who were then mercilessly herded over long distances to a collecting point called Fort Sumner on the Pecos River, where they were incarcerated for four years (1864–1868) before being allowed to return to their previous homeland. The architect and arch villain behind both the capture and movement of the people was Christopher "Kit" Carson, who vengefully watched the suffering of the Navajo with pleasure. Once they arrived at Fort Sumner, the Navajos chaffed under the control of General James H. Carleton, who was insensitive to their needs and suffering. All through the entire period there was rape, murder, and large loss of life, a part of the punishment for opposing the government.

A second school of thought gives a far different interpretation.[27] When the U.S. government waged its war against the Navajo, its military units were relatively ineffective, but not so the auxiliaries that roamed through the country. These groups, composed of Native American and New Mexican opponents who had been antagonized by the Navajo, looked upon this as an opportunity to make war with the blessing and support of their ally, the Americans. Their effectiveness was telling. Entering every nook and cranny of traditional Navajo lands, they ferreted out large numbers who either surrendered to U.S. forces or escaped into highly defensible locations in areas not regularly visited by their enemies. Kit Carson also advocated a scorched earth policy that destroyed food supplies and production while capitalizing on a state of imbalance and constant movement. This strategy was the only way to keep bloodshed to a minimum and yet force surrender. The deaths associated with the Long Walk from various staging areas was more a function of moving elders, women, and children hundreds of miles in the middle of winter because none of the collecting points were equipped to manage large populations of Navajos surrendering to get away from their enemies. Indeed, many talk about wanting to surrender to the U.S. military for protection.[28] Once Navajos had surrendered, the government had the responsibility to care for them. Unfortunately it was ill-prepared to handle the large numbers, and death stalked the inmates at Fort Sumner. Carson, an old and tired man who actually did not want to be involved in any of this, died two weeks before the government released the Navajos to return to their country.

Regardless of whose side of the discussion one might agree with, there is no doubt as to what Samuel had been taught. This is not to suggest that it was wrong. Very likely many of the things that had been passed down through the oral tradition did happen to his family members, fostering a fear of the white man and a reason to train hard for adversity. In the same respect, Samuel easily links both the seizing of children for boarding school and the livestock reduction of the 1930s to the Long Walk and Kit Carson. Although to people today this comparison may seem like a large stretch, in Navajo thought, both were examples of history repeating its cycle. Boarding schools represented "capturing" the children and turning them into white men. Indeed, in many instances, health practices in those days were at times primitive when it came to communicable disease, and there were many children in the early years who never returned home. The range riders were scouts, looking for the unwary prey that could be identified and sent off to school.

Livestock reduction was equally severe. In Navajo thought, such reductions not only removed their wealth by wiping out their herds, but it was a direct attack on Navajo people with the end result of killing them off. Oral testimony filled with metaphors of war and genocide paint a graphic picture of how Navajos meshed the two events, even though there were seventy years between.[29] The killing of the sheep is equated to the killing of the people; John Collier, head of the Bureau of Indian Affairs (BIA), becomes Kit Carson; and the horror of the slaughter in the pens is another attempt at genocide. So it is not by chance that after Samuel explains how his family hid their sheep, he says, "No wonder we survived the Long Walk."

CHAPTER TWO

Diné Language and Control

Boarding School and Enlistment

THE TWINS: SURROUNDED BY MONSTERS

That night the Twins lay in bed listening to their mothers talk in muted tones. Finally they garnered the courage to ask, "Who are our fathers?" to which came the reply, "You have none; you are illegitimate [yátaashki']." The young men persisted but never received a satisfying answer. The next day, however, the mothers fashioned crude bows and arrows for their teenage sons and told them to learn how to use them during play but warned them not to travel far from home because there were monsters (naayéé) about. The youth disregarded the advice, traveled east, and encountered Coyote, a spy for one of the monsters. After reporting what they had seen, they received a scolding from their mothers, who warned them not to make that mistake again, but each day they traveled in a different direction, south, west, and north, only to meet other spies—raven, buzzard, and crow—who returned and told the monsters of the boys' presence. The mothers were distraught. They warned the Twins that now they did not know how they could save them, the secret was out, and soon the alien gods would be there to eat them. To protect them, the women dug a hole under the fireplace, put the boys in it, and covered the pit with a large stone. They received the title of Łeeyah' neeyání, or Raised Underground.

Still the monsters knew there were young, tender children nearby and wished to find them. One day Changing Woman left her house in time to see the approach of Yé'iitsoh, the largest and most powerful of the monsters and son of Jóhonaa'éí, or Sun Bearer. He demanded to know where the boys who made the tracks around the hogan were now hiding. Undaunted, Changing Woman said there were none, that she had made what looked like footprints in the sand with the heel of her clenched fist then added the toes with her fingers just to pass the time. She next showed Yé'ii tsoh how she had done it, to the point that he was satisfied and left. Other alien gods approached the hogan so Changing Woman created winds in the four directions that stopped their advance. Early next morning the Twins slipped out of their home and started on a "holy trail" (Atiin diyinii) in search of their father.[1] Each placed his feet upon a short rainbow that carried them both safely on their journey.

ORIGIN OF LANGUAGE

At the beginning of mankind (Diné náhodideesdlį́įdí), the people "went around like sheep. Like sheep they did not talk."[2] They used their eyes to communicate their intent and made simple sounds to gain each other's attention. The Holy People watched First Man and First Woman lead the Earth Surface People. Wind (Niłch'i), who knew everything, wanted to assist them so offered his help. He proposed to enter the Diné and bring with him the ability to communicate, teach, and share ideas that would open their eyes to all. This made the People happy, knowing that they were now accepted by this Holy Being and that they could speak the langauge used by the gods (Diyin Dine'é bizaad bee yádeelti').

SAMUEL: OF SCHOOL AND LANGUAGE

By the time my mother had given permission for me to leave the Kayenta hospital school, classes were already in session in Tuba City. She tried to tell the government officials that she needed me at home to help and that she did not want me to go. Leading His Horse Around and an interpreter had come to visit her, insisting I enroll and reassuring her that I would be all right. She tried hard to tell them not to take me, but it was no use. I did not want to go and was very sad when I left, but another boy, William Weaver from Farmington, and I traveled in a car the seventy-five miles to the Tuba City Boarding School.[3] During that trip I thought about my mother a lot, worrying about how she would be alone without my help. I felt strong compassion for her and imagined how she would have no one to herd and care for the sheep now that I had left, even though she was very capable and knew how to take care of everything. My stepfather also had horses, a mule, and a cornfield to care for while he worked hard at other jobs.

But I also remembered that at planting time our neighbors from on top of the mesa helped and allowed us to use their plow and horses to work our land. This reassured me that my mother and father were in good hands; I also wanted to do well in my job. I knew that by leaving home for school I would learn things for my future life if I were to succeed in the white man's world, which in turn would be good for my family. Knowing white ways could open the door for the future, although I was still not sure whether to trust them or not. Still, they had given us food and supplies and told mother that she would have a house built for her, which put me at ease with them. After thinking through these issues, I was not afraid of the white man anymore and was anxious to get started learning and accomplishing something.

As Willie Weaver and I traveled to school for the first time, we talked in Navajo. Although the car made its way down the graded dirt road slowly, it seemed the trees whizzed by at amazing speed. The more I traveled these roads, the more I noticed that when it rained or snowed they became very muddy and that the few cars I saw on them slid off. The wind blew sand banks into the ruts, stopping travel on certain stretches. We arrived that fall afternoon at a strange group of buildings—the boarding school with a lot of children. I was scared; as soon as we got out of the car someone informed on us that we were talking in Navajo. It did not take long to learn how wrong that was.

The first thing I noticed was that many of the children were playing outside. All had been separated by sizes—the little children stayed in one place and had a different dorm than the middle-sized ones. I was put with the bigger, older children in a different part of the dorm and then met my dorm advisors. I could tell right away that the Navajo woman working in our dorm was strict, mean, and bossy. Each group had one adult assigned to take care of the students' clothes, laundry, mending, and to supervise the living quarters. There were also Navajo male dorm advisors in charge of the athletic program and daily morning exercises. Harry Sloan was the one assigned to my dorm. He looked at me in disgust as if he did not want me to be there. It seemed these advisors were trained to have nothing to do with Navajo traditions and language but instead were instructed to push it out of our lives. I looked like a traditional Navajo to Sloan, so he announced that we must always speak English and never Navajo. I was very scared and apprehensive of these dormitory advisors. Now we were to learn the white man's way.

The next thing the school employees did was to have me get rid of my plain store-bought clothes in exchange for an issue of three sets from the school—one for class, another for church, and one for play, as well as some all-purpose socks and shoes. I thought they were all right. At least I had new clothes and everybody else wore the same kind. On Sunday the boys put on a church uniform composed of white pants that tied in the front with a white shirt. Coveralls that buttoned all the way to the underneath side served as everyday clothes to work and play in. I also received blankets and sheets then was soon assigned a bunk bed. That evening we lined up to eat. Some of the older boys who understood and spoke more English received the title of "captain" and made us line up, something we did everywhere we went. They kept us in line and were our leaders. After dinner we went to the dorms to sleep.

We got up early in the morning and formed to do exercises, one of which was to march around the buildings. Then we marched to breakfast, ate, then lined up and marched to class. When I got there, my teacher, a white lady, put me in a classroom with all of the new students labeled Beginner Group B. I was the oldest and tallest one in the room. Those little children were very naughty and would kick me, saying things in English that I did not understand. The teacher reminded me again that I should not talk Navajo but only English. There was also to be no more Navajo religion and traditional ceremonies. "Learning English will help you in your future," she said. "The Navajo way will not help you; it has nothing so you must speak only English." This was very hard for me because I had always spoken Navajo and this new language was difficult to learn. I did not even know how to say "chair." Then I thought I would try hard to learn and speak English; that was the only way.

The first week in the classroom and in the dorm was very difficult. All the adults were very strict; the dorm advisor woke us up early in the morning to exercise; the teachers had spelling tests with fifty words every week; the bigger boys in the dorm were rough, made fun of me, and picked on me constantly, real bullies, while the little boys in my class were just plain naughty. Even my height became a problem since I was middle-sized for my age, but when I went to class I was the only tall boy there. I was very stressed and scared and wondered how I was going to speak only English. The three months of school at the hospital had taught me a few words along with the alphabet and some basic numbers. It was hard, but I wanted to learn and be like a white man. I made up my mind at that point to be just as good as or better than the rest of the students, trying extra hard in everything.

In the afternoon we took out sleeping mats like sheepskins to rest on. When I lay down I was taller than everybody else and so the others teased me, calling me giant. Every once in a while I would get kicked by the boys as they told me to move over. Once I kicked back and the boy started crying so I was punished by doing extra work. This often took the form of having to scrub the floors and walls or by having to stay in the dorm while everyone else played outside. Our class used to take walks, and the white teacher and I were the same height. The boys teased me, saying that she was my wife. One time we went to an apple orchard after the harvest and the trees still had some fruit on them. "Hey boy! Reach up and get me an apple," the children teased since I was a tall beginner and they wanted to pick on me. I got mad and threw one of them down. He started crying and told both the teacher and dorm advisor so they punished me and said not to pick on the little boys. That was something I remember from one of our walks. It was a rough beginning.

One thing that did not seem to get any easier at first was always talking English. Once in a while some of the smart children would get away with speaking Navajo, but often they were caught and punished. The new arrivals in Beginner B received some leniency because they did not know any English words at all. Still the teachers did not approve of it. After we were in school a while, we were not allowed any Navajo words at all. Beginner B was mostly five- and six-year-olds, while Beginner A was mostly eight- to ten-year-olds. There the teachers forbid all Navajo: "Talk English!" they yelled at us. Within three months after going through the Beginner B, then through the Beginner A group, I was in the second grade. This had the smarter boys and girls. Harry Isaac was there, too. I later married his sister, Lupita. Most of us were the same age, size, and height, but there were also some younger boys.

Our teacher, Ms. Handly, was very strict about our getting assignments done and turned in. She was mean and tirelessly enforced English-only, saying, "No Navajo, no Indian, no, no, no." Fortunately by then I was able to speak more words, but now we had to learn subjects. I ended up staying after school a lot. We were given tests every week. When it came close to exam time everyone was studying where there was light. Sometimes we stayed up at night to study in the washroom. I was sad and suffered greatly because I could not respond or ask questions about what I wanted to learn. My first year I was very scared; the boys often told lies about me, saying that I was talking Navajo, so I received punishment many times although innocent. That is how I began my schooling. I used to have friends that I hung out with and asked questions in Navajo on how to say certain things and they would teach me. There were others who told on me saying that I was speaking Navajo when they were nowhere in sight. The younger ones would get in small groups and tell lies on me about speaking Navajo while at the same time there were bullies in the dorm who picked on me by physically pushing me around and fist fighting.

I wanted to defend myself from them and so when school started that second year, I visited the sports coach, John Benally, and told him that I wanted to learn how to box. By that time my leg was fully healed. I joined the boxing team. John Benally, the boxing and football coach and silversmithing teacher, later became one of the original code talkers and an instructor at the Marine Communication School during the war. He helped me to become a very good boxer. I then beat up all the big boys who tried to bully me, but I never touched the little ones even though they were mean. After that no one bothered me again.

The first year was the most difficult. There were two languages available but it was very hard to speak only one and try to learn in it and so I devised a plan. Even though I was always hungry because we never received enough food, I saved the occasional apples, oranges, cookies, and cake and hid them in my pockets. We were always hungry for those kinds of sweets so whenever we had them, especially cookies, I paid the older boys, who were often bullies, to teach me English. I went with them on field trips, where they tutored me for long lengths of time. Sam Davis from Shonto became a friend as well as my tutor. When we were together I asked questions in Navajo about how to say certain things then he would teach me and I paid in cookies or apples. Whenever I watched him eat, I wished I was eating them instead of him, but that was his price for teaching me. I learned a lot of English.

I eventually started getting used to school life. In the morning the bell rang for us to get out of bed and wash in a hurry. Then we lined up for inspection.

Navajo students outside of the Tuba City Boarding School, 1919. The strict discipline administered by school authorities did not seem to bother Samuel as much as did the antics of his fellow classmates. It was in this crucible, however, that learning English became a major goal. (Photograph from Warren family photos, Northern Arizona University, Cline Library)

On school days we wore nice clothes and marched everywhere counting one, two, three, four. We made our beds, and the captains inspected our work. If they were not well-made, they stripped them and messed everything up so we had to do it over again. It never bothered me because I had to do what they told me, otherwise I would get more punishment. By this time I wanted to learn these things, take care of myself, and look good. This is how I began to feel, not wanting to make a mistake in my personal, outward appearance.

In Ms. Hanley's class we took spelling tests where I learned how to spell the words I was now speaking. She gave rewards of a pencil for making 100 percent on the test; this was at a time when pencils were scarce, so I was happy when I earned one. I always wanted to write well. There was a boy named Willie Roy who was very artistic and had the best penmanship. He showed me how to write nicely, and I learned quickly from him. After we left school I heard he had an art studio in Los Angeles but later died.

In the morning we went to classes, and in the afternoon we were taught trades so we could work after we graduated from school. I chose bakery and cooking. By the time I completed my second year, I had gotten used to the way the school did things. I stayed in the small boys' side and went to class with them for three years. The last two years I went on the large boys' side and finished school. I really did my best because I wanted to learn. I liked the large boys' side because we could speak Navajo and didn't get punished for it. That place was not strict at all. The boys even made coffee that they bought with their own money. I did not have any money, which made it hard. One of the teachers owned a large garden and farm, and he hired school children to work on it. This farm had chickens and pigs and lots of corn for their feed. After school some of the boys stole, roasted, and ate some of that corn, but I worked there and was happy to earn money—five dollars a month—which made me very proud. I also got involved in sports like basketball but was afraid to participate in football. So this daily routine kept us busy, but at times I was homesick for my mother and wished I could see her. Especially at night after I went to bed, I would get lonesome and missed her so much. Still, I began to like school.

I spent five years there and made it to the seventh grade. When summer arrived we were hauled home on a truck, and later a bus, with our few clothes in a cardboard box. When my mother first saw me as I arrived she would call me "My Baby," and I loved it. I was so happy to be home, to herd sheep, and work in the cornfield. Still, I had grown to like school, learning, and my teachers as well as the idea they shared that I would have a good life, a house, and a car. Officials also told my mother that she would be paid and have a house built for her. My older sister had not gone to school and remained home with my mother to herd sheep and later went to stay with our maternal grandmother, Asdzáán Hasbídí (Mourning Dove Woman), living at Pigeon Spring (Hasbídí Tó) in Monument Valley. My grandmother wanted her help so took her back with her, leaving just my stepfather and mother to herd. Little wonder my mother was so happy to see me. I worked on our wagon, hauled wood with my stepfather to the Wetherill Trading Post, and when we talked with the white men, I could communicate in simple English sentences. They wanted to know how I was doing in school and how I liked it. I told them I was doing well and how naughty the boys were. They were happy to hear that I liked it.

When I returned home, I also returned to traditional Navajo teachings and ceremonies. My mother noticed that I no longer prayed with corn pollen, and although she understood that I was not allowed to do that at school, she started to teach me again. She was the only one who made prayer ceremonies for me while I was at school, but all I could do while I was there was to pray silently in the way my mother had taught me according to Navajo tradition. She believed in her prayers; they were sacred words from the Blessing Way.[4] She would say, "Peace and harmony will be in front, behind, below, above, and all around you." She prayed for my protection and made medicine for me. These prayers were sacred to me also.

I listened to many of her stories. She knew and told many like Hataa' Baazhní'áázh (Journey to the Father) with spiritual feelings and understanding. It was not just a story to her, but a teaching that for some people is very difficult to understand and remember. Even medicine men today do not know the full length of it. I used to ask her many questions—about the characters and where it happened. She explained the meaning of its different parts and how the Twins were born in a sacred, holy way. I now compare it with the birth of Jesus Christ. Everything that is harmful leads to death before one's time. Each of us has a spirit or soul that needs to be taken care of, otherwise we get sick. Like a car when the battery runs down, our body has a heart, organs, and blood vessels so that when we stop doing what we should every day, that is the end. The elements of life—water, sunlight, wind, and earth—take care of our spirit.[5] Water is first in the elements of life and is very sacred. Fire is next, even though fire was used in making mountains that were cooled off with water. Mother Earth was then planted with all kinds of different seeds before water came down as rain and things began to grow. From some of the plants came fruit, then animals, including livestock. These are teachings from a truly traditional medicine man as shared by my mother, but as I grew up there were no male role models, not one man to personally teach me.

In the story of the Twins, the brothers, Monster Slayer and Born for Water, were born in the holy way. They showed us the way to avoid bad and evil things in their journey when they returned to their Father and were rewarded for their efforts. Today there is so much death caused by evil that the good teachings from the story are no longer being taught. Sometimes people add their own version to it, changing the intent and lessons from the narrative. Mother used to say that if this keeps happening, the people will have no more honor in life or for each other. All of these stories have strong teachings because they have spirits.[6] I have often wondered what could be done to share with our young people the true ways that these stories teach, but I am not sure what to do.

During this time I also learned of a variety of things ranging from other religious beliefs to trades. For instance I went to a church run by a husband and wife whose last name was McGaffin. They traveled around Monument Valley picking up people for church then conducted services in Navajo. From this I learned of Christianity. I also tried the peyote religion, became a member and still am, but I only use peyote when conducting a ceremony for someone.[7] This is also true of crystal gazing used for healing because it is sacred and so I use this power only when I feel that it is right.[8] During the summers, once I was older, I worked for a dollar a day in the Civilian Conservation Corp (CCC) after it moved into Monument Valley during the Great Depression. One time I earned eighty dollars, which I thought was a lot of money. I also learned how to buy things on credit and began ordering clothes like pants and shirts from the J.C. Penny catalog. Next I assisted Neal Bradley, who owned a truck, hauling coal and supplies for the store. He drove, and I went along with him many times. That is how I spent my summers, learning a lot of things.

For five years I went to school. I remember in the seventh grade I was playing basketball when a bunch of boys came running out of the dorms to us. They were excited and told us about the news on the radio saying that the Japanese had attacked Pearl Harbor and declared war on the United States. They were saying, "There's a war going on. There's a war going on." We all stopped playing and ran inside to listen. There was no television at the time; we turned up the radio and listened to the news, which also mentioned that the country needed young men to enlist. Several of the older boys volunteered for the various services not long after that. About that same time while I was away at school, a man from the agency, Hugh Burn, visited my home in Monument Valley to learn when I was going to be eighteen years old because the military was looking for young men to become soldiers. Mother did not mean to tell him but let slip that I was going to be that age on June 2. She quickly said that she was not sure about the day, but it was too late.

That spring two white men visited our home. Mother told them that I was needed in Kayenta to work and help with chores more than in the military, but they would not listen. "He's the only one I've got to help me with the sheep and horses." She also told them that I was going to train to become a traditional medicine man, but they did not seem to care. One of the officers said that I was needed to help fight in the war, that I was old enough to go, and that I would receive a letter in the mail as to what I should do. After trying to talk them out of taking me, she realized it was impossible so gave her approval for me to join the service. I now worried about my mother and older sister, wondering what was going to happen to them without me being around to help.

That spring when I turned eighteen, I worked at my mother's and stepfather's place hauling wood, caring for the horses and sheep, and working in the cornfields. During the summer I heard that my biological father, a medicine man, was singing and praying around the Oljato area and that the last day of the ceremony was in one day. So I saddled my horse and headed there for a visit since by this time mother let me go wherever I wanted. I got to the ceremonial site around sundown as my father performed the last night of a four-day chant for Hastiin Tso's (Big Man's) daughter. There were at least twelve men and six women in the hogan when I entered. The men sat on the south side and women on the north, so I began shaking hands with the people going around clockwise. My father called me Shi awéé (my baby) and told the people that I was his son. He explained that most of those attending lived around the Oljato area and were my relatives by clan. Soon the hosts of the ceremony brought in food, which I really enjoyed because I was so hungry and tired. After the meal the men and women told jokes and teased each other by making fun of their in-laws or by teasing each other about their cousins.

There was also a sweat hogan where I was able to ask my father some questions. One thing I wanted to know was where he had gotten his English name, Billy Holiday. He said that it came from my maternal grandfather Tom Holiday, or Man with an Aching Stomach (Hastiin Tsą́'dinihii). When Tom was a young man hunting rabbits, something frightened his horse that reared up, throwing him against a fence and cutting him along his belly on a post when he fell. It was a serious injury. Prayers, ceremonies, herbal dressings, and potions eventually healed his stomach leaving only a scar. His brothers, grandfathers, and uncles gave him a name that teased him for the scar and is loosely translated as "Boy with Belly Pain." When he got older and became a medicine man his name changed to Man with an Aching Stomach to reflect his age.

Later when Tom Holiday became a teenager, he and a friend were looking for stray horses in Monument Valley. They heard noises around Sand Spring near Totem Pole Rock. When they investigated they found white men at the

Tom Holiday, or Aching Stomach (Tsą'dinihii), sits before a sand painting of Monster Slayer. Samuel's paternal grandfather, this powerful medicine man was highly respected for his healing ability and traditional knowledge. (Photograph courtesy of Utah State Historical Society)

watering hole. They were lost Mormons who thought that they had no way out of this valley surrounded by canyon walls. The white men signaled for the Navajos to come over, and even though Aching Stomach and his friend did not know any English, they used hand signals and motions to communicate. The Indians soon realized what had happened. The Mormons had become lost while following a wrong trail to Salt Lake City. Most Navajos knew where this city was and so could show them the way. Aching Stomach put the Mormons back on the trail, went home and loaded his blanket, then assisted with their crossing the San Juan River and the travel beyond.

As the party started through the canyons, the Mormons wanted to know my grandfather's name. They would say theirs as they pointed to each other, "This is John, this is Bill," then signal to him to tell his. He said, "Tsą'dinihii," but they could not pronounce it so decided, "Let's give him a simple name. Tom, you're Tom," they said, and it caught on fast. While traveling, Tom's job was to let the horses out to graze in the evening, retrieve them in the morning, and saddle them for the day's ride. The party had a wagon used mostly for hauling supplies, but it fell apart and so they left it alongside the trail. Afterwards, they used only horses to carry loads. Somewhere near present-day Moab, Utah, they found many trails that were cleared of rocks with trees axed out of the way. They had reached the main trail to Salt Lake at the base of the La Sal Mountains (Dził Ashdlaii, Five Mountains) near Moab. Before separating, the grateful Mormons made a special dinner with lots of food for Tom to thank him for bringing them back to the trail and gave him a special paper. "Carry this with you. It has your name," they told him. "And for helping us along the way and bringing us back to the trail, your last name we will give you will be Holiday. That is a special name." This is how he received the name of Tom Holiday. That is the way it is told.

Also at this ceremony where my father was conducting was an important man named John Stanley. He worked as the livestock branding inspector, which would be called today a grazing committeeman. Everyone listened to what he had to say. He addressed the people, telling them that he had been around to the different areas and warning that because of the war a lot of the young Navajo men were being drafted and that some were even volunteering. There would be a lot of jobs for the older people; even the boys who signed up but failed for the military would have good employment. He talked about how the Japanese would next attack the continental United States, how many men had already enlisted, and how a boy I knew from Dennehotso had been killed in action.

After listening to the older men talk about this war, I decided to enlist in the military with the recruiter in Kayenta. This man told us that those who volunteered would have it easier than the ones drafted because of preferential treatment. The government would see to it that we were cared for even after we got out of the military by receiving money every month and that while we were enlisted, the armed forces would pay our mothers and fathers in war bonds. He even said that we would get homes with running water and electricity. I was excited about all the good things that I would receive, especially the part about having a house with indoor utilities like there was at the boarding school. My mother would not have to bring in wood or water. I knew enough English by then to tell the recruiter, "I want to volunteer" then registered at his office thinking about all the promises made. The man told me I would not have to worry about transportation or meals when it came time for me to go and that I was to report to his office every Wednesday to let him know where I was living. My mother was very sad when I told her that I could be called to go into the army at any time.

That summer I stayed around home helping my parents with farming and caring for the livestock. In the fall I did not go back to school but spent time working in the Kayenta area for the CCC. Most of the work was done with shovels and wheelbarrows. I was hired by a man named Weston Mark, who later became a range rider after the CCC work ended. Because I had learned to be a baker and cook while in school, I now also worked as a cook's helper for a dollar a day. The amount does not sound like much, but groceries at the store were cheap so I still had money at the end of a month.

One day a man and woman came to our hogan looking for people who wanted to work on the railroads, at ammunition depots, or at shipyards or go to trade schools. They were recruiting in the Kayenta area for a vocational education program and said that if I were interested in going a truck would pick me up within a week. This couple was representing a trade school operated by the government in Provo, Utah, where it made things for the military. They told of the different occupations that I could learn, such as cabinet maker for radios used in the military or a mechanic or welder. I wanted to go so the man wrote a note for me to take to a Mr. [Edwin Z.] Black in Blanding, Utah. From there I would be taken to Provo to attend the school called NYA.[9]

I agreed to take this training even though I had never been to that city. Willie Weaver, my friend from boarding school, was already in Blanding working in the fields and wrote a letter to me. I caught a truck hauling uranium ore to Blanding and arrived in the evening. It was dark and chilly in a town crisscrossed with all dirt roads and not many buildings. I stood there with a suitcase full of clothing and watched the lights come on in this unfamiliar place. After asking around for Willie, who no one knew, I found a nearby ravine, put on all of my clothes to keep warm, and crawled into my sleeping bag. The next morning I was very hungry so went to a restaurant where I saw my first menu. With the little money I had, I ordered pancakes for twenty cents—my first meal in a café—then went looking for Willie. There was a corner store where itinerant workers gathered each day to be taken to their job sites. Some labored in vegetable fields, others for farmers, others as sheep herders, while others chopped wood. I asked a white man if he knew where Willie Weaver was working and he told me that he was staying in the workers' shack. It was still early in the morning when I found him, but he got up and we walked to the store to find that most of the workers had already gone to their job sites. Some white men asked if we were looking for employment, we told them we were, so they put us to work by a store hauling dirt in a wheelbarrow. We made adobe blocks, mixing dirt, straw, and water with our feet before shoveling it into square wooden forms.

For about a month we worked there and earned seven dollars each. Then I told Willie about the trade school in Provo; he was interested, and so we both caught a ride one night on a lumber truck. Willie sat in the cab with the driver and I sat on the lumber in the back, nearly freezing to death. We did not arrive in Provo until noon the next day, found the school, and saw all of the students: Japanese, blacks, Mexicans, and a lot of whites. They were learning how to weld, perform auto repairs, build boxes for radios, and work in basic carpentry.

There were many young people of different ethnic backgrounds there. I was assigned a room with four other men: a Navajo, two whites, and a Japanese American. The next morning a clerk wrote down my name and address then took me to a big room divided into compartments where there were representatives of all of the different occupations. We were to learn these trades so that we could help in the shipyards or wherever we were needed to assist the war effort. I selected woodworking and went quickly through the various courses all the way up to construction. Usually we were building cabinets and frames for radios using the woodworking machines, which would be helpful in later years. The job was fairly easy because everything was already drawn in patterns. The radios fit together perfectly in the cabinets every time before being shipped off to Los Angles, California. I also worked in food preparation classes and in the bakery, since I had learned those trades while in boarding school. I really liked this training and its instructors and found the students friendly.

One day the clerk handed me a letter from the U.S. government recruiting office in Flagstaff informing me to report immediately to Phoenix for a physical examination. That same evening I bought my ticket and boarded a bus in Provo bound for Flagstaff. On board there were mostly white people—I was the only brown person there. They were making lots of noise screaming

Philip Johnston (*right*) and two marine recruiters working on the reservation, 1942. The war effort encouraged recruitment for both military and civilian employees, which for the Navajo, drew them off the reservation and into the dominant culture's workforce. (Photograph from Philip Johnston, Northern Arizona University, Cline Library)

and yelling. As a Navajo, I felt alone. Someone asked me where I was going and I replied into the military. We made a rest stop near a place called Cedar Ridge where there were a lot of red rocks. The day was just beginning so people walked around admiring the sunrise over the sandstone formations. Then somebody yelled excitedly, "What's that?" I looked to where they were pointing and saw a Navajo man emerging from his home. "A wild caveman just came out of that hole," they were saying. I noticed that he had emerged from a hogan covered with red dirt, but to the white men it looked like rocks except it had a doorway. To those on the bus, it appeared the Navajo man came out of this hole and so called him a caveman. I felt very embarrassed so did not say much for the rest of the trip to Flagstaff.

Once I arrived there, I met Ned Hataałii, who had been a captain in the Tuba City School with me and would later become the president of Navajo Community College. He, too, had received a letter to report to Flagstaff, and so we both rode on the bus headed for Gallup. While we were loading up, there was a group of drunk Navajos from the Gallup area also going to Phoenix for their examinations. They were big and loud, showing off, and picking on people while Ned and I were small and skinny and kept to ourselves. Eventually they settled down. On this part of the journey there were more Navajos and other nationalities than on the previous bus. Most of the passengers worked on the railroad and had been drinking. There were rough-looking Mexicans and white men as well as an old man who stepped off the bus and started coughing and spitting. That night we stopped at a hotel and everyone got drunk except Ned and me. He asked as we traveled which military branch—navy, army, or marines—I was going to join, with the idea that we should sign up together, but I did not yet know. Once we arrived we started our physical examination and I lined up in the marine line while Ned went into the navy one, so we never did stay together.

In Phoenix the government assigned us to rooms at a hotel, but a lot of the men set out to go drinking that night. The next morning after breakfast everyone went for their examination. Some of the men had disappeared while many of those who were there were hung-over and failed. As we randomly lined up, the doctors told us to take off all our clothes before they examined us. They looked us all over—in our ears, nose, and eyes—then told us to bend over. One of the doctors said, "I know that this is a Navajo." "How do you know?" asked another. "Because he has a sore ass." That particular doctor had examined Navajos with calloused, red butts before and had asked why they were like that. He learned that on the reservation not very many Navajos had saddles and had to ride bareback, giving them calloused butts. I was very embarrassed. Still, I passed my physical exam, boarded a train to San Diego, then took a bus to Camp Pendleton for boot camp. All of this time, I thought of my relatives and their children whom I had not seen for a long time. I wished that they knew what had happened to me.

Commentary: Worldview—Of Mothers and Monsters

Betsy Yellow, just like Changing Woman, knew that there were spies looking for those tender children, to be taken away and devoured by the white man's culture. Despite her protests, Samuel left his home for the foreign experience of boarding school, where trials and tests waited. When he and his companion Willie Weaver left that spring day in a car bound for Tuba City, it was anything but a "holy trail" traveled by the Twins. There were plenty of challenges for them to confront, but the traditional teachings used to protect and assist Navajos in the past were spurned by those trying to help and teach them now. Later, it was again Willie Weaver who accompanied Samuel on a different road, this time to Provo, that figuratively went in the same direction—instruction for and assimilation into another aspect of the white man's world. Shortly, he would travel yet another road to California to begin a foundational life experience as a code talker. With each step on his journey, there were forces pulling him away from the tradition and safety provided by Navajo culture.

One of the most fundamental changes in his life was the direct assault on the Navajo language, provided by the Holy People as a means by which the Earth Surface People would be known and were to communicate with those not seen. The emphasis Samuel places on his desire to learn English is counterbalanced with the crude enforcement of this wish by boarding school employees who did everything they could to wipe out any "Indianness," especially Navajo language and culture. Later Samuel points to the irony, as do many other code talkers in their accounts, that at first the government tried to remove the Navajo language but eventually would depend upon it as it became increasingly crucial on battlefields in the Pacific. At this point, it is important to understand how white culture viewed the language and how different it was in function and form from Navajo cultural beliefs and practices embedded within.

Anthropologists and linguists classify the Navajo language as part of a large group of speakers belonging to the Athabaskan, or Athapaskan, language family. There are three major divisions of this family: the Pacific Coastal, located in California and Oregon, with eight different tribal entities; the Northern group found in western Canada and the interior of Alaska and composed of twenty-three different branches; and the Apachean in the Southwest, consisting of Navajo, Western Apache, Chiricahua, Mescalero, Jicarilla, Lipan, and Kiowa-Apache.[10] Other Atahabaskan speakers live in Siberia, sharing with all a common ancestral prototype. For the Navajo with their Apachean relatives, the generally accepted theory is that they began migrating along the eastern flank of the Rocky Mountains from northern Canada around 1000 A.D. and by 1500 A.D. were unequivocally established in today's Southwest. Earliest physical remains definitely identified as Navajo and dating to the late fifteenth century are found in the Navajo Reservoir—Gobernador—Largo Canyon area of southern Colorado and northern New Mexico, a region generally accepted by Navajos as Dinétah (Among the People), their homeland and place of emergence from the worlds beneath.[11] Some historians and archaeologists push the date of arrival substantially earlier—to 1300 A.D. or before—citing among other things Navajo mythology that discusses at length their interaction and clan origins with the Ancestral Puebloans (Anasazi) before these puebloan peoples abandoned the Four Corners region and moved south by that date.[12]

An outsider's analysis of the Navajo language when compared to English would point out the emphasis it places on verbs, whereas English is more noun-adjective oriented. For example, when an individual picks up an object, the size, shape, composition, and general classification of that article will influence the verb to be used in Navajo whereas in English, this type of specificity is unnecessary. Anthropologist Clyde Kluckhohn summarized what he believes to be one of the major differences between the two languages: "The general nature of the difference between Navaho thought and English thought—both as manifested in the language and also as forced by the very nature of the linguistic forms into such patterns—is that Navaho thought is prevailingly so much more specific, so much more concrete."[13] Perhaps no Anglo anthropologist/linguist understands the Navajo language better than Gary Witherspoon, who would agree with Kluckhohn's observation, adding that for just the verb "to go" there are 356,200 distinct inflected forms.[14]

From the perspective of an outsider who is comfortable with English, this type of complexity is unnecessary. Boarding schools in earlier periods of history enforced the government mandate to prepare its students for assimilation in white society, meaning that antiquated, ancestral languages like this needed to be erased so that an individual could speak English, hold a job, and subscribe to the values of a mainstream Christian America. The 1930s, however, had seen a change to this devastating policy when John Collier entered as the new commissioner of Indian Affairs (1933). His vision went in the opposite direction, celebrating with Indian people their diversity and cultural expressions, including language, while promoting self-determination for tribes. This mindset had obviously not trickled down to the staff in the Tuba City Boarding School, who subscribed to the old philosophy. For Samuel, anything that smacked of Navajo was to be erased.

What, then, was the boarding school trying to remove? An explanation of the Navajo language from fluent speakers' perspective provides a glimpse at a very different worldview and means of expression. Much of what follows is derived from Witherspoon's groundbreaking analysis of the Navajo language. One of his basic premises is that "Knowledge is the awareness of symbol, thought is the organization of symbol, speech is the externalization of symbol, and compulsion is the realization of symbol. Symbol is word, and word is the means by which substance is organized."[15] To understand this complex statement, one must start where all Navajo explanations begin, with the Creation.

Navajo teachings say that the People emerged into this, the Fifth, or Glittering, World from four worlds beneath this one. Each of the previous spheres had a color (black, blue, yellow, and white) and a name: First, Second, Third, and Fourth Language, each of which had three subdivisions of speech, making a total of twelve language levels in all. Each level had its own forms of communication, each went from a simpler to more complex pattern, as did the forms of the inhabitants in each world: insects, animals, and Holy People. Once these beings arrived in today's world, First Man ordered a sweat lodge to be built large enough to hold the Holy People to include First Woman, First Boy, and First Girl and others to help plan for the future. Coyote, the trickster, remained on the edge by the door and did not participate until much of the thinking was finished and patterns for this world were established. The seasons of the year, phases of plant growth and animal life, forms of precipitation, heavenly bodies, illness and cures, and every other aspect by which the Earth Surface people should live were part of this plan.[16]

While specifics vary in different versions of this teaching—colors of the worlds, role of Coyote and other participants, and so forth, because of an oral tradition—all agree that there was a definite sequence within the process that moved from awareness to thought to word to reality or creation. The end result was, according to Gladys Reichard, a leading scholar in Navajo studies, a "Navajo dogma [that] connects all things, natural and experienced, from man's skeleton to universal destiny, which encompasses even inconceivable space, in a closely interlocked unity which omits nothing, no matter how small or how stupendous."[17] In simpler terms, everything is connected because the Holy People designed it that way, the primary means of which was through language. Song and prayer, preceded by thought, created all.

Everything in the Navajo universe—both animate and inanimate—has an inner spirit. Thus things like the earth and sky, lightning and thunder, rocks and trees have an inner form roughly glossed as "animate being that lies within" (bii'gistíín). Humans also have an inner form known as "in-standing wind soul" (níłch'í bii'siziinii), which enters the body at birth, leaves at death, and during life controls a person's thoughts and actions, giving rise to individual personality traits. "The capacity to think 'far ahead' and speak a language is acquired from the wind soul dispatched at birth, and it is this capacity that distinguishes humans from other animals, who have only calls and cries."[18] Thus, while everything has a spirit or soul, there are gradations in ability as to what each spirit can accomplish.

Navajo language reaches its greatest power in ritual and ceremony. Through prayer and song, thought becomes concrete, the creation of the world and the control of power are exercised, and order is achieved. In the Anglo world, with a few exceptions found in Christian dogma, words are merely a means of expression, not a way to control supernatural power. The opposite is true here. "In the Navajo view of the world, language is not a mirror of reality; reality is a mirror of language. . . . It commands, compels, organizes, transforms, and restores. It disperses evil, reverses disorder, neutralizes pain, overcomes fear, eliminates illness, relieves anxiety, and restores order, health, and well-being."[19] Conversely, language when used or directed with evil intent can create chaos and ugliness.

Power is at the foundation of both good and evil. These two qualities are inseparable for they are rooted in the same source. Like electricity, this power can be used to bless and protect the lives of others or curse and destroy those targeted for harm. Each person has within a desire for self-protection, but when this ability is taken to extremes, it can become evil and used to destroy others.[20] Language becomes the means that directs how the power is to be used. A phrase common in prayer is "the tip of my tongue. [This] symbolizes 'my speech' and means 'may I have the power to speak all necessary words of formula, prayer, and song in proper order.' By implication it means also 'may my speech be so controlled that I will not say anything not needed or use words which may attract evil or danger.'"[21] Through ritual the Holy People are compelled to participate, in either good or evil, bound by the sacredness and contractual ties of language.

In summarizing the role of language in the Navajo universe, Witherspoon returns to the previously mentioned premise of knowledge, thought, speech, and action or realization when he writes: "The Holy People first became aware of things through their symbols and then later went into the sweathouse and organized these symbols through thought processes. Next the organized symbols were spoken in prayer and sung in song. Through these songs and prayers the inner forms of things were organized and controlled; that is, they were told where to go, how to position themselves, and what functions to fulfill."[22]

A few final points. The application of these religious and theoretical beliefs is important to understand when listening to Samuel explain his life story. Starting with his language experience at school, we see an entirely different way of looking at the world now being imposed upon the belief system taught to him by his mother. While both Anglo and Navajo teachings are based on cause-and-effect relationships, there are different causes that bring about different effects or perhaps even the same effects. The gulf between the two views is as big as those found between science and religion. There are exceptions, but generally, science deals with the manipulation and control of elements and objects through reproducible laws that govern the physical world. Intangible spiritual laws have no place in theory-hypothesis explanations concerned with observable fact. To say that an experiment's outcome occurred because the Holy People willed it that way is an anathema to scientific thought. English language and the thinking behind it support this view that man is the actor who controls what occurs around him. The noun directs through the verb the action taken.

The Navajo language with its highly specialized verb orientation allows for a different type of categorizing of the human experience. The power of thought filters through every aspect of daily life—even to the point that it causes events to occur and physical change to take place. Whether a person thinks or talks about sickness and death or health and long life, it will occur.

A dramatic example of this is found in the films created by John Ford during his Monument Valley era. Many Navajo participants played the role of Indians waging war against the white man and so were "killed" many times on the set. Ford, often on the lookout for the stereotypical "Indian face" with high cheek bones, piercing eyes, and other facial features, placed certain actors in the forefront of the action, then directed they act out being killed in a final fight scene. Men like Frank and Lee Bradley, and John, Johnnie, and Jack Stanley—all from the Monument Valley-Kayenta area—played these parts. Many of them died relatively young in life, confirming to the Navajo that because they had acted out death scenes in the movies, their loss became a reality.[23]

Another important concept expressed through language is the ability to be an actor as opposed to being acted upon. Language and thought again become the important dividing line between the two. There are two different categories among animate beings, speakers and callers, which can be further divided into humans, different sized animals, insects, and plants. The rest—such as natural forces and objects as well as abstractions such as old age, hunger, and so forth—are inanimate. Each of these is ranked in such a way that something can act upon another thing of equal or lower status but not upon something in a higher order. For instance, with man on the highest scale, he can control and act upon a horse. On the other hand, if a horse kicks a person, it is because he allowed the animal to do it. The horse cannot control the man.[24]

In the following pages as Samuel tells his story, the Navajo language will prove central to his experience. Prayer becomes fundamental to his survival; at one point he declares that was all he had. It was prayer that sustained him in the intense combat—more than the bullets in his rifle. Another time he comments that the code talkers who were killed were most likely the ones who had not had the protection ceremony performed, suggesting that the power from words was absent. And when he later ponders how many enemies he had killed with his words, he is not just referring to the radio transmissions that proved so effective in defeating the Japanese. Words control and words can kill if they are used by a person who understands their power and how to apply it. Just as the Twins encountered and slew the monsters in their path with words and action, so too does Samuel use words for protection to control his physical situation. The inner peace that he attests of during frightening times is derived from his positive knowledge and view brought forth from the language and prayers he has received. Thus, "It is through language that man acquires the capacity to control the powerful beings and entities that occupy the fifth world. Without language man is greatly reduced in stature and his control of the world about him is greatly impaired. He becomes the acted upon rather than the actor, the created rather than the creator, the object rather than the subject."[25]

CHAPTER THREE

Training and Protection

Preparation for War

THE TWINS: ASSISTANCE FROM SPIDER WOMAN

They traveled rapidly on the holy trail until they spotted a plume of smoke coming from an underground chamber with a blackened ladder protruding above the surface. Peering down the hole, they saw an old woman, Grandmother Spider Woman (Na'ashjéii asdzą́ą́), sitting by a fire. Beautiful weavings and feathers hung about the room's walls. After inviting them in, she asked four times why they were traveling only to receive vague replies, indicating they had nothing better to do. Finally she said, "Perhaps you would seek your father," to which they agreed. "Ah, it is a long and dangerous way to the house of your father, the Sun." She now told them all she knew about him then filled four small bowls with white corn meal, seeds, and bee weed. Next she dropped a small turquoise bead in one for the oldest brother and a small white bead in another for the younger to give them courage in difficult times. The boys looked at what she had prepared, thinking that they would never get full from such a small amount, but as they ate the food in the bowls it replenished and by the time the Twins had finished, they were satisfied and had swallowed the turquoise and white bead.[1] She continued:

> There are many of the anáye [enemy] dwelling between here and there, and perhaps when you get there, your father may not be glad to see you, and may punish you for coming. You must pass four places of danger—the rocks that crush the traveler, the reeds that cut him to

> pieces, the cane cactuses that tear him to pieces, and the boiling sands that overwhelm him. But I shall give you something to subdue your enemies and preserve your lives.
>
> She gave them a charm called naayéé ats'os, or feather of the alien gods, which consisted of a hoop with two life-feathers (feathers plucked from a living eagle) attached and another life-feather, hyiná biltsós (hiinááh bits'os), to preserve their existence.[2] She taught them also this magic formula, which if repeated to their enemies, would subdue their anger: "Put your feet down with pollen.[3] Put your hands down with pollen. Put your head down with pollen. Then your feet are pollen; your hands are pollen; your body is pollen; your mind is pollen; your voice is pollen. The trail is beautiful. Be still."[4]

Finally she gave them secret names by which they could call each other during sacred occasions. Spider Woman felt satisfied that she had given them all that they needed to protect them on their dangerous journey to their father.[5]

POLLEN AND PRAYER

The Holy People had met often, establishing patterns, laws, and the order of songs for the Earth Surface people, but there were still questions not answered, such as how would humans live together and have peace in their life.[6] There must be a reminder, something of power to help them find long life and happiness. They held several meetings, but nothing was decided. Early one morning Changing Woman, mother of all, made her way to one of these gatherings at Blanca Peak, her dress wet with dew. As she approached, she heard a corn beetle singing and so she answered with song, found the small creature, and picked it up. From this insect she gathered the pollen and mixed it with dew before continuing on her way.

As the meeting started, Coyote, or First Scolder, in his normal hurry rushed into the group asking what was happening while trying to take charge. The Holy People were not impressed. "Do not say anything. Go away, First Scolder Coyote. You have no respect for holy things. What we are doing here is holy."[7] Undeterred, he countered by first denying the accusations then saying that he was the only one there who was wise and had the answer as to what people should live by. But it was Changing Woman who had the real answer. The Holy People turned to her to hear what she would say. Placing a basket made of the material associated with each direction—white shell, turquoise, abalone, and jet—she took white corn meal and dew then mixed yellow corn pollen with dew and proceeded to make sweet cornmeal cakes shaped in the form of humans. She sang sacred songs as she formed the material and blew on them with her breath. Talking God and Calling God assisted, blowing on the cakes, which gave them life.

The day proceeded, the figures uncovered, and three young men and three young women stepped forth. Changing Woman dressed all of them with pollen, blessed them with riches, and charged them to live on the earth. She instructed White Corn Boy, Yellow Corn Girl, Pollen Boy, Pollen Girl, Cornbeetle Boy, and Cornbeetle Girl that by doing so, this pattern of life would become permanent. Then came specific instructions:

> "You will speak for us with pollen words. You will talk for us with pollen words. You will not think evil about us, you will not speak evil about us, because I, I made you, my children, because I dressed you with corn pollen, because I dressed you with dews. I made you to be Long Life Boy and I made you Happiness Girl. I made blessing to be before you, I made blessing to be behind you, below you, above you, all around you, I made blessing to be. I made you, my children, so you will speak wisely with pollen in your mouth." [Changing Woman blessed and sang over them again before they left for the four directions. Once in position, they said:] "May we all live in peace." Saying this, they prayed for themselves. "Now you will live by that, my children," said Changing Woman. "All of your songs will end by mentioning long life. Now that is the way it will be, my children."[8]

After this the people dispersed, knowing that there was Happiness and Long Life in the four directions no matter how far they traveled.

EAGLE: THE MESSENGER

During the creation of the heavens and earth, the Creator made everything beautiful.[9] Mother Earth received the largest, most beautiful mountains. Sparkling streams of clear, sweet water cascaded over the rocks and filled lakes and ponds for the animals to drink and for the Holy People to enjoy.

Dark forests of trees, rich, lush grass, and a dress of beautiful flowers covered her nakedness. The animals were sleek, well-fed, and could not have been happier, while birds of all kinds filled the air with soft melodies and a sense of peace. Father Sky also had his beauty, with a radiant sun during the day that brought life and warmth to the earth and the soft, cool moon at night that gave a gentle glow so that creatures could find their way. The clouds provided shade and created ever-changing patterns in the sky, while bringing rain and snow to cool the earth, water the plants, and give drink to living beings. The sparkling stars at night added to this beauty as they stood in sharp contrast to the velvety black darkness when plants, animals, and Holy People rested. Both the earth and sky were things of beauty and blessing. And they knew it.

One day Mother Earth, in all her glory, told Father Sky that the Creator loved her most because she was the most beautiful and should therefore be in charge. Everything placed on her was there for her purpose and this made her important, the reason for existence. Father Sky was shocked and argued that it was his power and ability that allowed things on the earth to flourish. Where would she be if it were not for the sunshine and water to grow plants and bring life? She would be nothing but a shriveled ball of dirt. The two quarreled, each trying to prove their own self-importance but never listening to the other. Father Sky finally drew the line and threatened to withhold his power until Mother Earth recognized that he was master. Both refused to speak to each other, and any cooperation was out of the question until the other apologized.

This threw the inhabitants of earth into chaos. With no moisture to replenish life and nothing to cool the earth, the whole life cycle started to collapse. After four years Mother Earth moaned and groaned as the life ebbed from her and the land's surface with its creatures began to split, crack, and die. Her majestic mountains erupted into ugly volcanoes, the beautiful trees that had once grown straight and tall withered and fell, turning to stone (petrified wood), and the large animals—nah-ah-sheen (dinosaurs)—died, leaving behind their remains as fossils. The sweet water was now saline, poisonous gasses filled the air, fires raged, and chaos reigned. All of the creatures fought and turned the peaceful land into turmoil, while Father Sky watched his stars begin to fall and the heavens erupt with turbulence, lightning, and fierce winds. Nowhere was there peace or a refuge from the disaster.

More and more living beings died until there were only four things left: an eagle, cedar tree, mountain tobacco plant, and yucca. Each spoke to Mother Earth with the same message: "You were so beautiful at one time. Now you have turned ugly and everywhere there is chaos and destruction. All of your charm is gone. Why don't you plead with Father Sky and restore harmony between yourself and the heavens. Beg him to return with peace and prosperity." They pleaded and pleaded until finally she agreed to apologize. But his back was turned so that he could not hear the message. Somehow he needed to learn of the change. Eagle volunteered to be the messenger and approach the Holy Being. Flapping his large wings he began his ascent, circling, circling, circling upward in a spiral until he was no longer in sight. For four days those on the earth waited and wondered what the answer would be until in the distance a large cloud, heavy with rain, appeared to cool Mother Earth and restore life. Father Sky had accepted the apology and allowed Eagle to bring back this token of peace, forgiveness, and restoration.

In order to avoid this type of conflict from ever happening again, the two agreed that everything on the earth would be either male or female, bringing equality and balance to all that happened. There would be male and female mountains, rivers, trees, and clouds. A soft gentle rain is female, a hard driving rain is male. Jagged powerful lightning is male, sheet lightning female; all animals and humans are either one or the other; and even a person's body, regardless of sex, has both a male and female part as token of this agreement. Man and woman are equal but have different qualities and responsibilities. All is well, all is beautiful, all is balanced (hozhǫ́ na ha skleen). Mother Earth and Father Sky were once again in harmony, a harmony that remains to this day.

As for Eagle, he is the greatest of all birds and is still the messenger between earth and sky. He carries the prayers for those below to the one above and so his feather is a symbol and holds the power of connecting human prayer to the Holy People and the Creator. He is the only bird that has this power. He also is the only one who can choose if he wants to go through a process of regrowth to become young again. This is a painful procedure where the bird almost dies in order to get new claws, beak, and feathers as a part of the rejuvenation and restoration. Still, it is a very painful experience that the eagle may choose not to go through. Regardless of how old or young, every eagle is a symbol of prayer.

SAMUEL: SECURING SAFETY

Following the different physical examinations, the government loaded us on a train for San Diego, California, for Marine Corps boot camp at Coronado. From the train we took a bus where everyone on board was talking loudly and acting big. We thought we were really something, behaving proudly and bossy until we unloaded and our big, muscular instructors arrived. They were not laughing or smiling but looked mad and started yelling and cussing: "Line up, you shit birds!" We formed ranks then marched to the barbershop for a haircut. The drill instructor (DI) kept yelling at us even as the barber shaved off our hair, which turned my head white. They did not want anything left on anybody or else we were considered wild. Then they marched us to a place, had us take off all our civilian clothes, and issued uniforms. Mine were baggy. The helmets we received were round and very hard so that when we made a mistake the DI banged on it, making an irritatingly loud noise. Next we went into another room where we were issued boots and shoes, bedding, sheets, and blankets, which we brought to our tent. Then we received shots as each corpsman poked us quickly and roughly with needles, giving two or three shots in both arms at once. Our arms became really sore from all of these shots. Some of the recruits passed out, but the DIs showed no mercy. While we were still sore, we also had to qualify in swimming. I was with a Navajo friend who did not pass his test and required an additional two weeks to learn. I qualified with everything the first time and went through boot camp like that. But we were no longer individuals in control of our lives but robots who did what the instructors told us.

Day after day, we drilled. Every morning started with a DI coming by the door and saying only one time, "Get up!" We all had to jump out of bed, but if anyone remained lying there, the DI poured water on him. Each recruit had a bucket of water by his bunk for that purpose. Next we lined up and marched for about an hour. I can still hear the DI counting, "Hup, two, three, four." Then there was the obstacle course where we had to swing across a deep muddy puddle, climb over a high wall, and catch another rope to swing over more mud. Another wall was not too high, but after we climbed it, we had to jump off halfway down. The course was so difficult that a lot of the recruits could barely complete it and had to be beaten to finish. For a rest we would take our rifles apart, clean them, then

Future code talkers marching at the Navajo Communication School Training Center, Camp Pendleton, California, 1943. For some marines like Samuel, who had come from a background of hard work and exercise, the physical aspect of training was easy. Others found it grueling, suffering through days of endless drilling. (Photograph courtesy of the U.S. Marine Corps)

run the obstacle course again over poles, platforms, and walls, and continue with more physical conditioning exercises. Some of the men had flat feet that turned black from all of the use, which made it difficult to heal because of all the running and walking that kept us constantly moving. I would hear them moaning and crying at night in their bunks and felt sorry for them, because they had not come from demanding physical labor jobs like I had.

The boys who had been brought up on farms or the open range as cattlemen or in the woods as lumberjacks had a much easier time because they had physically worked hard. They had no problem with the obstacle course and other activities. For me it was relatively easy. While the other marines were suffering from fatigue and sore, aching muscles it did not bother me at all. I was in good physical condition from riding horses, running after the sheep, hauling and chopping wood, lifting barrels full of water, boxing, and playing a lot of basketball before boot camp. All the prayers, meditation, and physical labor prepared me for what I encountered and made it easy. After about two or three months of this physical training, we began target practice, where I earned marksman and, later in advanced training, expert with rifle and pistol.

At the end of boot camp there was a boxing match held between my platoon and the other platoons. Our instructors asked who knew how to box, and for some reason, without realizing what I was getting myself into, I raised my hand along with a couple of Mexican fighters who were good. They each won their match. Someone said that if I volunteered I would fight a professional boxer so they hoped I was good. When it was my turn, the fight managers put me against a white man who was a little shorter than me but a good fighter. I tried to be quick with my jabs, and so most of the time he missed me. At the end of the fight we both won $10, which is like $50 today and were told that we were even in our scores. Shortly after this my platoon graduated and went on for advanced training at Camp Pendleton.

To me, the military was much easier than BIA school because I did not have to worry about getting along with others; I was able to do the obstacle course easily as well as qualify with weapons and swimming without any problems. It was not difficult for me, whereas in school I had to deal with bullies who took away part of my lunch, forcing me to survive on what little was left to eat. As I went through this training and got ready to go to war, I was not frightened but ready to fight for my country. When my ancestors went on the Long Walk, many suffered and died, going far beyond what I was facing in preparation for this war. I believed that the Holy People guarded me, and my mother's prayers gave me strength to carry on. These were my real weapons to fight with.

I knew in my heart I would do my best and return to my mother, which I told her when she was very sad, crying even as I tried to comfort her. I told myself when I left that I would win using the modern weapons given to me in honor of my ancestors who suffered first. I did not start thinking about these things until I heard that the Japanese had declared war on the United States. That was when I thought of my ancestors who suffered on the Long Walk like my grandmother Asdzáán Bikiní, who told me stories about it and then in later life started reliving what she had gone through. She imagined hearing soldiers riding toward her, the clanging of their stirrups, and the earth vibrating with horses trying to run her down. She was severely traumatized and suffered mentally from these nightmares. I felt like I was doing a service for her suffering.

My family had given me objects to act as my shield of protection, making me strong and willing to fight for my mother and country. All that I had with me at this time were my memories and prayers, but later I received an eagle feather and corn pollen. When I joined the marines I often thought of my mother and heard her singing the protection songs and saying prayers, which gave me a lot of courage. I believed it and never forgot the sacredness of it. Having them in my head made me belong to these prayers. When she sent me away with tears in her eyes, she told me that the Holy People would watch over and protect me, and I told her that I would be kept safe and come home alive, but it was still hard to see her cry.

Sometimes I think of how strong and resilient my ancestors were to have traveled many miles for days at a time during the Long Walk, suffering from hunger, brutality, and poor living conditions. Many died, but others came home. I wanted to somehow pay them back for their sacrifice and fight with the modern weapons I was now given but this time win against the enemy. I was determined not to lose, and that is why I was not lazy but gave all my energy to learning while knowing I was shielded by my prayers and faith in the Navajo way.

After I completed boot camp, the marines assigned me to the communications school at Camp Pendleton near Oceanside, California. When I arrived I was glad to see John Benally, my former teacher in boarding school. He had been with the first group of Navajos recruited as code talkers, helped design the first code, and was now an instructor along with three other Navajo men I did not know. There were initially twenty-nine men, such as Paul Begay and King Mike from the Monument Valley area, as well as others from Tuba City, Gallup, and Fort Defiance who developed the code.[10] I was in a later group. I was told that a person had to have graduated from eighth grade in order to be selected. The men in this first group had that type of education and so designed and built the code, doing a good job. They were very intelligent in white men's education and Navajo traditional ways. The ones from Gallup and the Fort Defiance region seemed to have an advantage of the best eighth-grade education because the early white settlements were strong in those areas. King Mike and I from Kayenta did not have that advantage so were a little behind.

Shortly after I arrived I reported to an officer. "I guess you know the reason for coming here," he said to me, taking out a paper. "You will be learning to use the Navajo language in a different way. There are a lot of Navajos here in school. They are doing regular Marine Corps training, the same as other marines, but are also learning code. Some of them catch on fast. The reason to learn this use of your language is that the code cannot be broken by the Japanese. You will learn many words that pertain to military equipment and military terms, like airplanes and other things used in war. That is what you will be learning. This is a secret weapon," he told me, "so you have to be very careful with it too."

He explained how some Japanese had come to the United States and gone to school at our universities and studied American ways and language then took it back with them to Japan, using this knowledge during the war to break our codes. They knew the U.S. military could not hide anything from them because of their understanding of English. They understood everything and that was probably why Pearl Harbor had been attacked. The Japanese knew the right time to strike and how we would respond. So the U.S. military was trying to find new codes for sending messages.

At this time there was a white man named Philip Johnston whose parents as missionaries had lived on Navajo land when he was young.[11] As a little boy he did not have any white playmates and so played with Navajo boys. He eventually traveled all over the reservation, even going to ceremonies and dances; soon he learned our language fluently as well as Navajo ways and customs. That was how he was raised. When his parents moved away from the reservation, he went to school and became an engineer, living in Los Angeles when the war started. Johnston heard how the military was looking for a new code and so thought of using the Navajo language to encrypt messages. He went to see some Marine Corps generals, told them about the Navajo language, and after some successful tests, the marines organized the first group of Navajos as code talkers. They recruited men who passed the entrance test.

Then the officer interviewing me said, "So that's why you are here. This is a new secret weapon and is very unusual. The Marine Corps is going to use the Navajo language and it needs you. We have radios that you can learn to transmit on as you use this code." He also told me that there would be a couple of code talkers assigned to each battalion. One would work on the front line while the other received messages back in the battalion. Then we would alternate. While I was mastering the code, I also had jungle training and learned how to perform minor repairs on radios.

The actual training for the code took place with some of the original twenty-nine code talkers. These men were highly educated and also knew a lot about Navajo tradition and culture. I was intimidated by their great command of the English language and felt like I did not know very much and was still learning, but I nevertheless felt like a man. I, too, had been raised in the traditional culture and used the language just like they had and so on that part I felt equal. I was born into it, taught it, and lived it all my life, but I did regret that I was not as highly educated in the white man's way as the marines who came from the Gallup region. Those of us from the Monument Valley area had lived in humble circumstances with relatively little formal schooling, whereas the highly educated marines read well and that is why they were selected to teach. I got to know these code talkers, who were a lot older than me, but they kept mostly to themselves. Surprisingly, they were not willing to share any of their knowledge with us as to how to learn something the easy way.

In my group we had two Navajo instructors, John Benally and Johnny Toledo, assigned to teach the new recruits the code. The first thing I learned was that I had to treat this knowledge as highly secret. We were reminded of this every day. Even with other marines we were told not to share any part of what we were learning or doing. Our classroom was in an isolated area with heavy metal doors. As soon as we entered, the doors closed. Our Navajo teachers stood in front of the room, opened their books, and went through each word, emphasizing and covering every bit of it. The first column in our book was the English word as I would receive it in a transmission but then I had to know what to do with it. The second column was in the Navajo language which I would transmit. That was the secret weapon. The last or third column was the translation of the Navajo word that gave additional information. We were told never to talk about this information and that if we did, we would be taken out of the program and put in isolation in something like a dungeon or prison and have no outside contact of any kind. There we would probably suffer all kinds of hardships and not be released until the end of the war. That got me really scared because I wanted to go home whenever I could, even before the end of the war.

We worked in groups and did much of this training orally, but if a person did not understand something, he had to speak up and ask for it to be repeated.

It was essential for everyone to understand the code. If the spelling was not correct then the person had to go through the entire code from beginning to end until he had it right. For me as a young man, learning the code was not difficult while the written Navajo was easy to understand because I already knew the interpretation of it. There were capital letters like *WAR* we had to keep lined up as we wrote them. Even today as I write a letter *A*, I do it as a capital letter just as I had practiced and practiced when I was learning it. It was difficult at first but became easier as I became more familiar with English. I memorized all the code words, was able to write them down (and there were a lot), and passed my tests successfully on time.[12]

The type of question we would have to translate and transmit might be something like, "Japanese artillery is firing," written on paper, sent, and then I would sit down, translate it, then write it down as I received it on my end of the communication. Or I might be asked in Navajo for things that are needed, such as water or ammunition. So I translated the message from Navajo to written English. We worked in pairs, stayed in sight of each other at all times, and got used to how each of us operated. After a while it became easy. I finished my training and passed my test on the date we were supposed to have it completed; our instructors told us that we had done a good job.

It took about three months to become a Navajo code talker. The white platoon I was in was not aware that I was being trained as a code talker; only the radio men knew. Our assignment and language was top secret so the other marines did not question but only respected us and we respected them. There were other Navajos going through the same training, but the only one I knew was Dan Akee, who had attended the Tuba City Boarding School and was perhaps five years my senior. His maternal clan was Kiiyaa'aanii (Towering House) so we called each other "grandfather" and joked with each other because that was how we were related. Later I called him my hero and "shi-buddy." Like me, he practiced traditional ways and knew Navajo prayers. I do not believe he had a protection ceremony like I did, but the one that was done for me was for all servicemen, so he would be included in it. Even with the ceremony, some Navajos still died. It was nice that we ended up together in boot camp and communications school and eventually worked together in combat. One day they told us it was time to go. Dan and I were both assigned to the Fourth Marine Division, Twenty-fifth Regiment.

After our schooling we received a ten-day furlough. The night before I was to go on leave, a group of men got together to gamble. The Marine Corps did not pay a lot of money so I had about $70.00 when I entered the game, which I needed to buy a ticket for the train to Flagstaff and then pay to Frank Bradley for a ride on his mail truck which ran twice a week. I played in the evening until midnight and gambled away all of it. I heard a noise upstairs, went up there, found John Benally and borrowed two dollars from him. I returned to the game and started winning so that by morning I had $113.00. I remember that very well. That was how I was able to get on the bus to Los Angeles then catch the train to Flagstaff. I was a no-good man.

When I arrived home my mother and older sister invited my father, Billy Holiday, to come to my mother's hogan to perform a ceremony for me. He did a Prayer against Enemy (Naayéé'ii Sódizin), which combines elements from the Enemy Way and the Blessing Way. It includes protection while on the ocean, from big winds, and against all enemies. I was given an eagle feather ('ats'os) and corn pollen in a small medicine pouch at this time. Other medicine men assisted. Once I received these objects I kept them secret from others, but at times a person would see them and ask what they were. For instance, once when I was getting ready to take a shower, my pollen pouch fell out of my shirt and onto the floor. A white marine found it and wondered what it was. "What's this?" he said. "It belongs to the Chief," somebody told him. I just said it was for good luck and protection then put it back in my pocket.

The teachings behind these things are very important and are what kept me alive. They go back to the time of creation. In many respects it is like the Navajo code that I learned in the marines. One must know the story and then how to apply it, just as the Twins learned and applied that knowledge on their journey to meet their father. When you first learn the story it teaches you what you must know in your life to solve future problems. Just as I went to school after boot camp to learn the Navajo code, I already knew how to read in English and all I had to do was speak the Navajo language then I could understand what was being communicated. My mother taught me traditional ways and so by knowing the story of the Twins, I could figure out that code and its teachings, to know how to be safe and live my life in a good way. That is how the Navajos survived in battle. My protection ceremony blessed me with courage and safety before

Samuel Holiday at graduation from Navajo Communications School, Camp Pendleton, 1943. Graduates from the course had memorized the code sufficiently that even under extreme pressure, Navajo terms and military concepts were inextricably joined to provide a high degree of accuracy on the battlefield. (Photograph courtesy of Holiday family)

going to war. The stories provide a pattern of what to do, who the evil enemies are, and how to protect yourself so that they will not become strong enough to overtake and kill you.

There are many versions of the story of the Twins, and each has teachings for both adults and children. Children are holy like Monster Slayer and Born for Water, who, when they started on their adventure and left their mother, needed guidance and instruction on how to find the path to their father. As with people today, there were barriers everywhere that prevented them from growing into good, decent human beings until the obstacles were destroyed. All of the monsters that they encountered represent the distractions and evils of this life that will kill a person if he does not know how to combat them. One must have guidance to avoid these pitfalls. I heard this story as a child so I do not remember everything about it, just as with children today, who hear a serious story and act as if they were listening but pick up only part of it.

Let me give a couple of examples of how this Navajo code works. After the Twins left their mother, they arrived at the home of Grandmother Spider Woman, where they received warnings, advice, and objects to help prepare them for what they would encounter in their future. She represents wisdom for life. I do not remember the details, but she told the two boys of the many tests they would experience and how to overcome them before they could become warriors. That is like us as we struggle against many things in life before we become mature and stable. It was just like me going through boot camp, struggling but learning during different parts of the training before finishing and becoming a marine. In boot camp I learned to arm and throw explosives to destroy an enemy position. This is like the twin warriors who destroyed dangerous monsters like the Crushing Stones. We, too, must overcome things that could destroy our lives; in my case it was kill or be killed. Just as the Crushing Stones were going to smash Monster Slayer and Born for Water to pieces, preventing them from advancing on their journey, the boys were able to outsmart the rocks; they were not crushed, but passed through without getting hurt. If one thinks and does good things in life, the path will be clear. If one does bad things and has evil thoughts, his actions will lead to being crushed. This is how the story teaches us to overcome or avoid danger.

Other creatures in the story represent different dangerous encounters in our lives that destroy. For example, the Twins met 'Adah Hódziiłtáłii

(Kicks-People-Off-Rocks Monster), the one who kicked unsuspecting travelers off a cliff at Navajo Mountain when they tried to pass him. He lured Monster Slayer to him, calling him grandson. But the Holy Wind told Monster Slayer that if he did not go close to Kicking Monster, the Twin's life would be spared. Teachings like this warn of danger, like methamphetamines in today's society. If one does not listen and goes near the monster, it will take one's life. Kicking Monster would have sent Monster Slayer off the cliff to his death if he had not listened. One does not know how life will end or what bad things will attract a person. That is why prayer is there to guide so that no one will be left alone. God listens and answers prayers and is with us all the time. We have to learn these teachings.

Another monster, Naa' Yee'aghánii (Staring Eye Killer), represents all the evil that can drag one into poverty, such as gambling, prostitution, and drugs. There are evil people who stare at others with thoughts of hooking them on bad things. In Navajo the Staring Eye Killer is interpreted as a bad person who is sinful and envious. It might be when someone buys a new car and a neighbor covets it and tries to get it. There are also adulterous and womanizing men who abuse women sexually while other women become prostitutes. There are many teachings in this area, and if one knows these traditional stories it is easy to interpret them and be guided in the right direction.

People who wish to tear a person down so that they will not succeed in life can be overcome through prayers and Navajo ceremonies, but their power can only be understood by knowing these stories. From them an individual becomes strong against evil that might bewitch him. Once a person is under the influence of evil, it is difficult to escape. That is why a strong character protects one's spirit. As in the stories, life is a journey during which one finds things that are good and helpful but also that which harms. One's goal is to return to the Holy Father (HaTaa') by knowing these stories that provide safety. In the beginning the good things were put on the earth and at the same time the evil things were put here too. It is up to us to find the good and follow those teachings, the holy way. There is always a bad force working against the good force. These bad and evil forces will tie up the good and put a stop to it. There is a Navajo medicine for it called "wooltáád," which means "the unraveling."[13] When the evil force is used against a person, their strength in the traditional ways will weaken and they will lose their path. This is part of witchcraft.

The whole story of Journey to the Father has to do with the holy way and has teachings just like the stories of Jesus. He taught many lessons about our travels through life and then he left. Jesus, like the Twins, had a holy birth on this earth. It was similar to that of Monster Slayer and when they got older they both did away with evil enemies. In the Navajo way the Twins killed our enemies in war, but Jesus killed evil through words. The story of Monster Slayer and Born for Water is tied together with the story of Jesus. Their spirit and physical birth are one [the same]. The spirit inside of us takes care of us and is joined with the physical body. The spirit never sleeps, is always awake to keep us alive, while caring for the heart, the blood vessels, air, and water—everything inside of us. If it did not do this we would not know how to do anything for ourselves. Monster Slayer and Born for Water are two spiritual beings with physical bodies who are here to protect us just as is Jesus.

One does not know what kind of danger lies ahead. There may be sickness or physical harm, so there must be a plan. From these teachings one learns how to overcome or avoid danger. The most important and powerful element on our side is prayer, which should begin each day. Many people do not know these stories, even some medicine men, who tell you that they recognize there are teachings in them but do not know how to apply them in life. They do not know how to teach the Navajo Code as given by the Holy People. This is what and how my mother taught me. Other people keep it sacred and that is why some Navajos do not discuss it and keep it to themselves.

One of the main ways that the Twins stayed safe and knew what to do after they left Spider Woman's home was through communication with the Holy Wind, or Níłch'i. It was their guide who told them how to avoid being killed. Everyone should obey instructions from those who are teaching things that are good. In boot camp one listens to directions or else makes mistakes that harm. Everyone should be guided by the Holy People. There are medicine men who perform the Wind ceremony. They speak of a sacred white wind from the east, a blue wind from the south, yellow from the west, and a black wind from the north, which is the strongest one of all—very, very strong. Mother Earth controls these winds. There is also the Holy Wind, which is very strong and sacred and when part of it is made small, gives life to people and other living things from within the body. We cannot create life by ourselves without this Holy Wind, just as breathing is not in our charge.

When I was twelve or thirteen years old and in the hospital, I saw my first radio. I had never heard of it before, but I compared it to the Holy Wind that spoke to the Twins, telling them what to do as they traveled to their Father. That is what it seemed like to me. Just as the Holy Wind was a voice of warning as the Twins went through many dangers, telling them how to escape, the radio used the wind to give messages. The Twins came upon the monsters, and the Holy Wind told them what to do to avoid being killed. The radio from the box is the same as the radio that I talked into to warn soldiers of the Japanese who wanted to kill them, just as in the Twin's story. As radio operators, we did the same thing, warning others of danger. I thought that was how the spirits talked in the stories and how the holy people communicate with us. As earth goes forward with time, we make it run well with our actions. Other times we do wrong and shorten its life. A long time ago people lived in a sacred way, the holy way, but today people are taking life lightly and make fun of it (doo hashkał baa'oldah) while the sacred ceremonies are no longer holy to them.

My mother called the Holy Wind the Little Wind by which the Holy Beings talked to people. Elders would say, "This is what I was told" or "Something told me this," meaning the spirit talked to them. These were messages from the Holy One. If a person is serious about keeping things holy and sacred, the Holy People will work with you. Traditional Navajo ceremonies work with God. As you know the Holy People are a working force. The Sun uses its power in many ways; the Twins received communication from the Holy Wind; when I pray, that, too, is just like a radio. All these things are the doings of the Holy People.

Prayer was another thing that guided the Twins and was very important to me. As with the radio that transmits information about what to avoid, prayer helped me escape the dangers of war. My mother prayed for me using corn pollen because that is the traditional way. She pleaded for my safe return and for me not to die. She also had faith in the ceremonies performed for me before I went away to war. It is only when a person believes in the spiritual way that he will be guided and shielded by prayer. In the ceremony I had the words of the prayer said that the spirit of Monster Slayer would be with me as if I was a person who could not be harmed by dangers in my path. I look at the Hero Twins as representing the Spirit of God and the Holy Spirit. I studied the Bible and Navajo traditions and now hang on to these two teachings; whenever I am unsure of something, I join the teachings of these two ways together. Sometimes when I herded sheep I read the Bible and compared it with Navajo traditions. I would stay with the sheep, lie down in the grass, look at the stars, and think about these things. God and the Holy People made the sky, created the earth and everything on it. Believing these things kept me alive. I compare prayer and Christianity to traditional teachings and live according to them.

When the Twins visited Spider Woman, she gave them an eagle feather. As part of my protection that I carried with me, I received a small feather taken from a live eagle. The bird shares its spirit with you, giving protection against bad people, injuries, diseases, the Devil, and witchcraft. The eagle is the leader of all the birds and is a messenger for what is happening and what will take place in the future. He is a powerful bird, and that is why he is on U.S. money and our government is known by it. Leaders of the people are like eagles, leaders of other birds. It is very sacred to Navajo people, and so its feathers are found in many ceremonies like the Enemy Way and can be used to chase away bad dreams by fanning a person with an eagle feather. I have an eagle bone whistle used for healing and prayers in peyote meetings; it is called a spirit carrier. The eagle is always flying between earth and heaven.

My father gave me an eagle feather along with my corn pollen. The feather is called a live eagle feather and is very difficult to obtain. It can come from a flying bird that drops it, or from one that sits down and loses it. These feathers are very sacred, and prayers come true by them. People used to go hunting for live eagle feathers up in the cliffs where the birds nested. A long time ago, when I was a child, I saw men climbing to the top to take baby eagles from their nests. Once they reached the nest, they had to say a prayer. Now this type of collecting is no longer practiced. Feathers could also come from two birds that were fighting. When this happens both feathers become sacred and valued by the finder, who was usually a medicine man. Medicine men help each other by sharing these feathers. My father and other medicine men prayed for me during the ceremony. When I received the feather I was not told how it was obtained, but it had been tied in a very small knot just like one fastened on a string. The feather was small enough to fit in my corn pollen pouch. Medicine men who perform ceremonies this way choose what they feel would help the patient the most. There are also protection songs and prayers that one can say and sing when confronted with danger. That is why I was not shot but kept safe and protected. There were many Navajos who had protection like I did, but there were others who did not believe in these things and were killed.

When one is in nature these spiritual things are easily felt. As I herded sheep I would think about who made this world and how it operates. When I looked at the stars I would feel at peace and everything around me became beautiful. I prayed to the God who made this earth while others probably prayed in different ways, but I believe in Him and Jesus, who became the first healer/medicine man. Their work is sacred and holy. Now I look at some medicine men and know that they are not in harmony with spiritual things and are uncomfortable with them. I guess they have faith in what they do so I do not think very much about it anymore.

Commentary: Power, Protection, and Peace

Preparation for war in both traditional and contemporary Navajo culture requires two things: the physical aspect of running, riding, shooting, and being toughened for what might be encountered and the spiritual side that protects a man from potential harm. Just as the Twins had raced against the gods and eventually triumphed, so too did Samuel—with all of his boot camp training and, later, with use of the code and radios—prepare for combat. Yet it was the spiritual side that to him proved invaluable, being "shielded by my prayers and faith in the Navajo way." Time and time again he repeats that "having them [prayers] in my head made me belong to them," suggesting a two-way covenant between him and the Holy People. This view is central to Navajo thinking about how to successfully navigate the trials of life. Through the interaction of the Twins with Spider Woman, a pattern of preparation embedded in power and symbol readied them for combat. Samuel followed a similar pattern, as outlined in the myth that protected him during future combat.

After Spider Woman taught the boys from her knowledge of life, she prepared something for them to eat. Putting corn meal and other plants in bowls, she then dropped two precious beads—white shell and turquoise—into the mixture. The Twins ate what was in their bowls, ingesting the two objects along with the food. The white bead was a symbol of internal protection, providing courage and other mental qualities necessary for the future. Turquoise protects the outside and is worn by Navajos as a means by which the Holy People will recognize and assist them. Another object that can be swallowed during a Prayer against Enemy (Naayéé'ii Sódizin) ceremony is a small eagle feather so that the participant can face fear and have his spirit live on.[14] Samuel said that in his ceremony, these aspects were not performed although they are a common practice.

Next Spider Woman gave each of the boys a life-feather (iina) taken from a live eagle. These feathers were small, sometimes down, as was the one received by Samuel—small enough to fit in a corn pollen pouch. In the past these feathers were obtained by digging a pit to camouflage a man inside who secured a live rabbit outside as bait for an eagle. When the bird attacked its prey, the man grabbed its legs and pulled it down into the pit as a captive. Then the desired feathers could either be plucked and the bird released or it could be smothered with corn pollen and a hood. Another way to secure live eagle feathers was to climb to a nest and pluck a feather from a baby eagle.[15] According to Gladys Reichard, "The longer the bird struggled, the more potent were its parts in a ceremony. The feathers represent strength, speed and motion, deliverance; the pollen exposed to them stands for light and life, that is, the sheen of the feathers."[16] Some life-feathers were tied in a special knot before being placed in a corn pollen pouch carried by the person seeking protection. In ceremonies an eagle bone whistle that is called a "spirit carrier" is used to summon the Holy People and to send or carry prayers to them.

Eagle feathers are worn in the headdress of Talking God and Hogan God; twelve of the feathers were received as payment for helping Monster Slayer in defeating some of the monsters. Born for Water took eagle down to make prayer sticks, other Holy People to fletch arrows, still others for hair ornaments. "All the other gods received either tail feathers or down feathers from the eagles. Every sacred article was provided with some kind of eagle feather and the Navajo still use the sacred objects so trimmed to this day."[17] But it was Monster Slayer who was directly saved by his life-feather when a giant monster bird (Tsé nináhálééh) snatched him in her claws and flew to Shiprock peak to dash the young warrior against the rock, turning him into food for her young below. Instead, he floated gently to the rock with his life-feather and later defeated the monster bird.[18] Like Monster Slayer, Samuel depended on this sacred feather to keep him alive.

The prayers and the words the Twins received from Spider Woman gave the life-feathers efficacy. Without knowledge of the prayers, the power could not be set in motion. The concept undergirding this practice has already been discussed, but Gary Witherspoon reminds us that

> control of a particular diyin dine'é [Holy Person] is accomplished by knowledge of his or her symbols (particularly his or her name), knowledge of his or her offering, and knowledge of the smells, sights, and sounds which attract, please, and compel him or her. The correct songs, prayers, and symbols are irresistible and compulsive. A Navajo does not supplicate or worship his gods; he identifies himself with them and both controls their power and incorporates their power within himself.[19]

Gladys A. Reichard's title of her book *Prayer: The Compulsive Word* suggests that with the correct prayers, songs, and formulas, a person controls the situation, no matter how difficult or dangerous it may be.[20] Spider Woman gave the Twins, and Samuel received from his father, the ability to triumph in forthcoming struggles.

Although most of the ceremonies held to protect men going to combat were small and personalized (with perhaps one to three individuals involved), anthropologist Clyde Kluckhohn, who was heavily involved in research with Navajo informants during the war, encountered a ceremonial blessing on a large scale. Around May 24, 1944, a medicine man performed a ceremony for 150 servicemen and those working in war industries. The singer used a picture of each of these individuals in a collective ceremony held for their well-being. "This man, a famous Singer, sang ancient war songs, and Christian Navajos were encouraged to add their prayers to the tribal chants. After the all-night ritual, prayer feathers adorned with turquoise were planted to help assure the warriors' safe return."[21]

But how were the Holy People to know who they were? As First Man, First Woman, and others formed the things of this world, first spiritually then physically, those creations received a sacred and secret name that would be used to identify their spiritual essence. So, too, when Navajo infants are born—both boys and girls—they may receive a sacred name that is known only to them and close family members for ceremonial purposes. Often these are associated with war, such as "He Returns with the Warrior," "He Went Out to War," "She Meets the Enemy," or "[She is] Going to War."[22] Through this title spiritual connections with the Holy People are assured. During the blacking part of a war ceremony, the use of this name may either prepare an individual about to set out or purify a person returning. Animals, plants, and insects also have spiritual names that control power. If an individual is working against a person or group with witchcraft, the ceremonial name can also be used to sicken, curse, and kill. For that reason, few people are to have this inside knowledge of a person's spiritual identity.

Some families do not bestow a sacred name but may identify their child for an action, physical characteristic, and so forth that has no spiritual power attached to it. Others may have three or four names but only one that is a war name. An example of this change in names occurs with Monster

Slayer, who was first known simply as First Born. Later he was known as Reared in the Earth because his mother hid him underground from the monsters roaming about. When he had his first war ceremony, it then changed to One-Setting-Out-for Slaughter—a sacred name used in prayers. Later, after his visit to his Father, he received the title of Let Down on a Sunbeam, and finally after his cleansing of the earth, Monster Slayer.[23] This same process occurred with Born for Water.

Samuel mentions a number of times he used corn pollen when praying. This fundamental concept is found throughout Navajo culture as one provides both an offering and a summons for the Holy People to recognize the prayers of an Earth Surface Being. The word for prayer is *sodizin*, meaning "my tongue must be holy," while that for pollen is tádidíín, literally translated as "holy knowledge or light," signifying that the words spoken are true and acceptable to the Holy People. Although in the past there were different types of pollen taken from flowers, shrubs, and trees, the primary one now comes from corn, which is shaken from the top of the stalk into a bowl, with the larger material sifted out and removed. The remaining fine powder is then placed in a small buckskin pouch. When praying, a pinch is removed from the pouch, first placed on the tip of the tongue, then the top of the head, then cast forward. Washington Matthews commented, "Pollen is the emblem of peace, of happiness, of prosperity, and it is supposed to bring these blessings. When, in the Origin Legend, one of the war gods [Monster Slayer] bids his enemy to put his feet down in pollen he constrains him to peace. When in prayer the devotee says, 'May the trail be in pollen,' he pleads for a happy life."[24]

The means by which prayers and thoughts are transmitted is through Níłch'i, comparable in many respects to Christian beliefs of the Holy Ghost. This important essence participates with humans in two different ways. In Navajo thought it can be personified just as the Holy Ghost is, an incorporeal personality who warns, guides, teaches, and protects an individual facing danger. The second belief is that it can serve as a medium to transmit information, comparable in some ways to radio waves—an invisible, powerful means of communication. The word itself is interpreted variously as Holy Wind, Little Wind, wind, air, breeze, or spirit.[25] Although some people speak of níłch'i as a very slight breeze, there is no mistaking it for níyol, another name for wind. The former is strongly associated with spiritual communication whereas the latter is much more physical and does not transmit messages from the Holy People. Thus, níyol is what one feels blowing against one's face whereas níłch'i speaks to a person.

Indeed, without this Holy Wind, there would be no life. Myths describe how, at the time of creation, the first people had no wind in them so they were weak. Then different colored winds—black, blue, yellow, and white—came from the four directions and entered the bodies of humans and animals, "giving strength to men ever since for this was nature's first food and it put motion and change into everything, even into the mountains and water."[26] Hair on the head, hair in the skin, swirling patterns of fingerprints and footprints, and the breath of life are proof of this wind's existence. During the fourth month after conception, this holy wind enters the body, giving animation to the fetus.

It also brings death. Some of the winds argue as to which one will enter the child and be able to claim it as its grandchild. Once the wind enters, it carries with it an expiration date, after which the person will no longer be able to live. Some people say that a medicine man can ceremonially replace the old air with new in a patient who has had a heart attack, giving a renewed lease on life.[27] Níłch'i inside a person communicates with the air outside of the body. When Holy People provide warnings and help a person to learn through this spiritual means, they should not be taken lightly. Claus Chee Sonny believes the gods want humans to know the songs and prayers, but this can only be done if the "Wind people want to communicate them to you."[28] He explains that this is the reason that some people fail to learn the songs and prayers even though they try very hard. The gods simply do not want some individuals to have this power. When treated respectfully, however, Níłch'i accurately communicates future events. Talking God, Growling God, and Sun Bearer placed throughout the land many of the Holy People "who were to be prophets and teachers of men in the future. The wind acted as messenger between these spirits and the people."[29] Divination and protection by the gods is based upon being respectful and spiritually sensitive to their communication.

Many Navajo myths tell of the Holy Wind whispering in the ear of a protagonist in need of assistance, warning of future problems, or helping with protection. As the Twins fought the various monsters, Níłch'i was there constantly directing their next action in order to defeat the enemy and death. This same invisible power is transferred in Navajo names for some of today's common appliances, denoting how they were first perceived to function. Although Anglos understand their working in a physical sense, the understanding of the Navajo view was based in their sacred teachings. Most Navajo speakers today may not analyze their term's underlying meaning, just as in English few people think of the root of "good bye" as meaning "God-be-with-you." But it is there. Keeping in mind the definition of Níłch'i as the Holy Wind, look at the following names. Radio is translated as either níłch'i hataałí , wind singer, or níłch'i halne'é, wind that speaks. An antenna is níłch'i báyaa'ahi, the rod that stands for the wind's words; radio waves is níłch'i; television is níłch'i naalkidí, wind that moves (performs) around; and telephone is níłch'i bee hane'e, wind that you speak by.

When Samuel entered combat, he depended upon his radio (níłch'i halne'é, wind that speaks) to carry his words and both destroy his enemies and protect his friends. He will mention on a number of occasions that he wondered how many people he killed with his words and that his ability to speak code was a secret weapon. Indeed, at one point when discussing the code, he would refer to the Navajo words and their translation as the secret part of his weapon. Certainly he understood his ability to transmit radio messages from a pragmatic standpoint. There is no missing the practical application when sitting in a shell hole surrounded with black volcanic sand on Iwo Jima. But the traditional context with which he viewed his role should also not be missed. As Witherspoon pointed out, "In the Navajo view of the world all entities which have the capacity of self-animation are directed and controlled by the power of thought. The power or energy source of all life and animation is located in the air, but the director and controller of all animation is the mind."[30] As Samuel prepared to enter combat, he and his radio controlled and directed actions through the air that would both save and take life.

CHAPTER FOUR

Traditional and Contemporary Combat

First Encounter: Kwajalein

THE TWINS: THE-ROCKS-THAT-CRUSH

Shortly after leaving the home of Spider Woman, the Twins came to the Rocks that Crush (Tsé' ahéénídiłii), two high cliffs with a narrow cleft between. An unsuspecting traveler would approach the opening, the rocks would separate, then once the person entered between the two cliffs, they would smash together, killing their victim. "These rocks were really people; they thought like men; they were anáye."[1] Four times the boys tempted the rocks by putting their feet down and then withdrawing them quickly to see the rocks slam shut, foiled in their attempt to crush their victims. Exasperated, the rocks questioned who these young men were only to receive the reply, "We are the children of the Sun . . . and we go to seek the house of our father." Holding up the feathers and repeating the prayers given them by Spider Woman, the Twins safely passed between the subdued rocks and continued on their journey.[2]

OCEAN AND WATER DANGERS

Water Monster was angry. Someone from among the Holy People had stolen her two babies and she wanted them back.[3] The Holy People had just escaped the flood waters destroying the Fourth World beneath and entered into this, the Fifth, or Glittering, World only to find that these waters were also rising. The people had merged onto a relatively flat land that sloped toward the ocean and so it would not take long before the place of emergence, where they had come into this world through a hollow reed, would soon be flooded and the land base covered. First Woman realized that Water Monster, who controlled the rising tide, was angry for a reason: something had been stolen, and someone needed to discover what it was. After many of the Holy People had been searched, First Man discovered the two babies hidden under Coyote's coat. Following a sharp scolding, Coyote gave up the infants so that First Man and First Woman could return them to the Water Monster.

The ocean began to recede, leaving swamps, marshes, and other bodies of water filled with sea and fresh-water life, much of which was different kinds of monsters. Two of the most dangerous were a "great toad-like creature with spines of sharp horns along its back, while on the far side [of the land mass] lived a long scaly monster with double rows of sharp teeth."[4] There were others inhabiting the sea. "In the ocean was the great Sea Serpent that caught people in its coils and there was the *Ch'indii* with eight long arms, and there were fish with sharp teeth, besides enormous clams that could eat a child in one bite. These ocean monsters did not come on the land to trouble the First People, but when storms lashed the waters into great waves that rolled over the ground, people and animals were washed away and never seen again."[5] When the marsh dwellers and the sea creatures learned of the people on the land, they hungered to eat them. Something had to be done for protection.

First Man and First Woman decided that if there were guards placed in the four directions, then warnings could be given so that the people could flee from the monsters who lived in the marshes and who, at times, ventured on dry land. A number of birds volunteered for the duty, but the grebe, with its shrill cry, received the responsibility. The monster toad and the one with spines on its back were the most troublesome, and so the grebes devised a plan where they would fake injury and lure the two monsters across the ground toward each other. The scheme worked so that eventually the two met in the center of the land and began fighting over the right to be in that territory, totally forgetting about the grebes they pursued. The struggle was long and violent, with "blood splattering all over the land so all the rocks turned red and they have remained red to this day."[6] Eventually the two became exhausted and returned to their homes to die. "Hundreds of years later, men with picks and shovels came to uncover these fossils and take them to museums where people who come to see them are amazed at their age and size."[7]

There was still the issue of the sea monsters, who lashed the ocean enough to cause it to wash over part of the land and carry away people into its depths to be eaten. There were too many of these creatures to be killed, and the land was too large and flat to create a protective sea wall. First Man had an idea and the necessary power to create a larger more permanent barrier, but he needed the animals to assist him in getting four stones—white crystal, blue turquoise, yellow jasper, and black jet—found in the middle of the ocean. Many volunteered to help, but all were found wanting until a small, humble duck said that he would accept the task. Most of the others jeered him, explaining that he could never complete the task, but First Man thought differently, gave him a powerful medicine bag, then sprinkled him with pollen from bulrushes growing by the side of a lake. "This he did so small Duck need fear no harm from the deep dark water. But First Man had no magic words or powerful medicine to give this bird to use against the slimy Sea Serpent, Scaly Fish, or the black Water Monster."[8] He would have to do it through his own power.

Small Duck left the safety of land and flew to the center of the dark waters of the ocean. Tucking the medicine bag beneath his wing, he dove into the sea and descended until he reached the first mountain deep below and found the first stone, a white one, and placed it in his bag. Before the sea monsters realized he was in their domain, Duck swam to the mountain of the south then found and took a blue stone, thence to the west and a yellow stone from a mountain, and finally a black stone from the mountain of the north. But now the Water People from beneath knew he was there. As Small Duck ascended, a long, shiny serpent with open jaws approached him. The bird shifted directions only to have a large scaly monster with many teeth take up the chase. He thought of dropping or at least lightening his sack to get away, but he could not slow his efforts long enough to do it as a third creature, a great brown monster with three long arms joined in and almost captured him. Finally the duck broke the surface of the ocean just as the great-fish-with-many-teeth lunged for him. That monster missed, but Scaly Fish bit down on the duck's tale, securing only a mouthful of feathers as the bird soared into the sky.

Hawk, flying high above the land, was the first to see the duck's return. The animals and First Man greeted the exhausted fowl and inspected the four stones that had come from the mountains beneath the dark water. They were just right. First Man took them, placed one in each of the cardinal directions, then blew on them, enlarging their size and stretching the land between so that there would be a wall of white mountains to the east, a blue mountain to the south, yellow to the west, and black to the north. Next each of the four Wind People blew against the mountains, pushing them back, stretching the earth's surface, "leaving mesas, small hills, valleys and desert land where they had been standing. . . . Now when all this was finished and the First People felt safe from the ocean waves and the hungry sea monsters, they began looking around to see what had become of Small Duck."[9] Having lost his tail, he was embarrassed and hid in the marshes. First Man knew of his sacrifice and pronounced that this bird had proven to be the bravest of all the creatures in the difficult and dangerous task that frightened and almost killed him. "'He brought us the four stones that now stand like a great fortification between us and the dangerous waters. From now on, no one of us shall ever try to harm Small Duck or destroy his nests.' And to this day, that law is carefully observed by the Navaho people."[10]

SAMUEL: COMBAT ON KWAJALEIN

Following my ten-day leave, I returned to find that Dan Akee from Tuba City and I were to work together in the Fourth Marine Division and that we were to get ready to go overseas and fight. There were many tents set up where combat training was going on. I do not really remember how long we stayed there, perhaps a week, before we left. Navajo code talkers were dropped off among the different combat elements, and Dan and I were assigned to the Twenty-Fifth Regiment. The code talkers worked in pairs, one pair being on the front lines, with others held back in a safe area to receive. Dan and I were one pair who were to work at the front. There were also about eight white radio men who shared the task of carrying the radio. They were tough men—one was a wrestler from New York—who served as wiremen, runners, and communication specialists. These were the white men I knew best.

I enjoyed being with the marines in our unit. We got along very well and respected each other, even teasing each other like brothers. Everyone was friendly, just as within a family. The only people on our level who knew about our special training as code talkers were the white radio men, but none of them knew about the codes. The rest of the men had only been told we had a dangerous weapon to destroy the enemy and the things they used against us. The marines were ordered not to ask us questions but just be friendly; our weapon was very confidential and should be left alone, so they understood we had a special task and knew what we were doing. Other than that, I was an ordinary man just like them. In my platoon I was greeted with, "Hello Chief," and worked closely with the radio men, but the rest of the marines pretty much stayed with their own tasks. I kept everything in my heart; no one knew, and I did not share, any information about my beliefs and practices. Outside of my heart we joked around, played cards, dice, and had fun. Once it was time to get serious, then the fun ended and I kept to myself. My power to use this weapon came from prayer, which I always remembered to do, but I never prayed in a group with other Navajos. When praying I often remembered those fighting alongside me and servicemen in all the branches. I prayed for our safety.

I saw and visited the ocean for the first time when I was at Camp Pendleton. As I thought about it, I knew there was life in the ocean, that it had a lot of waves, and that it was very colorful. My mother did not really explain what it was like except that the ocean surrounded us. Once I had joined the marines my father prayed, mentioning rain, the ocean, and all the creatures in them for their help and protection as he talked to the Holy One. He prayed first to the male side and then the female part of the ocean, asking to keep me safe as I traveled these waters.[11] Traditional Navajo prayers mentioned that it, and everything in it, was made by the Holy People. There were caves, rocks, pebbles, and plants that looked like trees, and the fish were all pretty.

Before I left Camp Pendleton I had an all-day pass and so spent two dollars to go into an underwater aquarium, where I watched the ocean through a glass and saw a big whale with its baby swimming around. I told myself that I would someday return and bring my children and mother to see it, and later I did. The ocean is a sacred place and has a prayer. In it there are living things, so as I watched them, I talked and pleaded with those creatures and asked them to do me no harm. That included the whales. God created and designed a good thing in the ocean, which amazed me to see, so I blessed myself with it, now that I would be traveling on it in danger. I just thought that it was all in the hands of Diyin and how he dealt with water in general. I didn't think deeply about it because of the prayers and the medicine that was made for me before I left home. I was blessed with all the forces of water.

We were packed and ready to go then just waited. Officers told us we could be called to depart at any time, but we were never told when. One night around midnight trucks arrived, we loaded our gear, and drove to San Diego where we boarded a ship. For days we sailed before anchoring about two miles off the Hawaiian Island of Oahu near Pearl Harbor. We were there for three days to refuel and receive supplies while some officers boarded our ship before leaving for the Marshall Islands. No one else went on shore before departing. Again we set sail where there was nothing to see except an ocean that never seemed to end. I only thought of what my father had said during my prayer ceremony, reminding me that there were living things of all kinds in the ocean, including fish of all kinds and sizes, and that I should respect their life. There would be many dangerous things and the landscape where I landed may have some great mountains that could hurt a person and that when I prayed I should pray for them and feel their spirits so they will not harm me, just as I did while on the ocean.

As we neared our objective the officers put out maps. We surrounded tables as they pointed out where we were going to land. They showed us the location of an airport and some communication buildings. As I looked at the map, I thought about the power of the ceremonies performed for me. I imagined the caves from which the guns would be firing and thought about how the code talkers would help win the war and how the marines depended on us. I was not scared so volunteered to be in the first wave to land. The officers shared the plan, telling us who we were assigned to and the estimated number of Japanese soldiers to be encountered. The intelligence report was right. If we had landed on the side where the guns were pointing, we would have lost many of our marines, but instead they had us come in on an open side where our target was visible and we were much safer.

On February 1 we landed in the Marshall Islands on a series of small coral islands known collectively as Kwajalein atoll. I went in on Beach Green Two located on Namur where the Japanese had built a communications center. From the base on Roi the enemy sent aircraft to attack American B29 airplanes bombing against Japan. We climbed down the side of the ship on cargo nets and into landing craft that took us to the island so that we could move inland toward our objective: the radio station. I wore a small

The war in the Pacific was highly dependent on naval forces to deliver men and equipment to a series of objectives as part of the "island hopping" strategy. Naval gunfire and carrier-based aircraft softened enemy positions before the marines headed to landing beaches. (Photograph courtesy of the U.S. Marine Corps)

backpack the size like those that school children carry. It held food, such as crackers that swell when you eat them so they fill you up, a gas mask, a first aid kit with medicine to seal off gunshot wounds, and water. Those were the main things because the pack could not hold much more.

The marines went ashore on the south side, or backside, because the Japanese had all of their big guns pointing to the north; I was in the first wave with the group headed toward the Japanese communications center. It was a small island with the land looking all torn and blown up. There were some dead soldiers, but we moved past them as if it did not bother the other marines, some acting as if there were no dead bodies. Earlier, there had been heavy shooting in this area, with firing now in the vicinity of the communications center, letting us know that others had already reached that position. As we neared the radio station more shooting broke out around us. Our company scattered but kept moving toward several buildings made of concrete. The radio station was huge but badly destroyed by naval gunfire. I could see it had been blasted so that now rebar stuck out where the concrete had been peeled away. There was more sporadic gunfire here and there ahead. We took three or four prisoners, but the rest of the enemy had been killed. The shooting continued for about five hours then slackened to only Japanese snipers, who remained hidden for maybe two more days. There were also those who went into hiding after being shot. We sat around a lot and slept with our clothes on, always ready, remaining vigilant all the time, night and day, watching for snipers. But I knew that we could do this job and win. We had a lot of ships and weapons as well as the advantage. Eventually it quieted down.

I felt very sad seeing the dead Japanese even though it was war. I could not do anything about the lost lives, and so I tried not to pay much attention to it. There were also dead marines, some of whom were wire men I knew from working with them in communications. Others had been runners during the night. I was very sorry for them. It is a different feeling dealing with the dead in war. In the past there were many ancestral warriors who were given permission to kill an enemy by having a ceremony done for them before the battle. You must kill sometimes to protect yourself. I, too, had been given permission to kill the enemy by being a marine, so to see a dead body was not scary; I just felt sorry for them. My protection came from the ceremonies that had been performed for me. In a war you think, "I will kill the enemy before he kills me," just as if a mean dog attacks so you have to fight back. The enemy was not that close, but we all had to think and protect ourselves and we each had a gun to kill with. You only think of your own safety and not the other person's. I had to be on alert for myself against my enemies.

There were also natives who lived on the island who the Japanese forced to do labor for them. They were generally uninjured and unarmed. We could see women and children in safe places while the fighting was going on around them in their homeland. Our medics or corpsmen helped both the wounded and the civilians, no matter what nationality or age, whether children or adults.

I manned the radio and listened to all the messages passing over it. My job was to report how intense the shooting was so that the guns on the ship could fire on the enemy. Dan Akee and I were always together, listening to other code talkers on the same frequency requesting water and ammunition or reporting if they were pinned down and could not move forward. Also if there were injured and wounded we helped implement a quick transport plan to get them to the hospital ship. No one wanted prolonged suffering from gunshot wounds or other injuries for these men. Life was important and needed to be saved. We settled in and began working with the radio, sending and receiving messages. By listening to other code talkers transmitting their information, we often knew more than the officers, who liked to be stationed with us so they could be aware of what was going on. We had our first victory there in a relatively short time. It required four days to conquer the whole atoll. This was the first time I saw what combat was like.

After capturing the islands, we went back to Maui for rest and more training in jungle warfare. There we met the new replacements. When we were resting we mixed and talked with the other soldiers and took it easy, enjoying good food and rest. We joked around and got along very well with the other men. But when we were in actual war, it was different because we had to be on guard and very serious about what we were doing. After four months in Maui, the next operation started. This time it was Saipan.

Commentary: Waging War—Model from the Past

Samuel Holiday, as a Navajo man, descended from a long line of warriors who had waged combat against traditional enemies such as the Ute, Hopi, Comanche, Apache, and later the Mexicans and Americans. The old way of war preparation, travel, and combat held sway until around 1870 when completion of the Long Walk era and settlement on a reservation put an end to men participating in war as a primary responsibility. Much of the associated practice fell into disuse. Fortunately, W. W. Hill in 1933 collected information from elders who remembered the old ways and published them in 1936 in a now-classic work entitled "Navaho Warfare."[12] Although Samuel was not aware of many of the things that Hill wrote about, many of the underlying beliefs and a few of the practices transferred into what he encountered in preparation of and participation in his first battle. What follows is a synopsis of Hill's findings that explain the Navajo's old warrior activities and their relevance to Samuel's experience.

Hill starts by pointing out two fundamental concepts that affected Samuel's preparation and later conduct. The anthropologist comments that the ceremonial aspect of war "was the most important part of any military undertaking" and that travel through enemy territory and the country itself "was potentially maleficent [so that] . . . a great amount of ritual was performed during the course of an offensive movement."[13] When a Navajo person moves beyond the limits of a safe, protected environment, such as the lands bounded by the four sacred mountains consecrated by the Holy People, danger lurks. Crossing one of the four sacred rivers placed in the cardinal directions opens the door to foreign elements and trials that are primarily controlled by supernatural means. Once beyond friendly territory and in that of the enemy, precautions must be taken. These precautions apply not only to actual combat, but also to concerns with witchcraft, strange powers, reduced ceremonial efficacy, and the unknown or unpredictable. The Holy People know of these concerns and can assist but must be respected and given offerings in placating that which is harmful.

Samuel's concern with the ocean is an important example of how he viewed potential danger in travel upon it and how ritual was part of his protection from that danger. Known as Tónteel, or Wide Water, the ocean has its own teachings and makes its own demands. The two stories offered at the beginning of this chapter illustrate the type of monsters and creatures that live beneath the sea. They can be harmful to man. Another story alluded to previously was when Coyote stole the two babies of Water Monster, who caused the waters to rise and forced the culprit to return her offspring. This water creature's anger was unpredictable as she sought revenge. Water today is still respected and believed to have latent anger and power that can be used against a person who fails to act appropriately. Whether in lakes or streams or the ocean, water can quickly become angry and destroy a person, drowning one in its depths, sending its waves to capsize boats, and washing over land far beyond its bounds. Coyote, as a creature familiar with the powers of water, can bring rain to bless the land or cause the waters to lash out in destruction. Like water, he is unpredictable and controls its forces. An appropriate offering and prayers can placate the tempestuous spirit of both and allow one to travel in peace and safety.[14] When Samuel pleads with the ocean for smooth sailing, blesses himself with it, provides an offering, and uses its power to protect him, he is creating an ally and assuring his safety.

Seth Bigman from Monument Valley joined the marines in 1943 but was not a code talker. Still, he traveled extensively on the ocean, and upon his return he had an old medicine man interpret what he had encountered in a mythological sense. Seth recounts this experience:

> "The mother has sent out her child to go on the warpath," he [the medicine man] said, "the same way as Mother Earth [Changing Woman] sent out her warriors to defend her. The rainbow is the defense of Mother Earth, where the land and water meet. One of the rainbows is sitting vertically, that's the rain, and one is sitting horizontally, that's the ocean. When you go through the rainbow to war, that is the defense of Mother Earth." And of course the weapons that the warriors defend her with would be the colors of the rainbow.
>
> My old medicine man said to me, "We have only seen the rainbow where the land and water meet vertically, but you have seen both horizontal and vertical, you have gone to war through both rainbows."[15]

The rainbow, a means of protection as well as transportation for the Holy People, symbolizes their power and ability to bless. Passing through the rainbows bestows that power upon the traveler.

The Pacific Ocean is male and has a sacred name used in ceremonies to help control its influence. This name is used when making offerings. Because of the ocean's tremendous power, everything that lives within it also has the same power. Samuel mentioned some of the creatures like sharks, whales, octopus, and so forth that are large in size and obviously dangerous, but so, too, are shellfish such as crabs, lobsters, and clams and so should not be eaten. Traditional teaching says that if one eats any food from the sea, that person can take on the qualities of the creature eaten—if not immediately then in the future. Creatures from the ocean are not made for Earth Surface People. If one eats crab or lobster, his hands will become claw-like and he will walk very much like those creatures, bent over and ambling. Eating fish from the sea causes a person's lips to swell and the face to take on the same appearance.

Things that come from the ocean are controlled by the ocean, have the power of the ocean, and should not be used, particularly as food. The one major exception is the ocean's wealth found in abalone and white shell—two of the four elements that comprise ntł'iz, or sacred stones, provided as a male offering just as pollen is for a female blessing. The reason that they are used and highly desired is that two of the elements hold the power of land (turquoise and jet) while the other two hold the power of water. Within the abalone and white shell are all four of the sacred colors—white, blue, yellow, and black—central to Navajo teachings and ceremonial practice. Coral, another example of Ocean's wealth, is also acceptable as are turtle shells used in ceremonies because they, too, have a glittering inside. But fish and water snakes can cripple a person, and alligator-skin handbags and shark-skin boots should be avoided. Even Changing Woman, when she finished her travels about the earth, went to her home in the west near the ocean, some say to an island in the ocean, as part of a punishment because she challenged her husband, Sun Bearer.[16]

For the Navajo warrior of the mid-nineteenth century, the ocean was far away whereas enemy Ute and Pueblo territory was much more of a concern. There were several different ceremonial approaches that could be used—the Monster Slayer Way, the Enemy Way, and the Yei Hastin (Yé'ii Hastiin) Way—the primary difference between them being the songs and prayers offered. Monster Slayer Way, the oldest ceremony that is based on the teachings, sprang from the practices of the Twins. The leader of the war

Samuel (*front row, second from left*) poses with cousins and nephews belonging to a traditional song group called Tó Dinéeshzhee' (Fingers of Water—the name for Kayenta) at the Shiprock Fair (2009). Their dress is that of a nineteenth-century warrior, the cap in the old days being adorned with owl or eagle feathers—predatory birds known for their skill in hunting. (Photograph courtesy of the Holiday family)

party was the one who knew the ceremonies and songs and could spiritually navigate his followers to a successful conclusion. The warriors, like Samuel, had been raised with physical rigor—snow baths, long runs, diving into icy water, sweat baths, emetics, weapons training, field craft, and lack of rest—always with the adage: "Wake up, be lively! If you are not up early, the enemy will come and kill you while you sleep. . . . [If they did not do these things] the first thing that came along would kill them because their systems were filled with ugly things that they should have gotten rid of: they would be quick tempered, have weak minds, be unable to stand life's hardships, and therefore disgrace their families."[17] By the age of seventeen to twenty, a young man was ready to participate in war.

If a man wished to become a war leader but had not yet had the necessary training, he would approach a medicine man who had this knowledge and accompany him into enemy territory, where they would build a sweat lodge in which instruction began. The novice would then learn "the most important things pertaining to war, the secret names of the enemy, and the songs and prayers which were used before making an attack."[18] For four days, the instructor and student remained, learning the names and prayers, something that could not be done in friendly territory for fear that someone in the family or a relative would die, an epidemic occur, or the enemy attack. Once the information had been mastered, the young man was ready to organize and lead a war party.

Following the recruitment of warriors who wished to go against the enemy, the men spent from three to five days preparing. Songs and prayers first sung by Monster Slayer and now offered in a sweat lodge would bring protection and success if performed properly. Offerings of pollen and ntł'iz ensured the assistance of the Sun and Wind People in providing protection to the travelers. Their weapons and equipment were similarly blessed as the men gathered without women for their spiritual preparation. Many warriors wore a close-fitting cap, similar to those used for everyday use except that just before engagement with the enemy, the wearer attached a special plume from either an eagle or owl tail feathers. "This protected the wearer just like the badge of Saint Christopher."[19] In addition to this, a warrior may wear a wrist amulet made of bear, mountain lion, eagle, and owl claws to provide strength and power or a small medicine bundle with the "shake offs" from a bear, snake, thunder, and cyclone along with a "live" eagle feather. These shake offs were made from pollen that had been placed on a creature or from a place that was representative of these animals or elements. Once it had been put on this representative and the appropriate prayers said, the pollen was collected, combined, and put in a medicine pouch to provide protection. All of these elements had strong supernatural powers described in the teachings that spoke of their ability to protect, making the warrior invincible. A shield may have eagle feathers sewed around its edge, giving the object similar powers that "will protect you from the enemy and help you kill other Indians."[20]

Although Samuel did not go through this war preparation to the same extent as those warriors of the nineteenth century, there is no missing the parallels of offerings, the role of pollen, the power of the eagle, and the idea of carrying a medicine pouch filled with sacred materials for protection. Much of this practice derived from the Twins, whose power was evoked by prayers that would establish a pattern and urge: "Step into the shoes of

Monster Slayer. Step into the shoes of him whose lure is the extended bowstring. Step into the shoes of him who lures the enemy to death."[21] Protection was one aspect; killing the enemy with supernatural means was another. Just as the Twins used words and songs to destroy their enemy, so did those participating in a war party. Clyde Kluckhohn in his study of witchcraft tells of an account given to him about a group of Navajos waiting one night to capture a flock of sheep guarded by Mexicans. The leader of the Navajos used witchcraft, shot a feather from a basket into the Mexican leader, and said, "If we hear a noise, we've got him."[22] The man gave out a yell and by the next morning was dead, causing the other Mexicans to flee. Thus witchcraft that is dependent primarily on songs, prayers, and words can cause death and is just as real as the arrows and bullets fired for the same purpose.

Once the war party entered enemy territory, the leader began his chanting and prayers against the enemy, inviting others in the party to offer their own songs. They sang for the animals they had come to steal or the revenge they would exact. To encourage success strict rules of conduct were followed; good weather conditions were sought, such as wind and snow to cover tracks and muffle sound; and members of the war party had to have the ability both to understand the seriousness of the undertaking and to put all thoughts of home behind them. There was even secret "war talk" used only during hostilities.

> When the warriors entered the enemy's territory, the leader told the men to use certain words other than the usual ones for the animals and objects that they hoped to obtain. This was called "war talk" and "not talking plainly." The Navaho never practiced this "war talk" in their own territory because it was believed if they did that an attack from the enemy would follow. This restriction lasted from one to three days of the journey. When the leader decided that the appropriate time had arrived, the party lined up in a row facing the enemy's country. At the coming of dawn, the leader began a song in which the rest joined. At a certain part of the song all turned toward their own homes and the tabu [taboo] against "not talking plainly" was removed.
>
> The leader told the men not to urinate in the brush. He also warned them that should they become separated and wish to communicate with each other, they were to use prearranged calls such as those of the coyote, wolf, whip-poor-will, or screech owl.[23]

Anthropologist Gladys Reichard, like Hill, was aware that this special use of language existed but was unable to obtain many examples. She believed the reason for this was because of the power these words held and the desire not to use them when not in war. The one example she gives illustrates the complexity inherent in this system. "Even if a horse is meant, if it has kicked or thrown a person, in this changed language [war language] it may be called 'merely a life feather' a circumlocution flattering to the horse and signifying its identification with supernatural speed and lightness."[24] She next cites Berard Haile, who wrote of a story in which Monster Slayer sent Turtledove to report on two traveling warriors. The bird returned saying that the men "did not go anywhere unless they spoke a language called 'irritably they speak.' [Haile:] This term is explained as a sort of 'twisted language used by warriors.' Either the word symbol was slightly changed in the code or a special meaning known only to fighters was given to the words. Monster Slayer's war band advancing on Taos, spoke only in the war language."[25]

Hill, Reichard, and Haile performed their research prior to World War II before there was any suggestion that the Navajo language might be used as a code to defeat the Japanese. They looked to the past for their examples instead of the future. There is also no indication that when forming the Navajo code talkers there was any discussion of past practices. Certainly the impetus behind the earlier "war talk" was rooted in the spiritual side of the language and was based in the idea that using euphemisms and other ways of expressing future events or characterizing the enemy was done not so much to hide the communication from a physical enemy as to say things in an inoffensive way so as not to offend the spirits or to state boldly what was to occur.

This supernatural or spiritual aspect of war continued when the war leader, following his instructions to the group, sent two men from the camp to determine the outcome of future events by "listening." Navajos considered this the most reliable form of divination, although stargazing and hand trembling were also used. With listening, the two men moved about one hundred yards from their group in the direction of the enemy to listen for noises that would indicate success in their raid—such as the sounds of livestock or of animals running—or to see a vision of some type that showed them obtaining their goal. On the other hand, if they "heard the cry of a crow, screech owl, hoot owl, wolf, coyote, or any other 'man eating' bird or animal; heard the footsteps or conversation of the enemy, or heard someone shout as if he were hurt (this is believed to predict the death of one of the members of the party), these were considered bad omens and the party would turn back."[26] Through Níłch'i, the Holy Wind, the future was known.

As the war party moved closer to their intended target, scouts went ahead to detect enemy activity. Just before the attack, which was usually at dawn, the leader—dressed in his war gear, including moccasins with Big Snake painted on its soles and his medicine bundle and eagle feather tied to his cap—moved from the group. Alone, he sang songs, offered prayers, and called the enemy by their secret name to again ensure success. "The prayers are like this: he starts with the enemy's head and mentions all the different parts of his body right down to the ground, and ends his prayer in the ground. This is just the same as burying the man."[27] He then returned to his warriors, reported his efforts, and encouraged the men to prepare by painting on themselves designs of snakes for power, bear tracks for fierceness and bravery, and human hands to represent a man. If the leader has performed his part of the ritual successfully and the warriors are prepared spiritually by following practices taught in the accounts of the Twins and Holy People when they first waged war, then "everyone knows and feels that they will be lucky."[28] Soon the attack commenced.

Although much of this detailed practice performed in the mid-nineteenth century was a thing of the past, the Navajos recruited into the Marine Corps a hundred years later shared some common elements. Rather than using the war talk derived from traditional teachings, the Twenty-nine (with three additional men added during the communications training phase) received the task of developing their own code. The course for code talkers, resulting in a military occupational specialty of 642 Radio-Telephone Operator, required176 hours of instruction. Included in this instruction was printing and message writing; Navajo alphabet and vocabulary; wire tying, splicing, and laying; telephone and switchboard operation; pole climbing; voice procedure; message center operation; and familiarization with radio and wire equipment to include telephone EE-8, and radios SCR 300-600 and the TBX; as well as Marine Corps organization.[29] At first held at Camp Elliot and later Pendleton, this thirteen-week course followed hard on the heels of boot camp.

The first Navajo code talkers had the additional duty of developing a new code system transmitted by voice on the battlefield. Members of the first Navajo group given this task belonged to Platoon 382. The customary leave of ten days following boot camp never materialized. The men arrived at Elliot then received their mission to prepare an alphabet using Navajo words as phonetic equivalents. They had to assign names to military equipment and operational terms, keep the code words short for rapid transmission, and commit it all to memory. All of this was kept totally confidential within the group, with no mention to their white marine buddies or word sent home to family members. Failure to keep this secret information internal resulted in dire consequences.

Chester Nez, a member of the First Twenty-nine, or Platoon 382, provides the most complete eyewitness account of what this experience was like for Navajo participants as they created their secret "war talk." In the beginning of July 1942, the Navajos arrived at Camp Elliot, were given an isolated building with guards around it and bars on windows, and were told by an officer to get to work. They were released from the facility at the end of each day.[30] A Navajo alphabet became the starting point. After some discussion, the marines decided to use an animal, plant, or object familiar to the Navajo experience. Thus, *A* became "Wol-la-chee" (wóláchíí), or (red) ant; *B* became "Shush" (shash), or bear; *C* became "Moasi" (mósí), or cat; and so forth. Soon the code talkers added other phonetic symbols for the frequently used letters so that *A* would have two added (axe—Tse-nil [tsénił]; apple—Be-la-sana [bilasáana]), *B* would have two added (badger—Na-hash-chid [nahashch'idí]; barrel—Toish-jeh [tóshjeeh]), and so forth. In five days, the alphabet was finished and the more challenging aspects of the code undertaken.

The vocabulary of the code, like the alphabet, came from things that were encountered or resembled what was found on the reservation or within the Navajo experience. Some words were an exact translation of how it might be said in Navajo, whereas other things demanded more creativity. Eugene Crawford recalled later:

> There were days that I thought my head would burst. All the memorizing and frustration trying to find Navajo words that would fit things like "echelon" and "reconnaissance." Sometimes we would spend three or four hours on just one word! It was the hardest thing I have ever been asked to do. Looking back, reservation school was easy compared to building the code. Reservation school did prepare me, in some ways, for what we were faced with, so I guess it wasn't a total waste.[31]

The Navajo are noted for keen observation, providing names characteristic of an individual, new situation, or object, and so this talent could be put to use. But the problem now was that these men did not have enough of a military background to be able to picture the necessary characteristics. Nez explained the situation as follows:

> Certain military terms would be used frequently—so frequently that we didn't want to waste time spelling them. Those words needed direct translations. We men barely off the reservation, were not familiar with military terms, the names and capabilities of various ships and planes, types of artillery and other equipment. Words like "echelon" or "battalion" stymied us. We also had to figure out a way to indicate various officers—"captain, "major," "brigadier general," "colonel," "first lieutenant," "second lieutenant," "major general." How were we supposed to find equivalents for all of those?[32]

At this point, the three additional Navajo men previously mentioned—Felix Yazzie, Ross Haskie, and Wilson Price—joined the code talkers to bring their military experience to bear in devising the code. They later remained with the original Twenty-nine and deployed as code talkers to various islands in the Pacific. For military designations, the clan system was used: corps became "clan," division became "salt" (clan), regiment became "Tabaha" (Edge Water clan), company became "Nakaii" (Mexican), and so forth. A brigadier general was a "one star," a colonel was a "silver eagle," a captain was "two silver bars"—all based on what their physical rank looked like. Airplanes and ships followed function so that a dive bomber was a "chicken hawk," a fighter plane "hummingbird," and a patrol plane a "crow"; a submarine was "iron fish," destroyer a "shark," and an aircraft carrier a "bird carrier." Some of the more creative terms found in general vocabulary included the following: amphibious was "frog," bombs were "eggs," parenthesis was "rib," route was "rabbit trail," and torpedo was "fish shell." In this initial code there were 263 terms; the final code at the end of the war in 1945 had 623 words and sixty-three different renderings of letters in the alphabet.[33]

Once the initial code was completed, practice and field trials followed. A standard rule was that although written materials outlining the code could be used in training, none were to go into the field in combat, requiring that everything be memorized. Official correspondence emphasized that even though Navajo marines worked hard and long on difficult tasks without grumbling, that "when teaching the Navajo alphabet and vocabulary, it must be remembered that the process is one of pure memory work and only by constant repetition and drills can the student become proficient in the use of the Navajo language for tactical message transmission."[34]

Thus no supporting aides were allowed outside of training. There were two reasons for this prohibition. The first and most obvious was that there was great concern that a written copy of it would fall into enemy hands and compromise the entire system. Indeed, the Japanese had been so effective in breaking every other code that the United States used that there had to be some assurance that this would not happen again. Nez confidently explained that after he and the others developed the code, "We felt sure we had a code that even a native Navajo speaker would not be able to crack. Our classroom was unlocked and we code talkers went out on maneuvers to test the code and to practice, practice, practice."[35] For weeks expert American code breakers tried to crack what the Navajos had developed but to no avail. The acid test came, just as Nez stated it would, when the Japanese held prisoner a Navajo soldier.

Joe Kieyoomia was a Navajo from Arizona who enlisted in the U.S. Army in March 1941. Following the Japanese attack on Pearl Harbor and the surrender of his unit in the Philippines, he survived the Bataan Death March before being shuttled around to a series of prisoner of war camps in the Philippines then to other camps in Hatashi, Matashima, and Nagasaki, Japan. From April 9, 1942, to September 4, 1945, his official status was that of prisoner of war. He was convinced that the Japanese took a strong interest in him initially because they believed he was of Japanese ancestry and just trying to deny it. Perhaps he would see the errors of his ways and join their cause. As the war continued and the Navajo code talkers went to work, the Japanese were baffled by what they encountered on the airwaves. Kieyoomia, interviewed years later as part of the Doris Duke Oral History Project, described his experience:

> One evening I was brought to the commanders' quarters for questioning, and they asked me again, for the hundredth time, if I was an American. I told them I was an American Indian, but that only made them angry. "You are American Japanese! Why are you fighting against your own people?" the commander shouted. The interpreter, a guy named Goon, understood that I was an American Indian, but

> the interrogator didn't. When I refused to confess that I was Japanese, the interrogator hit me with a club, broke my ribs and then my wrist. When I refused to confess again, they dragged me back to the barracks and threw me in a cell.
>
> We had a British doctor named Whitfield who examined me but all he could do was bind my ribs and give me aspirin. Later that night the pain was so intense they took me to the infirmary. It wasn't much better there. They laid me flat on the floor with only a thin straw mat under me and checked me every four hours.
>
> Sometime later that month, Goon must have figured out that the talkers on the radio who couldn't be identified must be Indians. They were having a tough time deciphering the code, and they finally figured that I might be able to help them. When they first made me listen to the broadcasts, I couldn't believe what I was hearing. It sounded like Navajo, just not anything that made sense to me. I understood my language, but I could not figure out the code they were using. That made the interrogators very angry!
>
> They stripped off all my clothes and threw me out on the parade ground to coax me into cooperating. It was very cold out there, and my feet began to freeze to the ground. They left me out there about half an hour then clubbed me back into the radio room. My feet were bleeding from being torn from the ground, but I still couldn't help them. They were trying to keep me alive to get something out of me. I liked hearing the Navajo language: it gave me hope. It told me that American forces were getting close, and I felt like I would be liberated the next day. If it hadn't been for the code talkers, I would have been put before a firing squad.[36]

The beatings and mistreatment continued, but Kieyoomia could not decipher the code. Eventually the Japanese transferred him to a camp in Matishima, sixty miles south of Nagasaki. A day later, America dropped its second atomic bomb, forcing the Japanese to surrender. Kieyoomia soon was repatriated and spent four years in different veteran's hospitals recovering from malnutrition and dysentery and undergoing surgery to correct his poorly healed arm. In 1949, he returned home to the reservation.[37] Joe Kieyoomia remained faithful to his country, the enemy received no assistance, and the Navajo code was never compromised.

For the Navajo code talkers about to enter battle for the first time, practice was essential. The tension, stress, and fatigue accompanying extended combat operations are not only physically but mentally debilitating. Radio transmissions must be delivered accurately over a long period of time; a radio operator cannot be fumbling around for a particular code word temporarily blotted from his memory. In secure areas, the men would quiz each other on how to transmit certain information and how to spell out words, almost like a game. When one considers the amount of radio traffic transmitted during the battle for Iwo Jima as well as the intensity of the fighting, automatic yet accurate transmissions become paramount. As William Kien, a code talker from the Fourth Marine Division who fought on the Marshall Islands, Saipan, Tinian, and Iwo Jima, said, "Throughout the war against the Japanese in the Pacific, we code talkers had to brush up on our codes at every opportunity. When the fighting got bad, words would fail us for a second; it was a good thing we [Navajos] have so many sounds in our language."[38]

Distribution of code talkers throughout the U.S. Marine Corps evolved so that by 1945 they were an inherent part of various organizational elements. With a total of seventy-six per division, the distribution was as follows: six per signal company, two per reconnaissance company, four per regimental headquarters and supply (H&S) company, two per infantry battalion H&S company, two per artillery battalion H&S company, two per engineer battalion, two per tank battalion, two per pioneer battalion, and two per shore party team. The marine memo detailing this list ended with a reminder to the reader that "The full value of the Navajo Talkers will not be appreciated until the Commander and Staff they are serving gains confidence in their ability. The Navajo language is the simplest, fastest, and most reliable means we have of transmitting secret orders via radio or over telephone circuits exposed to enemy wire-tapping."[39]

As Navajo code talkers received their initial training, the war in the Pacific against the Japanese intensified. Of the original thirty-two men, only two remained behind to train new Navajo recruits joining the ranks; the rest had been spread among various marine units. American and allied strategy called for a two-pronged offensive, one part going through the southern and southwest part of the Pacific, the other in a more central drive. The main objective of this "island hopping" was to seize strategic islands while by-passing others to obtain bases close enough to bomb Japan. The primary goal was to force the Japanese homeland into submission, forcing it to vacate all of the lands it had been seizing for years. The Americans' opening salvo came on August 7, 1942, when the First Marine Division landed on Guadalcanal in the Solomon Islands as part of the southern Pacific thrust. There they encountered heavy fighting that dragged on until February 1943, with both sides enduring heavy losses. By mid-September the Navajo code talker program received its baptism by fire. Soon Japanese on other islands began to hear this mystifying Navajo language that stymied any type of decoding and translation.

Samuel Holiday joined the fray in the central Pacific thrust, taking him to Kwajalein atoll, a series of eighty-five islands that extend for sixty-five miles. The primary target was two islands—Roi-Namur—connected by a causeway. The islands shared one of the world's largest landlocked lagoons, ideal for refueling and making naval repairs, while the 1,200- by 1,250-yard Roi held the principal airfield in the Marshall Islands. On Namur, an atoll of 800 by 900 yards, stood a concrete radio station, an administrative building, and an ammunition storage facility. An estimated 3,000 Japanese soldiers defended these specks of coral.[40] Two days prior to the invasion three battleships, five cruisers, and nineteen destroyers pounded the islands with 2,655 tons of explosives, pock marking the landscape with shell holes and leveling many of the defensive positions. There were three designated landing beaches on Roi—Red 1, 2, and 3—and three on Namur—Green 1, 2, and 3. Samuel went in on Green Beach 2 because it was closest to the concrete radio station where he was to establish his radio net.

The fighting on Roi was brief but violent. The marines quickly took the airstrip, now covered with disabled aircraft. Many of the Japanese defenders fled to Namur, where there was better protection from naval gunfire and bombing. Within six hours, the commander declared Roi secured and shifted his combat strength to Namur, where the fighting grew intense. The three concrete buildings were badly damaged but still standing. The Japanese defended their positions bravely for twenty-four hours, launching a banzai attack and repeatedly forcing the marines to fight from shell hole to shell hole. Four Medals of Honor were later awarded for individual acts of bravery.[41]

Code talker Keith M. Little, who served on the same island campaigns as Samuel, recalled an incident most likely occurring on Namur:

> During a lull in the battle for the Roi-Namur atolls in the Marshall Islands, our outfit was pulled off the front lines for some rest. The

> battalion command post was set up in a shell crater adjacent to a steel-reinforced concrete building. The men in the platoon were lazily enjoying the brief rest period when someone noticed that the heavy steel door of the building was very cautiously and slowly opening. Most of the guys trained their carbines on the door. Out came a Japanese, naked except for what looked like a g-string, with his hands in the air.
>
> The platoon leader immediately ordered everyone to hold their fire, but apparently some trigger-happy marine didn't get the word and took a pot-shot at the poor guy. Then twenty or more carbines blazed away. The Japanese took off and saved himself by diving into a shell hole.
>
> With all of the shooting going on, the platoon leader was shouting, "Cease fire. And goddamn, if you can't hit the bastard, leave him alone!" Suddenly the shooting stopped.
>
> Horrified at the poor marksmanship exhibited by the men in his platoon, the platoon leader unmercifully derided everyone. "What kind of Marines are you anyway, when you can't even scratch a target ten feet in front of you?" One shy Marine resolved the embarrassing situation for everyone by saying, "Sir, I was only shooting at the man's head." The rest of the men agreed that they, too, were aiming in that direction.
>
> The Japanese was coaxed out of the shell hole, given food and clothing, treated, and escorted to the rear. He was none the worse physically, except for a few minor scratches sustained in his desperate dive into the shell hole.[42]

The final phase of the assault—securing the outlying islands in the northern two-thirds of the atoll—required another three days to accomplish. At the end of four days of fighting, seizure of the Marshall Islands had cost 190 marines killed and 547 wounded; 264 prisoners were taken and 3,472 enemy troops were killed.[43] Samuel's first taste of combat came to a close as he boarded a ship going to Maui and a much needed rest. His next exposure to combat would be even more trying. But he had signed on for the duration, and like fellow code talker David Patterson who fought on Roi expressed it, "When I was inducted into the service, one of the commitments I made was that I was willing to die for my country—the U.S., the Navajo Nation, and my family. My [native] language was my weapon."[44]

CHAPTER FIVE

The Hard Edge of Combat

Saipan and Tinian: Protection Made Tangible

THE TWINS: SLASHING REEDS

The Twins next encountered a great plain covered with razor-sharp reeds called Lók'aa adigishii that had only one safe passageway through. As with the Crushing Rocks monster, when the boys pretended to move forward, the reeds rushed together to kill them. Four times the Twins feigned entrance, frustrating the monster, who demanded to know who they were. They explained that they were on their way to the house of their father then said, "We have power of our own."[1] Pulling out their feathers, holding them in front of them, and saying the prayers that Spider Woman had given them, they passed peacefully through the field of danger. A similar occurrence took place further in the journey when the boys reached a morass of cane cactus (Hosh dí tsahiitsoh) that could tear people to pieces by piercing with poisonous thorns anyone foolish enough to travel through them. Four times the Twins faked entrance, four times the cactus failed to touch them so enquired who they were. They offered the sacred words and were allowed to pass. The Cactus recognized their supernatural protection saying, "You do have strange powers like your father. May you travel in safety and find him."[2]

SAMUEL: SAIPAN—MOBILITY AND PROTECTION

We again boarded ship and departed in a long convoy composed of aircraft carriers, battleships, and transports. The code talkers had given each type a Navajo name.[3] As we sailed we practiced communications between ships. I was ordered to go to Colonel Jones's quarters to receive messages, so I ended up talking with the big shots in his office while waiting for incoming traffic. I sat there comfortably, they gave me a drink, and I talked and joked with them. Usually when we were around high-ranking officers we had to jump up and salute them, but here they acted just like regular guys. Their life was very different from that of the normal marine. Some things, like fresh food and alcohol, were hard to get on the ship. One night a corpsman brought us some pure alcohol so some of us got drunk. Other times someone would bring fresh vegetables like onions from the kitchen and we ate them with bread.

As we traveled it would occasionally become very windy. Heavy storms with strong winds hit us, rocking the ship as it swayed and rolled with the waves. The antennas and radar above moved back and forth, and if a person did not hold on, he would slide across the deck. Finally one night we neared Saipan. I could see the explosions and hear all the firing as battleships continued to pound the beaches and shore. In the morning of D-Day, I first saw the island of Saipan, with Tinian to the right as we arrived off shore about 9:00 A.M. There was lots of gunfire, with both sides shooting back and forth, bullets hitting the ocean with water splashing everywhere. Some of the marines who had fought in earlier engagements like Guadalcanal talked about how the Japanese had been grabbing up islands in the South Pacific and how we would really have to watch out for suicide bombers attacking our ships. On Tinian there was a big airport, with three others on Saipan. There was shooting everywhere, with smoke rising from the islands. I could see smoke stacks on buildings in the distance, but between us and those stacks were sugar cane fields and a town with houses and trains. To one side was another village that belonged to native workers enslaved by, but not sympathetic to, the Japanese.

Dan Akee was in the first wave; I was in the second to land on Yellow Beach One. The noise from the beach and in the sky sounded like a bull fight. I saw U.S. airplanes chasing Japanese airplanes between Tinian and Saipan. We also watched a dog fight overhead. They were chasing each other, and every now and then you could see a Japanese zero billowing smoke then crashing into the sea, breaking up when it hit the water. Everyone cheered and clapped, but it was very scary to watch. On shore along a mountainside, the smoke swirled all around with sand flying into the air from the direct hits by our battleships and aircraft as they pounded targets.

In the meantime, Dan Akee was on the beach with the first wave radioing back, "We can't advance. It's really rough and hard moving. There's lots of marines killed and wounded. There's heavy enemy fire from a hundred to a hundred and fifty yards ahead." It was very scary watching all of the bombing and gunfire from the ships, especially knowing that was where we were going. Once I got started in the actual fighting it was different; the fear just went away. Then it became my job to kill or be killed and that was how I thought of it when I went ashore as courage replaced fear. I knew then that the enemy was close and wanted to kill me so anger took over. I wanted to charge and kill them all as I joined the battle and forgot being afraid.

Near evening the second wave went ashore. Climbing down the cargo nets and into the small landing craft was frightening, with men fainting and the boats bobbing on the waves as the storm continued. Some men looked sad from fear, just as it was in boot camp, but now there was much greater reason. Somehow I did not feel that way as I climbed into the boat. The wind and waves rose high, the ocean raged and rolled as the main ship and the landing craft rocked back and forth. Finally the smaller boats were loaded and the second wave headed for Yellow Beach. Towards sunset we had a little ways to go to get to the shore, about fifty yards or more, when strong wind, waves, and maybe the bombardment turned over our boat and two others. I threw my pack off, but it caught on my gas mask hooked to my belt. I tried to release it, but the pack did not break free. I struggled in the water against the heavy weight dragging me down, fighting for air while trying to move forward. It felt like I was full of water as I began choking, almost drowning. The waves washed over me but I focused my effort to reach some trees along the shore. My lungs hurt, they could not get enough air, and every time I took a deep breath a wave swept over me. I swam close to the shore, got my feet on the bottom and tried to walk, but the waves knocked me down and the undertow pulled at my feet, throwing me back then pulling on my gear. Someone from shore patrol helped me up after cutting the straps from my pack, letting the water take it as he dragged me to the beach. My throat hurt, water drained out of my mouth, while I lay there coughing and watching the sunset. I must have passed out for a little while, slowly recovering but still dizzy, sore throat, tired, and coughing. As I rested there I thought of my mother, corn pollen pouch, and sacred eagle feather in my pocket. They gave me strength and protection so that the Holy One heard my prayers. That day, the prayers that were said for me before I ever left for war saved my life, unlike the two or three men from my boat who drowned and I never saw again.

Some marines watched me lying there and asked, "Who is this?" I struggled to my feet and one of them said, "Oh, there's the Chief." The men in our platoon who had come in the boats that capsized were spread far apart and many did not have packs or rifles. I knew we had to get back together and so we quickly identified members of our platoon and gathered what we could from the beach. The shore patrol knew where our company was located and gave us directions as to how to reach them.

By evening our reassembly was complete, but now we were pinned down by heavy bombing and sniper fire. Our front line had advanced slowly, the first wave pushing inland about fifty yards from the beach to a hill where they dug their foxholes. I moved to Dan's fighting position, feeling it was in a good, secure place. Another group had advanced ahead of us, but I still heard rifles shooting here and there, with big artillery rounds and mortar shells being fired from along the beach. It was very cold that night and the only equipment I had was my combat knife. I stayed wet and frozen the whole time and did not get warm until the sun came up. Then it became blazing hot.

That morning the fighting continued with intensity. The Japanese and our battleships were pounding away at different places. Dan and I received messages from the other units on the front line saying the fighting was hard and the going rough, with a lot of marines getting killed. Those of us who did not have any rifles or packs were told there were plenty scattered around the beach. One of the marine wiremen named Berman said, "Let's go down and get our packs from the shore." When we reached the beach there were heaps of packs that had washed in, been collected, and stacked alongside piles of rifles. It looked like bulldozers had dug some big trenches and dragged logs over part of them to provide overhead protection. These positions were reinforced with posts covered with sandbags. Men in the area carried wounded marines into these impromptu first aid stations, where doctors operated before evacuating the men to ships off shore. There were also dead bodies on stretchers outside of these shelters.

I took a backpack from a nearby pile and a small M-1 carbine to replace the heavy M-1 rifle I had carried before. I liked this lighter model

An invasion beach on Saipan, 1944. Cluttered with men and equipment and initially under fire, this staging area between the troops pushing inland and offshore naval vessels played a vital part for success. Two times Samuel almost lost his life in this area—once when landing and again when leaving. (Photograph courtesy of the U.S. Marine Corps)

that held sixteen .30 caliber bullets. I only took one hand grenade because they were heavy, but I did take a lot of extra ammunition. Just as we started back three tanks that had unloaded from a boat started inland. They were crawling along and provided cover so we followed them for about 100 yards from the beach until the Japanese spotted them and zeroed in mortar fire on these moving targets. We were unaware that the enemy was still hiding in the trees along the shore watching us.

Suddenly there was a boom when a shell fell right beside one of the tanks. We dove for some trenches the Japanese had already dug near a bushy area. Berman jumped into one a ways from me and I dove for another close by. We lay prone with shells falling all around. There was a blast not far off, then another closer, another even closer. "It's coming toward me," I thought. Before I realized it there was a loud boom that knocked me out. I awoke buried in sand. Panicked, I jumped up; Berman grabbed me and dragged me down into his trench. When I eventually came to my senses, I realized I was covered with sand and began brushing it off of my face, out of my hair, and digging it from my ears. There was a loud ringing sound, my head felt really big, and there seemed to be noises inside. My head was spinning as numbness crept into my left side.

After a while the enemy stopped shooting; I got up and staggered around. Berman offered to take me to a first aid station, but I said, "No, no, no! I'm all right." We returned to our group as I kept telling myself that I was not harmed even though I knew something was wrong. I told Dan Akee how I had almost gotten killed and that I could not hear correctly because of the noises in my head, but there was nothing much I could do even though I was very sick, shaken, and in pain. In Navajo these feelings are called hwii'hasdeeł, meaning a person is physically hurting in every fiber of his body. This is believed to be very harmful, even taking away a part of life. When it happened to me it lessened my hearing, but I thought it was temporary so never told anybody that I was hurt, even later when I was discharged from the service. With hwii'hasdeeł the feeling comes back every time a person thinks or talks about it. When there are two sounds it seems like I cannot really hear them clearly, turning it into a bunch of noise in my head. When people talk in a low voice I cannot tell what is being said. Other times I cannot hear them even if they are yelling, unless it is at a certain level and tone. If there is a lot of talking and noise I get mixed up. Surprisingly, I could understand clearly both the Navajo and English languages through earphones as I sent and received radio messages, but without the earphones it was difficult. I can still feel the boom and hear the firing around me and have regrets for going to that spot moments before the Japanese fired the shell. I wish I had stopped running and stayed by the shore a little longer.

The third day on Saipan, June 17, Dan received a message that a large Japanese convoy composed of battleships and aircraft carriers was headed for us and that some of our battleships and supply ships had already left for safer waters. Those ships were crucial to the taking of the island—we received ammunition, food and water, and protective gunfire and evacuated our wounded out to those boats. There was no battleship or hospital ship in sight. It felt like a child depending on parents who were now gone and there was no place to get help. That is how it seemed. We were very dependent on those ships that supplied us with drinking water and ammunition, especially ammunition. I thought we would suffer greatly without them. We all were scared, even the white marines. In the distance we heard naval gunfire, which worried us more since the fighting on the island was already fierce and now it appeared that we had lost some of our protection. A number of days later another message arrived saying that our forces had intercepted the Japanese aircraft carriers and that the enemy convoy was wiped out. When I heard that on the radio I felt a huge relief. This information was transmitted through the Navajo code so that the Japanese would not have access to accurate information.

For four or five days there was continuous shooting around us. At night overhead Japanese planes dropped bombs on the island. We used to call them Dishwasher Charley. Dan Akee had advanced with the front wave, sending messages back to me and other code talkers. In some locations the fighting was really bad. "We are being attacked," the radio operators reported. Then our unit received orders to take the Alito Airport, and I went with them to help. The Japanese began shooting at us from the airport then started running into the jungle on the far side. The marines shot at them, but I just watched until they were gone and we had taken the airport.

The Japanese evacuated a number of holes leading into a series of underground rooms. "Let's go down there," a marine buddy said, so I went with him, he with a pistol and me with a rifle. There were several big rooms connected together. We entered the first one and found where the Japanese had stored a lot of food like dried fish and canned goods along with some pots and pans. Everything was neatly stacked. There was also some pilot clothing with fur inside that were either hung up or stacked. We continued to walk for what seemed like a long ways, carrying our weapons and hand grenades at the ready. Elsewhere we found beer stacked around as well as a bottle of sake, which we drank. As we walked underground for a while we could hear shooting overhead. By the time we had explored these rooms and returned to the surface, the Japanese had retreated and our platoon had caught up to where we were, having killed a lot of the enemy. I sent radio messages back to our captain, telling him what was going on before our group returned.

Our patrol entered the frontlines and rejoined the company. We brought in several Japanese prisoners, stripped naked, with two or three guards watching over them. The big mortar and artillery shells the Japanese had shot at us had blown craters here and there, which now held water two to three feet deep. Some marines were already bathing in them. The day was very hot, the air sticky, I was covered with black from gun smoke, sand from combat, and I just did not feel well, being sick with fever. Washing in cool water would help. I was still hearing loud noises in my head and my body felt funny from the earlier explosion, so I walked to the shell hole and removed my clothes to wash and relax in a pool. By that time all the white marines had gotten out and gone back to the company, leaving me alone to bathe. Suddenly I felt a sharp sting in my back, looked up, and there stood a marine with a bayonet sticking me. I spoke up and said, "Hey, hey, I'm a marine. I'm a radio man." He was really mad and said, "Get out of the water, Jap." I raised my hands, left the crater, and tried to tell him who I was, but he did not believe any of it. Our commanders had warned all of us that the Japanese were very, very tricky and to never take a chance but just shoot them. The enemy was known to take uniforms from dead marines then infiltrate our lines with knives and bayonets to kill unsuspecting soldiers. The marine guard thought I was Japanese, and to make it worse I did not have any clothes on, just like the prisoners. I thought about this as he pushed me toward where the captured Japanese were detained. Luckily not too far away someone I knew saw what was going on. A group of our men were sitting around smoking, cleaning rifles, and eating when one of them came over and said, "Hey, hey what are you doing with my chief?" He explained that I was one of the Navajo radio men; Captain Kendall, our company commander, also verified that I was a marine in his company. The guard let me go and I hurriedly got dressed. The other marines were all laughing about it, teasing me because I looked like the enemy saying, "Hey, join your buddies over there."

This same problem of mistaken identity happened a second time a few days later after our unit advanced with another battalion. George Chavez and a second code talker were in that unit, and since I knew George well and was homesick to talk to other Navajo marines, I decided to visit him. As I walked over to see him, along the way I saw a pair of Japanese shoes, the kind that had a separated big toe. I picked them up, but as I neared George's position I fell in the mud. As I sat down to clean off my boots, two marines from the other regiment jerked my gun away, grabbed me by both arms, and yanked me up. I quickly yelled out, "I'm one of you from the other regiment, don't shoot." One of them poked a rifle in my back, saying I was a Japanese infiltrator. He was really rough, jabbing and calling me a damn Jap. I raised my hands when he told me to and tried to tell him that I was one of the radio men on my way to see George Chavez, but he did not know him even though they were in the same battalion. Again, luckily,

Japanese prisoners captured on Saipan. Twice while on this island, Samuel was captured by fellow marines mistaking him for an enemy soldier. Later in life he told of how degrading these experiences were. (Photograph courtesy of the U.S. Marine Corps)

somebody said, "George is over there," so the guards took me to him, rifle still in my back. George recognized me with a "Yá'át'ééh," and we talked for a short while. When it was time for me to return to my company, I went with an escort. For a number of days after, I was still sore from the bumps and bruises received from the rough handling.

I was not the only one to have this problem. Everyone received instructions not to walk around at night since that was when the Japanese tried to infiltrate. One night a Navajo code talker (name omitted) shot a Navajo marine (name omitted) as witnessed by another Navajo. The man doing the shooting told others that he had shot a Japanese soldier, but the next morning the men looked at the supposedly dead Japanese only to find that he was really a Navajo. Any one of us could be easily mistaken for a Japanese, especially at night, so we were very careful not to go by ourselves.

As our unit moved further into Saipan, we encountered a mountain that we paralleled. We moved to the front line, where I got back with Dan Akee and continued to send and receive messages night and day. The company commander ordered the unit to dig defensive positions, so Dan and I made ours on top of a hill. The other marines were making foxholes around us but lower behind the hill. Dan and I were so busy digging that we had not noticed that we were the only ones left on the top of the hill in our sector. We had dug in deep and it was getting dark, so we decided to stay. There was shooting and bombs going off around us, people occasionally yelling here and there, and the Japanese making banzai attacks on other parts of the line.

By this time the army had landed and was positioned to our right, marines on the left. The army soldiers were green, new to this battle, had just advanced, and were filling into different parts of the line. At least that was what we heard on the radio. Flares lit up the ground in front of our positions, and the army would start shooting at loose farm animals that had gotten away from their civilian owners. On our left side along a rock formation there was a lot of brush, where marines were positioned to guard against the enemy sneaking into our area. Every once in a while they would start shooting, followed by a Japanese scream or yell. I raised my head to look around, suspecting an attack by the enemy. Dan said to me, "Don't be crazy. Don't stick your head up too much or you'll get shot." I got kind of upset with him and thought that no one was shooting this way. "Let me see." I put my helmet on my rifle, raised it up, and immediately someone opened fire at it. Above my foxhole and all around, I could hear ricocheting bullets hitting the ground, kicking sand into our hole. I lay prone in my position and decided not to raise my helmet again.

Later that night, there was heavy fighting with the units on both sides of us. We just laid there and listened. Nearby a marine spotted a Japanese soldier sneaking through the lines who was quickly shot. He began yelling and screaming not far from us, gasping, moaning, and making funny noises with a gurgling sound. At first it was very loud, then it grew softer until after about two hours, silence. The next morning we went over to find him and saw that he had been shot in the lungs and died. The noise and blood had been coming out of the hole in his chest, with more blood and spit trickling from his mouth. I still hear the noise he was making, which bothers me to this day.

Every once in a while flares lit up the whole area when the Japanese staged banzai attacks. We were lying in our foxhole when there was a thud and Dan groaned like he was hurt and scared. My first thought was that he had been stabbed or shot. Chills ran through my body, thinking I was next. A flare lit the sky so I slowly turned my head in his direction, expecting he would be all bloody, but to my relief, I saw a big bullfrog on his back apparently trying to save his life too. We both laughed softly so as not to be heard. He explained the frog's landing on him had almost knocked the air out of his lungs. We chased the critter off and continued to stay down. For a moment I had really gotten scared thinking that Dan was wounded; I had a lot of close calls but those did not bother me as much as the thought of Dan getting hurt.

From this same position during the day, we could see what used to be houses but now were only piles of boards. The Japanese had moved out of this area and so some of the marines started to look around. The local people had farms with pigs, chickens, goats, sheep, and horses that had been let loose. One of the marines started yelling, "Hey, hey, in the boards I found a Japanese sling shot." I looked at it and saw that it was just like the ones I used to make. Under those same boards were some chickens that had gotten scared, run into the pile for protection, and now sat there with their heads sticking out. I started shooting at them with the sling shot and never missed. Other marines asked me to kill chickens for them, and soon men from other outfits were asking, too. I do not know how many chickens I killed, but I do remember the men next asked, "Do you know how to fix them," so I did that too. We also killed and butchered a calf. The soldiers ate a lot of meat and the same evening they milked the mother cow. They did crazy things like that. These were just young restless guys, eighteen, nineteen, twenty years old who were always hungry, so they really enjoyed any fresh food, especially meat. We spent three days in that position and feasted on boiled or roasted chicken or calf every meal before we moved on.

After the area had been cleaned and tidied up, Dan Akee came to our foxhole and told me that Captain McCain wanted me to go on a reconnaissance of an enemy position located between two peaks of a mountain. The Japanese were firing artillery from a hidden emplacement in that area and were targeting men, supplies, and boats landing on the beaches. Dan came back in the morning and said, "We are supposed to go over on top of that hill farther up in front to spot the Japanese artillery then radio back their position to our artillery, so that it can fire on them." I told him, "Only if one of us went with a white radioman because we might not make it if we went together. I have already been stuck with a bayonet and captured twice by our own men. So if we went by ourselves we would be taking a chance of being mistaken for Japanese and shot." Dan went back to the captain; I waited. He took a long time and I worried, wondering why they had given him those kinds of orders. It just did not seem right; we usually had one code talker on the front line and the other one with the company headquarters, but now they wanted us to go together.

I was sitting alone in the foxhole thinking about what was going on when Dan returned and told me to come and meet some people. The newly appointed radio chief named Foos, a tall man from our platoon, introduced me to a couple of white men I did not know. One of them, a short, young, blonde marine, was a rifleman; the other would carry the radio. I was told, "With these two men you will move forward, get on one of those hills, and spot the Japanese artillery. It is already on the map but we need to confirm its specific location and assign a target number." The three of us looked at the map to select a route and see where it was, then started off. The commander had the marines along the front line notified of our mission and that we would be passing through their positions, but once we left, all communication to headquarters was to be in Navajo. I was told not to let anyone else know about it.

The short rifleman took the lead as scout, running up ahead then motioning us forward. Up the specified hill we went but not to the top, for we had already spotted the artillery. The marine in the lead came down to us and told me he had identified the target with map coordinates. I radioed this information back to another code talker located with the marine artillery. For about five minutes we waited before hearing one shot and an explosion on the enemy location. I radioed back in Navajo, "Right on, right on the target." Then the marine artillery pounded the area. I do not know how long they were shooting, but by the time we returned to our lines, I could see a lot of dust and smoke rising from behind the hill.

Then it was like nothing happened. I returned to my foxhole and the two other men went to theirs, so nobody knew about it except for a few marines. I did not even tell Dan what had happened. I had been warned back in the States by my instructor John Benally to keep things a secret. "Don't let anyone know who you are. Nothing. That's the way you should go around," he told me so I did not tell anybody. To this day it is like a dream.

One or two days later we advanced to where the Japanese artillery that we hit was located. There were sandbags, rifles, and bodies all over the place. Some of the big guns were lying on their side with sandbags stacked around them. The dead Japanese had body parts scattered all over from our artillery's direct hits, and the smell of gun smoke and rotting flesh was everywhere. These Japanese looked like Navajos with their brown skin and black hair. I felt strange looking at them and must have stared at them a long time because one of the marines pushed me and said, "What's the matter with you, Chief? Are you afraid of dead Japanese?" Looking at them really made me feel sad. I wondered how many people we were killing because of the code talkers' work. I had not realized how much damage we were doing with the Navajo language or how many people were dying. I remembered what my mother had said about not killing anything without purpose. This meant not even killing a lizard or plant and here we were killing human beings. It was sickening, but it was war so we moved on.

I had not thought about Navajo traditions very much while on these islands. I was in war in a land of war with people trying to kill me, and so I did not think about these things but only winning. When we captured this land it would be ours. A long time ago the warriors who went into battle captured Utes or Paiutes at Navajo Mountain and Inscription House. Even the women were taken. That is how I thought about this situation. Navajo warriors brought Paiutes back to our land and they became Navajos called "Dinétsoii" (Yellow People). In war it is all right to capture the people you fight and conquer. This war was far away and we were conquering everything, making it like a prize to be won. It is our native heritage land that we honor forever, where we were born within the four sacred mountains. We belong there. That is how the Holy People made it. Their teachings are sacred, and we honor them. The important thing is the sacred mountains and the United States of America.

We continued to advance on Saipan. I worked with another commander named Major Muir who had a habit of calling me Geronimo from the first time we met on the ship. One day most of his company got together on a hill slope where we talked about moving down into a valley. Then he said, "Hold it, hold it. Geronimo grab some hand grenades," warning there were snipers below. I took some and started with our company into this valley where several houses lay shattered from artillery fire. There were lots of trees and caves, and even though the area had been heavily bombarded, I still did not believe it safe. Many small holes led to large underground rooms that could still have Japanese hidden in them. As the company advanced, the major told the platoons to stop and wait. "Come on Geronimo, bring your grenades and let's check for snipers."

Three code talkers on Saipan, *left to right*: Corporal Oscar Iithma, Private First Class (PFC) Jack Nez, and PFC Carl Gorman. Teams with men paired together facilitated communication as one man became used to working with his buddy. (Photograph courtesy of the U.S. Marine Corps)

He walked ahead of me spraying bullets and throwing grenades into the holes and collapsed houses, anywhere one could hide. We walked through bushes and around big rocks; I felt like the enemy was there watching me, so I looked closely at every hole and bit of vegetation. There were some bushes that were a very different shade of green and a little bit fake-looking. In Camp Pendleton our instructors taught us about camouflage and there was a part of the bushes that looked like someone had traveled through them. I had also learned a few simple Japanese phrases such as "Lay down your arms" and "Come out with your hands up. You will not be harmed." As I looked into the vegetation, I saw a small hole so spoke some Japanese then threw a hand grenade in. It exploded; dirt and smoke poured out followed by a Japanese soldier. He raised his hands, pleading for something in his language. In the meantime, the major, a big man, dragged another one over with his arms around his neck and told me to take the two captives to our unit where an intelligence man in our company who spoke Japanese would interrogate them. The major instructed me, "If they pull any funny business, shoot them," and with that I motioned the prisoners forward.

As I started back, the major continued throwing grenades and firing. I began thinking that if there was the slightest problem I would shoot both men because they were tricky and might run off to cause more trouble so I sure did not want them to escape. They walked ahead of me, hands behind their heads. About 200 yards out from the company, there were men sitting around watching me. When I was within earshot they began teasing. These white guys were saying, "Hey, that Japanese is on our side" and "Which one is the Japanese? Have the Japanese taken a Navajo radio man prisoner?" I was embarrassed.

We secured Saipan in twenty-five days, in spite of the fact that there were a lot of snipers who kept us jumpy. The last part was the northern end of the island. While our platoon was mopping up the rear, the major wanted me to be with him again ahead of the element. "Come with me, Geronimo," he said. Just then a tall Japanese soldier came out of some bushes. We at first thought he was surrendering but then he started running. A second later he was shot up, but he still ran another twenty-five yards. As we neared the northern part of the island called Marpi Point, the commander ordered the platoon I was moving with to stop a ways from a rocky height. Looking ahead I could see people from a village running to the edge of the cliffs. Some of them shot at us while others remained near the edge. I could hear loudspeakers pleading with them to surrender, trying to get the civilians not to jump.

We were told to stop a ways from them in order not to crowd the prisoners with the ocean to their backs. Beneath the point of the cliff were black rocks sticking up like knives in the sea, the waves hitting and splashing against them. Many children and women with babies stood in this group, one woman fixing her hair before running out of the crowd for the cliff. Some civilians grabbed and stopped her before she jumped then dragged her back into the crowd. Another woman threw what looked like a baby wrapped in a blanket into the ocean while others began committing suicide. I was told that some of the women had thrown their children down then jumped, but others had changed their mind. I also saw a tall Japanese prisoner run toward the edge, but the guards shot him. On the other side of the cliff and behind the village were loudspeakers and Japanese prisoners pleading with the people on the cliff to surrender and be taken care of.

SAMUEL: TINIAN—SAVED BY A FRIEND

After we secured Saipan on July 9, Tinian was next. We went ashore from a landing craft on the evening of July 24. Every once in a while Japanese planes took off from the island, but they went down in smoke. The first wave encountered heavy fighting; I was in the second wave. Marines were pinned down by artillery fire, the enemy's airfield was destroyed, while other reports came over the radio announcing what was happening before we ever arrived. Day and night code talkers sent messages, perhaps a few thousand, identifying targets and reporting casualties. We moved to the shore amidst heavy artillery and small-arms fire, which prevented us from advancing and forced us to dig in and wait out the night. A lot of marines from the Twenty-fifth Regiment were killed there on the beach. Dan and I were in a foxhole surrounded by thick brush. On our right and left was small-arms fire close by.

Early in the morning, just as it was getting light, a heavy enemy artillery bombardment started again. We watched more of our men being killed. Ahead of us another company advanced, and I could hear them shooting. When the bombing stopped I heard someone calling. We were still in our foxhole but I kept listening to "Help, help." I tried to get out, but there was still too much shooting. Dan warned me to stay down. He was always taking care, watching out for me. I eventually was able to leave our position as other marines climbed out of their foxholes to see who was injured. I walked toward the sound, hearing a call for help and crying. There was a big tree that had burst from an enemy shell, under which marines were lying in a foxhole. They had been showered with shrapnel from the shell that hit the tree. Two of them were dead, but a third man was alive with a cut across his stomach. The gash was large, his guts spilling out, and he could barely speak, but I think he still knew what was happening. He had his hand over his wound, trying to push his intestines back in. The corpsmen tried to help, but the man died shortly after. I went back to the foxhole with Dan but will never forget how sad I felt. Sometimes I thought I should get a notebook and write a memorial for him to send to his parents, but I did nothing. I still think about that young man.

By this point, members of the first wave had advanced across the island and captured the airstrip on Tinian. They had been in the heat of battle and taken a beating before sweeping toward us as we moved forward to meet them. It had not taken long to secure Tinian. We made camp near a rocky hill and prepared to receive our first hot meal in a long time. There was going to be lots of fresh meat brought in from the ship. While the mess staff was cooking, Dan and I climbed a hill on the side of a cliff. On top there was a large cave with some smaller ones beside it. In front of the caves were scattered tin cans and food scraps where the Japanese had tossed them as they were living in and fighting from this position. I started to enter with my rifle ready, but Dan warned, "Better not go in there. They are waiting to shoot you." "Okay," I said, and we went back to camp. While we were eating Dan and I sat talking with some other marines and mentioned, "There's a cave up there, but we did not look at it very closely. Dan thinks there's Japanese in it." Three of the men wanted to go and investigate so after eating, we went back up the hill.

By the time Dan and I reached the position, the three white men had entered. Suddenly there was a loud bang, then a second, then rifle shots. Soon we saw one of the marines, our radio chief, carried out, one leg dangling and torn. He had gone directly into the cave, where the Japanese attacked him with a grenade. Quickly a corpsman cut off the injured leg and sent him to the Red Cross ship on the ocean, but three days later we learned he died. Dan had saved my life earlier when I wanted to enter the cave.

During the fighting on both islands, it was my prayers and pollen that kept me safe. I used corn pollen all of the time to say my prayers because the Holy People made it and it was my connection to the Holy One. I kept it very close to me like a wife. My mother's prayers were answered and protected me from drowning and being injured by mortar shells. Prayers are real and protect you, but also I did not always pray because I was not scared some of the time. I know that other Navajo marines prayed and had ceremonies done for them before going overseas. After this last incident, I told Dan Akee that he had saved my life and that he was my hero. I said this over and over again.

Commentary: Island-Hopping—The Navajo Experience

When Monster Slayer and Born for Water encountered the Slashing Reeds Monster, they depended on their spiritual power received from Spider Woman to navigate their way to safety. The same was true of Samuel when he landed on Saipan, a forty-five-square-mile island covered with dry jungle, mountain ridges, and networks of natural caves. There were also extensive meadows of sword grass, whose sharp blades grow taller than a man and can easily cut human skin as one passes through. A medical officer in his pre-invasion briefing explained just how deadly this landscape was for those fighting in it:

> In the surf beware of sharks, barracuda, sea snakes, anemones, razor sharp coral, polluted water, poison fish, and giant clams that shut on a man like a bear trap. Ashore there is leprosy, typhus, filariasis [parasitic worm infection], yaws [skin disease], typhoid, dengue fever, dysentery, saber [sword] grass, insects, snakes, and giant lizards. Eat nothing growing on the island, don't drink its water, and don't approach the inhabitants.[4]

Add to this approximately 30,000 Japanese soldiers and marines embedded in jungle, meadows, and a few small towns, defending the headquarters of the Japanese Central Pacific Fleet, the Thirty-first Army, and Northern Marianas Defense Force, and one can understand the invading force's need for prayer and protection.

The task of seizing this largest land mass in the fifteen-island chain known as the Marianas was given to the Fourth and Second Marine Divisions and the Army's Twenty-seventh Division, all under the command of Marine Major General Holland M. Smith. A total of 165,672 attack and garrison forces prepared to take the island that would then place American B-29 bombers in range of every part of the Japanese homeland as well as cut the enemy's supply and communication lines in the Southwest Pacific.[5] Two days before the invasion, fifteen battleships began shelling the island and did not stop until the two marine divisions began landing troops on June 15, 1944. In the first twenty minutes of the invasion, 4,000 men on two beachheads disembarked from 350 amphibious tractors in heavily defended enemy territory.[6] Still, the Japanese expected the landing elsewhere, and so even though they rained effective fire on the amphibious tractors moving toward the island and placed mortar and artillery fire on the beaches, they did not have their infantry forces placed in opposing positions. By the end of the day, parts of the Twenty-fifth Regiment, Fourth Marine Division, which Samuel joined in the evening, had penetrated 700 yards inland, while other elements encountering less resistance had gone in much further. Samuel, however, indicated that his element was much closer to the beach. "The First Battalion, Twenty-fifth, on the extreme right, continued to receive withering enfilade fire from Agingan Point. The enemy was making a determined effort to smash the invasion on the beaches. Wrecked tanks, burning amphtracs, dead marines, and aid stations filled with casualties, were mute evidence that the Division had a tough fight on its hands," just as Samuel recalled.[7] By nightfall some marine elements withdrew from their forward positions to consolidate into a unified defense, but still there were gaps in the line, and the enemy held commanding terrain to the front. Parts of the Twenty-fifth Regiment received an enemy attack that pushed them back 400 yards—territory that had to be reclaimed the next day.

The first four days, June 15 to 19, of the invasion were the most demanding and crucial. The enemy's forces had maneuverability and cohesive forces to wage a campaign against the more closely contained American elements. On June 17 the U.S. Navy received word that a Japanese fleet was heading toward Saipan, and so for six days the men on shore had no naval gunfire support, reduced supplies—especially ammunition—and no place to evacuate wounded as the transports moved to safer waters and the battleships left to confront the approaching enemy. Once the fleet returned from the Battle of the Philippine Sea and announced that it had destroyed five vessels, including three aircraft carriers and 402 planes, the troops were elated.[8] It was, however, a disaster from which the Japanese Imperial Navy struggled to recover. Even with the naval absence, the land war continued, and on June 19–20 the Twenty-fifth seized the commanding terrain of Mount Tapotchau, a key position in the Japanese defense. From this high ground the enemy had delivered deadly direct and indirect fires. With its capture, the marines continued to move inland while using this high ground for observation.

On July 9, following twenty-five days of relentless fighting, the Twenty-fourth and Twenty-fifth Regimental Combat Teams hoisted an American flag on a telephone pole on Marpi Point as the mopping up of enemy forces continued on the nearby airstrip. A few hours later Marine Commander

Smith declared the island secure. Yet Marpi Point continued to be a problem as Japanese soldiers interspersed with civilians encouraged suicide by leaping off its cliffs. This mixing of 20,000 civilians (75 percent of whom were Japanese, the rest Chamorro and Korean) with Japanese soldiers had been an issue from the outset of the battle.[9] Now it was part of a large-scale finale. Samuel's witness of this event testifies of the desperate Japanese attempt to salvage honor in a hopeless situation. Just as tragic were the 5,981 killed, wounded, and missing marines from the Fourth Division representing a loss of 28 percent of its strength while the enemy had 23,811 known dead and 1,810 captured.[10] Months went by as small pockets of resistance were either eliminated or surrendered.

The thirty-nine-square-mile island of Tinian lies three sea miles southwest of Saipan. Although smaller, Tinian's three airfields were important objectives to seize. Rather than assault the larger beaches on the southern end of the island, which the Japanese had fortified in anticipation, the Fourth Marine Division seized two smaller beachheads—one being sixty-five yards and the other 130 yards wide—on the northern, undefended end. U.S. troops massed artillery fires on the southern end of Saipan, launched fighter aircraft from its captured Aslito Airfield, and used the island to stage the assault; thus, Saipan played a handy role in defeating its neighbor. On the morning of July 24 the attack on Tinian began. By that evening the entire Fourth Division was on shore and had established a front 4,000 yards wide and 2,000 yards deep at a minimal cost of fifteen dead and 150 wounded.[11]

By late evening and early morning of the next day, however, the Japanese had repositioned themselves and launched a massive offensive against their invaders. Supported by armor and artillery, enemy forces began aggressive and well-planned attacks up and down the marines' line, in some cases penetrating for a short time before being repelled. This hard-fought battle was the most intense encountered on Tinian, breaking the offensive back of the Japanese defenders. The next day, the marines counted 1,241 bodies, with an estimated 800 more retrieved by the enemy—casualties of the intense fighting. Following this battle, there were sporadic planned skirmishes, but most of the resistance boiled down to rooting the enemy out of cave and bunker complexes. By August 1 the Second and Fourth Marine Division with the U.S. Army's Twenty-seventh Division had secured the island of Tinian, with the Fourth losing 290 men killed and 1,515 wounded. The Japanese suffered 9,000 dead and 250 captured, with

13,262 civilians rescued and under military control.[12] With the fall of Guam a little over a week later to other U.S. Marine, Navy, and Army forces, the three main Japanese-controlled islands in the Marianas were now liberated by the Americans, allowing the bombing campaign against the Japanese homeland to begin that November.

Samuel's role as a private first class (PFC) radio operator in the seizure of Saipan and Tinian provides a detailed look at how Navajo code talkers operated in the field. While he recounts a lot of interesting and useful information, there is also a lot left unsaid about the general experience of other Navajos serving in this capacity. There are also gaps in understanding even his experience, because as a PFC, he would not be aware of the bigger picture. In addition, his focus was on his role as radio operator, and he was trying to recall details about events that occurred so long ago. Thus, for instance, Samuel was often unclear about who was receiving his radio transmissions, how many code talkers served in a particular operation, and what the experiences of other code talkers were like. This uncertainty is not surprising given the fact that of the 420 code talkers trained during the life of the program, many did not see combat, and those who did could not talk about their experiences until the government declassified the system twenty-three years later—a long period of time that allowed much to be forgotten and many of the code talkers to pass on without leaving any account. In fact, there have been relatively few official interviews with those who do remain. Indeed, the autobiography by Chester Nez, one of the original Twenty-nine, is the only full-length biography that gives a more complete perspective.[13] There is a fair amount of official military documentation about the organizational side of recruiting, training, and employing code talkers but only bits and pieces from the Navajo perspective.

This issue raises another point: how characteristic was Samuel's view and experience? He came from a highly traditional background that encouraged him to interpret events through the teachings of older Navajo culture, whereas many of his comrades came from a Christian belief system honed by the dominant culture's school system. Although all of the Navajo code talkers spoke the Navajo language and understood Navajo cultural beliefs, there appears to be a broad spectrum concerning who practiced these beliefs and how they practiced them, based on their upbringing. So while each code talker had his own individual understanding and practices, how much of it embraced traditional beliefs? The same is true of their combat experience. There were obviously common denominators in fighting against the determined Japanese foe, but each island and unit had its own peculiarities. Compare the six-month campaign to seize the mountainous jungle terrain of Guadalcanal (August 7, 1942 to February 7, 1943) with the seizure of a relatively bare coral atoll named Tarawa during a three-day battle. In both cases approximately the same number of Americans (1,600 and1,700, respectively) were killed, whereas on Guadalcanal there were twice the number of wounded (4,200) than on Tarawa (2,100). Still, given the length of time and fighting conditions, there were dramatic differences.

What follows is an attempt to consolidate information provided by code talkers who make reference to traditional Navajo practices they used on the different battlefields in the Pacific up to the invasion of Iwo Jima, which is the topic of the next chapter. Using Samuel's experience as a baseline, with Chester Nez's full account then adding other code talkers' views, one can see the role that Navajo culture played for at least some of these men. Where each of their experience falls along the spectrum of totally traditional to mostly Anglicized is difficult to determine. What can be said is that those cited felt a close enough bond with Navajo beliefs to incorporate some aspect of them into a highly modern form of warfare.

Samuel's assignment as a code talker led him to a variety of combat experiences: sometimes he was relatively divorced from actual combat in order to communicate with higher headquarters about general conditions and specific needs, and sometimes he was in the thick of fighting. The Saipan campaign was the most fluid on the battlefield that he would encounter. Following the initial acceptance of the code talker program after proving its value on Guadalcanal, a list of their responsibilities in combat identified crucial needs. Their primary responsibility was as "talkers" because the coded language was dramatically faster than using any mechanical or written device, both of which had been broken, or deciphered, by the Japanese. For code talkers it was just a matter of speaking it on one end of the radio or telephone system and writing it down on the other. They also worked in message centers and occasionally as couriers, because headquarters feared they might be captured and the code compromised. Suggested level of assignments included two (a pair of men) per infantry battalion, four per infantry and artillery regiment, four per engineer regiment, two per engineer battalion, and eight per pioneer battalion, with others being assigned to signal companies (eight), tank and scout companies (six), and other elements, with a total of a hundred per division.[14]

Chester Nez provides the clearest account of how this system worked on the battlefield. Although he did not fight in the same campaigns as Samuel, it is safe to assume that the general employment of code talkers was fairly comparable throughout the Marine Corps.

> We men worked in pairs. Officially, two pairs of men who partnered together were coupled into a group of four, and two groups of four worked together with two rotators, bringing the total number in each band to ten. Generally, we sailed together on the same ship. When we reached an island, four of the code talkers in our band remained on board ship and the other six disembarked. Our positions—land versus ship—changed with different campaigns. Once ashore, the land-based men stayed in touch with those on the ship and with each other so everyone knew what was happening.
>
> I spent most of my time onshore, actively sending messages. And I, like the other code talkers, stayed in communication with all the talkers as much as possible, regardless of assigned groups. We'd report what was happening in battle around us. We'd let the rear echelon know when we needed reinforcements and give them the hot dope on whether a particular strategy was working. If someone screwed up and our men were targeted by friendly fire, we'd send a message through requesting a halt. That type of message was always heeded when sent by Navajo code, because the Navajo men receiving our messages knew the Japanese could not fake them.
>
> Our staying in touch had another advantage: if a man heard an error being made in a transmitted message, he'd click the transmit and receive buttons on his TBX radio several times. That click acted as a signal, telling the transmitter to recheck and retransmit his message. When messages were flying, it was difficult to tell where the click came from and to determine which message might contain an error. But we were fierce about deciphering any problems and correcting any misunderstandings. People make too much of how difficult the code was. We knew it like we knew our own names, so it wasn't difficult for us. But every man worried about making some sort of error. The strain

> of having to be perfect ate at us. It weighed upon us every minute of every day and every hour of every night. Every bit of information had to be accurate: where the Japanese were, which way they were going to move, how many men they had. No one wanted any mistakes to get through and to endanger our own men.[15]

Even by the first engagement at Guadalcanal the American codes had been compromised to the point that the Japanese understood what the Americans were going to do. By the time of the battle on Saipan, the shackle code for encrypting map coordinates had also been broken.[16] To help deteriorate American capability to communicate, the enemy would also intercept radio signals and make horrific noises or tap into the landline of a field phone and quietly listen undetected. Jimmy King from Shiprock recalls that on Peleliu, the code talkers delivered their own messages just working through the interference. "Even when the Japs got on our frequency, I would break in on all of them, all the units, and say, 'Let this guy that's humming and singing and yelling and cussing—disregard what he is saying and just tell him to go kick Tojo's ass in Navajo then say message to follow to all units.' Then I would send the message. They were beating tin cans and drums and blowing horns into the mike when they got on our frequency."[17]

One white marine recalled just how important this ability to transmit was on Saipan. During the give and take of battle, the Japanese abandoned a series of positions and retreated several hundred yards to their rear. The marines occupied the vacated foxholes then notified headquarters of the change in location. Soon artillery shells started raining down on the friendly forces—those higher in rank did not believe the radio transmission, thinking it was just another Japanese trick imitating their enemy. A second round of fire landed even closer. Then headquarters inquired if the shelled unit had a Navajo. "The Marine said he will never forget the message that was sent by the single Navajo in the battalion, although he couldn't understand a word of it. A few minutes later, he and his comrades saw a cloud of smoke rising from the Japanese positions. They had been saved from being 'clobbered' by their own artillery by that Navajo message."[18]

One code talker on Saipan had a different experience in terms of how this important asset was employed. Shortly before the island's fall his unit encircled a town filled with Japanese soldiers and civilians. An army unit also encircled the objective, but that night, the enemy staged an attack that broke through the army's position and mixed in with the marines. Confusion reigned as friendly and enemy forces engaged in combat in the dark, neither one quite sure at times who was in front of them. The Japanese captured friendly artillery pieces, but there was no ammunition available for them to use. Not until the next day was the situation clarified and the enemy force defeated. One of the code talkers involved in this situation later observed:

> Very little code talking was possible during this emergency on Saipan because things were moving too fast. It seems to me that the use of the code was most effective when the Marines were up against something—when we were sitting in one place too long, and wanted to move on. When lines were established and planned strategy could be carried out—to take the next hill, the airport or what have you—that's when the code talkers were in greatest demand.[19]

Samuel's experience of twice being mistaken as a Japanese soldier was another experience not uncommon to a number of Navajos. The impression is that especially during a moving, fluid situation this type of mistaken identity could occur frequently. Three examples to compare with Samuel's experience are offered here. Take William Toledo, for instance. When he was at Camp Pendleton, he went to his assigned unit in the Third Marine Division and met the men he would work with. He later learned that they thought he was a Japanese interpreter and that was why they had been told not to ask any questions or talk very much to him. Eventually the men learned that he was Navajo. The second day on Bougainville, there was a serious case of mistaken identity as the marines pushed into the jungle from their initial beachhead. Men from different elements became separated then rejoined other elements as they moved through the brush. The communications men were also interspersed with the riflemen. Suddenly Toledo felt the sharp point of a bayonet in his back, with a marine telling him to raise his hands. After a futile explanation, Toledo went with the marine to his colonel, who explained that this "Japanese" dressed in marine clothes with marine dog tags was truly one of them. The captor faced a strong chewing out while Toledo's foxhole partner received the assignment to stay with his buddy and never let this happen again.[20]

Chester Nez had a similar experience. He recognized that his hair and skin color as well as a slight build gave him an appearance that closely resembled that of the enemy. One day while on Guam he studied a young Japanese prisoner in a stockade then understood how fellow marines could draw that conclusion. He also felt sympathy for some of the Japanese dead and one officer in particular who killed himself before the stunned radio man. And when another Navajo code talker brought in six Japanese prisoners on Peleliu, Nez felt pride even though the white marines made the most of it, joking "Hey Chief, did you hear? One of your guys brought in some Jap prisoners. . . . We thought he was a Jap bringing in his own men. We should have said, 'C'mon over here Chief. Let me see your dog tags.'"[21] Nez contemplated:

> At first I couldn't understand it. In my opinion, the two races—Japanese and Navajo—looked nothing alike. But later, after staring eye to eye with that young Japanese prisoner on Guam, I understood. But I never did understand why so many American troops thought our Navajo transmissions were Japanese. I guess Navajo just sounded foreign to them. Our language and the language of the enemy sounded nothing alike. . . .
>
> The title "code talker" had not been coined yet, since most of the Marines did not know of our secret function. But other Marines had been warned not to call us Navajos or Indians. No one wanted the Japanese to draw any dangerous conclusions. So "Chief" stuck.[22]

Nez also knew what it was like to be on the receiving end. One evening on Angaur Island, he and another code talker received orders to report with their equipment to a tank 250 yards away. They started on their journey when a group of army soldiers surrounded them with rifles and pistols pointed at the two. Nez tried to explain who they were, that they spoke excellent English and so could not be Japanese, and that they were just following orders. As a last resort he asked one of the soldiers to go to the communications center by the tank to find someone to vouch for them. One man left and came back with an officer, who had Nez released and told the captors to report to him later.[23]

The final example comes from Jimmy King on Cape Gloucester. During an interview in 1971, he recalled the following incident:

> It was raining. The monsoon had struck and rained all through the night. The last order of the day was that there should be no light, not even a cigarette. Even in the jungle they didn't want any light. So while I was in the dark black feeling my way around, I ran into a fellow who asked me for the password. I think it was "lame duck," anything with an "L" in it. So I said my password but he said "Say it again." I said "Lame duck" and he replied "You son of a bitch," and then stuck a bayonet right in my back, ready to kill me. I was going to be shot right away. Straight ahead there was a foxhole that I fell into and in it there happened to be a man that I knew named Sergeant Curtis from Kalamazoo. He asked, "What the hell is going on?" so I told him "They think that I'm a Jap. They want to kill me." Then my friends in the foxhole started firing their machine gun so I stayed there for half the night.
>
> The next day they [his unit] sent some runners out to find me since I was missing and took me back. Then they said, "Well you guys, it's too dangerous for you guys to be out there, but somebody has to deliver this message—that radio is knocked out. We're going to string this line. You will have to follow that line, inch by inch. Somebody's going to have to crawl there and make it. Right or wrong, you will deliver this message. It's an order." Yes sir—whether it was raining or shining, we crawled to deliver this message. And that is how we did it.[24]

Detainment by friendly forces was dangerous enough, but capture by the enemy was lethal. Statements made by code talkers indicate that the Marine Corps took steps to protect their Navajos from being captured by, if possible, keeping them away from the fluid part of a battle where capture was more likely and by also assigning a bodyguard. The reality was that in a mobile conflict, these safeguards were not always practical. If a code talker were captured, the entire code could be compromised, and so to prevent this, a white marine buddy was often assigned to accompany his Navajo companion to prevent his being confronted by friendly troops as well as being captured by the enemy. If the latter became inevitable, there is good indication that these men had instructions to kill the code talker. Nez said, "I don't know whether our bodyguards had orders to kill us rather than allow us to be captured. The Marine Corps has been asked if this was so and they did not deny it. I believe that an American bullet would have been preferable to Japanese torture. At any rate no code talker was executed by his bodyguard."[25] In other situations the intent was more direct. Kee Etsitty recalls a Colonel Robinson approaching a group of code talkers and handing them a .45 caliber pistol with the instructions: "This is for you code talkers. . . . You don't use this pistol on anybody. This is for you, when you get captured, that's when you cock that thing back, put it here [gesturing toward his temple], goodbye."[26]

Protection through traditional practices was a vitally important aspect for many of the code talkers in combat. Samuel's dependence upon the ceremony he had at home and his pouch with corn pollen and feather were important in sustaining him during the fear and trials of combat. He was not alone. Chester Nez, who considered himself primarily Christian, still exhibited great faith in a medicine pouch's power to protect. He tells of being on Guadalcanal, in combat for the first time, and each morning before sunrise crouching in his foxhole with his companion, Roy Begay, offering prayers. Each would take the medicine pouch that connected them to home and the prayers of their relatives and would take a pinch of corn pollen, touching their tongue then the top of their head then gesturing to the east as they offered prayers. Chester explained about his medicine pouch:

> It protected me and gave me confidence that I would survive. I rubbed the tiny black arrowhead attached by a wrap of rawhide to the outside of the bag. A white rock and several other small objects tucked inside had special meaning for me. The bag also held corn pollen, taken from the tassels of corn plants back home.
>
> Roy's medicine bag was different from mine, but they both had the same purpose: protection. No two medicine bags were identical, because their contents were personal, but one ingredient was always the same—bright yellow corn pollen. The other elements were specific to the person who owned the bag—perhaps a small piece of turquoise or other small mementos. No one talked about the contents of his medicine bag. Someone who disliked you could use their knowledge of the bag's components to cause you harm. Only people real close to you, like your children, should know about the contents of your medicine bag. There's a lot of power in those things. It's something you don't play with.[27]

Code talker W. Dean Wilson, who fought on Tarawa, agrees, adding that a person had to have faith in what he practiced, "otherwise they don't do any good. . . . You have to respect it in order to [have the power protect you]."[28]

Not all protection for Navajos in combat was carried on their person. The prayers and ceremonies performed at home were additional sources, as Samuel testified. He felt their power though he was halfway around the world. Others had similar experiences. Sidney Bedoni from Navajo Mountain who served on Guadalcanal, Vella Lavella, Saipan, and Okinawa spoke of how his father insisted on having an "[eagle] feather made for me" that remained with the family. "We're just going to pray to it, the same as you're here. But the feather that is made for you stays here."[29] The feather was tied in a knot and when prayers were offered, corn pollen was sprinkled on all four sides, with the prayers being carried by the four winds in the cardinal directions.

Chester Nez experienced how effective this practice could be. One day he and Roy and some other code talkers were quietly passing time when Chester heard sheep bells, but there were no animals around. One of the Navajos commented that someone back home was praying for those marines. Chester then commented that he often heard these same bells around noon. "Even thousands of miles from home in conditions I could never have imagined, it was comforting, the sound of the sheep and goats coming in. . . . I felt sure they continued to pray for me and burn sage or chips of cedar, fanning the smoke over their bodies. Their prayers were carried across the miles as pure, bright chimes of the bells. The clear tones told me that I was still in good faith," even though he had not been able to attend his own Blessing Way ceremony.[30]

Nez shared other spiritual practices undertaken by Navajo marines. Among them he tells of men sending home some of their unlaundered-from-combat uniforms to be used in protection ceremonies. Because they had worn and sweated in the material, a part of them was still in it and so could be used as a proxy in their absence. In the same respect, pieces of clothing or hair taken from dead Japanese soldiers were also sent home so that medicine men could perform ceremonies to spiritually confuse, defeat, and kill the enemy.[31] A similar practice is part of traditional Navajo witchcraft where one "works against" another through using something that belongs to the intended victim.[32] Conversely, because of this belief and practice, Chester felt "it was dangerous enough getting your hair cut during peacetime, when you could be sure that the hair was properly disposed of. During battle, I sure didn't want to take a chance."[33] For other Navajo marines it was not an issue. Later, a haircut on board ship where the clippings could be taken care of properly was no problem for Chester. The difference between those who had concerns and those who did not depended upon how each had been taught.

Code talker Alex Williams was raised by a traditional family. He spoke of his ceremonial preparation as well as his spiritually working against the enemy in combat. Before he left for the war he had a two-night protection ceremony. The first evening he was alone with the medicine man, who performed predominantly songs and prayers. The next day was fairly quiet as the recipient took a yucca bath, was dried with ground corn meal, and then donned clean clothes with a lot of necklaces, bracelets, and other forms of wealth. The second evening family members joined in and spent all night in song and prayer. The medicine man used eagle feathers to sprinkle the marine with herbs mixed with water for protection.[34] When Williams was on Pavuvu Island, he and five other Native Americans—a Zuni and four other unidentified Native Americans from Oklahoma—staged a "war dance." The men took a picture of Hitler and one of Tojo and sang against them as two of the men danced. At the conclusion, one dancer stabbed Hitler's picture, the other Tojo's. Exactly how much in keeping this was with traditional practices is questionable, but it certainly was a form of Native American expression.[35]

A final example of the spiritual side of combat comes from Samuel Tso, who tells of one night when he was asleep.

> That night I was dreaming about an Indian maiden. I can still picture it: her hair dripped down, all down, almost to her knees; wearing buckskin coat, and she said, "Here, take this and wear it, and you will come back to us." I was dreaming then, and when I was dreaming that I was reaching for it, and I was saying something to her. And I guess that's the time my buddy kicked me and woke me up, and he says, "Hey, Sam, are you having a nightmare?" It was so real that I just got up and sat at the edge of the foxhole, thinking about it. After a while they went for breakfast. All of them went over there. I just sat there, thinking about my dream. When they came back, they saw me still sitting there. And they asked me, "Hey Chief! Are you still there? What's the matter?" I think all I said was, "Oh, I'm thinking." I didn't bother to talk about it. After a while they had mail call. You see, I never go to a mail call because my father and my mother and the

> rest of them, they don't know how to read and write. I wrote to them but I never received any letter. They [fellow marines] went to the mail call. After a while there was a guy running back and he lifts up a letter and says, "Hey, Chief! You got a letter, you got a letter!" He came running, came running close to me, and all of a sudden he says, "There's something in it." So he brought it to me, and as soon as I got the letter, I looked at the return address. Nothing. So we opened the letter, pulled it out . . . Oh my gosh! That dream . . . in my dream . . . the thing she was handing me to wear—it's in that letter! "Hey, I'm supposed to wear this." So I put it on my neck. As soon as I put it on my neck, all fear dissipated. All I could say was, "I'm going home. I'm going home."[36]

The Navajo code talker experience was as much mental and spiritual as it was physical. The power, prayers, and protection these men enlisted on their behalf so they could perform the challenging tasks of communicating in combat played a significant role in their effectiveness. Although not all of them followed the traditional practices examined here, there were those who drew upon other religious beliefs for their strength to overcome trials. The adage "there are no atheists in foxholes" may not be true in all cases, but the emphasis Navajo culture placed on religion certainly encouraged recognition of a spiritual side to what was encountered. This reality was just as true for Samuel Holiday as it was for many of the other Navajo code talkers.

CHAPTER SIX

THE FINAL CRUCIBLE

Iwo Jima: The Code Talkers' Triumph

THE TWINS: SHIFTING SANDS

The final test before reaching Jóhonaa'éí's home was with turbulent, rising sands at a place called Séít'áád.[1] Accustomed to engulfing its victims by whirling about and burying them, this monster of desert sand awaited the unsuspecting traveler by laying placidly under clear skies. When the boys approached, the dunes became increasingly agitated, demanding, "Who are you?" The reply: "We are children of the Sun, we came from Dził na'oodiłii, and we go to seek the house of our father."[2] They repeated this four times, the sacred formula given them by Spider Woman. The Twins then passed peacefully through this danger and continued on their journey.

With each test on the holy trail, the Twins became more knowledgeable. Finally they saw in the distance the home of Sun Bearer, a square-shaped turquoise building located beside a large body of water with all kinds of pets and creatures belonging to the god.

> Water Monsters, Water Horses, White Egrets, Brown Herons, White Nostril Monsters, and black, white, yellow, and glittering Monster Fishes all of which were the pets of the Sun. . . . [The Twins] began to sing and the Wind arose. After four songs the Wind had increased and stirred the water, lashing the waves until they drove the monsters underwater. They [the Twins] were then enabled to jump across the water by means of their rainbow so that the spies of the Sun did not notice them.[3]

Before entering, the young men had to pass between four different guardians of the passageway. There stood two large bears, facing each other and preventing anyone from entering. Beyond them were two serpent guardians, then two winds, then a pair of lightning to stop intruders. The boys, now confident, took out their sacred feathers and pointed them at the fearful guards, repeating the prayer of protection given by Spider Woman. They passed each pair unharmed and entered into the majestic home of their father.[4]

SAMUEL: THE DISAPPOINTMENT OF IWO JIMA

After we secured Saipan and Tinian, our unit went back to Maui to a rest camp, where we trained again for three months. It was located not too far from the town of Waikiki, where banana trees grew wild everywhere. Still, the training was intense. As code talkers we practiced transmitting and receiving, but there were no new codes to learn. There were many tents set up for us, and we received new marine replacements to fill the positions of those who died on Saipan and we obtained new equipment and weapons as well. Our training continued to prepare us for fighting on the next island. One of the things we practiced was what to do in case our ship was hit during combat. Exiting under emergency conditions included standing with our feet together, knees locked and straight, then jumping into the water. This taught us how to enter the ocean safely to avoid being hurt by a board or other debris on the way down. We also practiced throwing hand grenades and did a lot of hiking for long distances. The Navajos were good hikers, which had been proven early on. One of the favorite stories I heard occurred at Camp Pendleton before the code talkers first deployed. The Navajos and white men who were in training for the first time had a competition hiking for about twenty-five miles. The white marines ran very low on water while the Navajos had a lot left in their canteens. This was because the Navajos were drinking the sap from a plant they called k'aabiizhii that grew along the way. They were familiar with this cactus-like plant as something that could be eaten for food or drunk for water in the desert at home. So the Navajos sucked moisture out of this plant, sipped a little bit of water from their canteens, and let the truck following behind pick up the white marines who could not hike any longer.

The Hawaiian island of Maui was so beautiful and the natives friendly. When we arrived they greeted us with leis. They were very scared, believing that the Japanese were going to return and attack them again since they had wiped out the aircraft carriers and ships earlier. The local people were happy to see us and said they felt safe with us there. When we went to a cafe to eat they served us huge steaks and soon learned that we could eat a lot of them. One time I went by myself to Waikiki. In the morning I saw some navy sailors and avoided them. A lady came over, took me into the kitchen, and tried to talk with me in her native language. I told her that I did not understand. "Oh, I thought you were a local boy," she said. "You look like one." "No, I'm an Indian," I told her. "Where are you from?" she asked, then served me all kinds of dishes. I really had a big breakfast that morning; before leaving she placed a lei on me.

After setting sail from Hawaii our ship stopped at Saipan for a week or two. The island was greatly improved since I had last seen it, with good roads traveled by army trucks and a working airport. It was a sight watching our B-29s taking off for their runs against the enemy. While there, Dan and I sent and received messages, one of which announced that our B-29s were bombing Japan. We also heard of B-24s and other aircraft and submarines working against Iwo Jima and how they were taking pictures of the island. To this day I do not know who the code talkers were that I was sending or receiving messages from or even where they were located. They could have been stationed on an airplane, submarine, or aircraft carrier. But every time I sent messages the big brass would say to me, "Chief. Don't tell anybody!" I think that Dan and I knew more about the operations than most of the troops.

The leadership did not officially tell us anything until we were on our way to Iwo Jima. Our commanders said that the next place we were going would be very tough. There was a Japanese commander who had been trained in the United States and knew how Americans fought. As the leader of the enemy forces, he would be very difficult to defeat. Now officers showed us pictures of the beaches with camouflage bunkers and pillboxes. There were also relief maps with markings on them laid out on a table for us to study. In briefings we learned that the Fourth Marine Division would land on Blue Beaches One and Two and Yellow Beaches One and Two as written on the map, approximately one-and-a-half to two miles to the right of Mount Suribachi. The maps also showed where the coast was heavily armed with artillery, anti-aircraft guns, mortars, rockets, camouflaged pillboxes, and block houses connected with tunnels and underground rooms used for storing food and ammunition. All I knew was that I was going to war again and felt numb. I really prayed for all the protection I could get and depended on the prayer ceremony that had been done for me. I prayed a lot and kept the feather and the pollen given to me in my possession all the time and never took them off.

On the morning of February 19 we arrived at Iwo Jima, and I watched the island at the southern end near Mount Suribachi as I prepared to board the landing craft. I could see bombers dropping their loads on Suribachi and fighter planes firing bullets along the shore. After the planes did their work the battleships began shooting. Smaller gun boats were also firing at the beaches, with smoke and black dust rising all over. One of the marines from our company pointed farther up the island saying, "That's where we're going to land." The battleships were doing a good job of pounding the caves on the side of the rugged mountain.

During this time the Japanese did little shooting. Not until the first wave hit the beach did the Japanese open fire with every weapon they had as the marines landed along the shore. I went in with the second wave at Yellow Beach One. As we approached it I saw two or three landing craft resting on their sides with bodies of marines floating in the water and lying on the sand. Once on the beach I crawled up a steep bank not far from the landing area. The sand was like ashes, like walking in an avalanche of snow. It was so loose and slippery going uphill that it was hard to move forward as I struggled to the top wearing my pack. Jeeps, landing craft, and tanks were also getting stuck. Around us the sand flew into the air as bullets hit the dirt.

There had already been a lot of marines killed, so we crawled through the bodies. I wormed my way to a marine, shook his feet, asked him about the enemy and if we should move on to find a foxhole. He was already dead. I patted him on the back and said good-bye then moved up through the bodies until I was almost at the top of the slope. Bullets continued to pass over my head while I watched artillery shells explode among the marines' supplies and landing crafts, causing big clouds of black dust to rise as debris flew upward. Smoke made the sun red. The rest of the landscape was dusty gray while all I could smell was smoke and rotting flesh just as on Saipan. This was war, and I had to go through it. I saw the bullets hitting the sand directly in front of me along the top of the slope. I thought that if I tried to go over this ridge I would not have a chance of surviving, but I also was not safe where I was. The vibrations from the explosions made the ground shake all over. Battleships were still firing at the hillside, but the enemy guns would not stop. The earth moved and shook, dead marines were scattered here and there, and we did not know where the Japanese were shooting from amidst the hills, rocks, and cliffs. Even though there did not seem to be anything blocking the way, we could not pinpoint enemy locations. There were some small trees toward where the mountain stood up, but where we had landed it was flat with a lot of little hills, giving the Japanese broad fields of fire to wipe us out, while much of the enemy artillery shot at us from the caves on the side of the cliffs and rocks.

Close to the beach was a hill where some marines were just sitting. I moved away from this group and started for another hill. Men were running from shell hole to shell hole to avoid the shooting that was all around. I ran forward and found a marine and tried talking to him saying, "Hey, what's going on? Shall we go forward?" I then saw he was moving, but badly wounded. I spied a group of marines sitting in a hole about twenty feet away. Before I could move, that position took a direct hit, sending a helmet high into the air. I do not know how many marines were killed with that one round, but there were others who just kept moving forward toward an airstrip that was our objective. Some had found protection behind a rock wall and were shooting from it while others used flame-throwers. There was so much noise along the coast and all the way to Suribachi that it seemed like everything was shooting at once.

By now the black clouds of dust covered the whole island. It was all such a horrible sight. Even the sun seemed sad. When I got on the first terrace, I looked out across the flat area. There were small and large craters made by different size shells from the bombings. I could see marines running for those holes so I decided to run for one of them, too. I passed two or three already filled with marines yelling at me to jump in with them. By now I was being shot at, could hear bullets going by with black dust spurting all around me. I jumped in a crater already occupied by a group of marines and sat down to catch my breath. Inside some were just standing around not paying any attention to the firing going on, as if they did not give a damn. I sometimes felt that way too. I was not worried about the small bullets but only the big bombs. One of the men, a big marine with a large mustache and chewing tobacco, kept looking at me. He must have thought I was Japanese. I don't think any enemy could have scared me as much as he did. It was a good thing there were two radio men I knew because I thought he was ready to attack me until he eventually calmed down. One of the radiomen in the crater said to me, "Chief, we are going to set up our radio here," so we established our communication station about fifty yards from the shore, which the Japanese continued to shell, but they never touched us. I began to operate the radio while the other two radio men reinforced the sides of the hole with sand bags; others helped turn the crater into a command post. By the time the sun went down we had built a good fighting position in which we remained for a couple of days. That night our company made its headquarters with us, turning it into a regular information booth. We gave one lost marine directions to his company.

For two days, Dan and I manned our radio and shared the position with our two white marines—one a radio man, the other a wireman. One of them kept telling us what he planned on doing after he returned to the United States, while the other said he was going to do important things to help his family and himself. Then they asked me, "What about you, Chief?" I told them that I was going to visit all the states. The ground troops made slow progress in the beginning, and so we remained where we were. I would sit there with the officers and call on the radio for water, ammunition, and medical evacuation. In the meantime, a crippled B-29 aircraft in need of a mechanic landed on the island. They found one who fixed it in about forty minutes, and the airplane was off again. The landing strip needed additional work as more and more airplanes began to land there.

The code talkers I trained with were strict with what they said to each other. I never knew who I was talking to, and I did not talk much to others if it was not official business. I know that there were a few communicators on the hospital and battleships and in airplanes who had special assignments. If there was a top secret communication, like from an airport to the carrier or to the hospital, sometimes a commander required a code talker to transmit the message. We used earphones and could hear very clearly even when the Japanese intercepted our calls and began talking on our radio frequency. I could even hear their breathing in my earphones, but I tried to listen only to our radio transmissions. The shooting around me did not disturb incoming traffic. I never worried about the radio breaking because I usually had a repairman with me, so if something went wrong he could fix it. Other white marines had assignments as runners and telephone wiremen so that these land-line phones could be used for local calls. The radio was used for critical long-distance communication in battle areas with code talkers. Some of these telephone men were brave heroes, and a lot of them were killed hauling phones around the battlefield. That's how they were.

After a while the marines advanced across the island. My job was with the radio and so as our units moved forward, I remained for most of the fighting in a command post probably about 200 yards from the beach where I first landed. In order to clear many of these enemy positions that were well-camouflaged and deeply entrenched, we really needed artillery, the big guns. The marines would request their assistance, keeping the code talkers on the radio day and night. When I was needed by the group I was working with, someone called my name and told me what I had to do. I would call another code talker located with the artillery, who would then give the message to an officer located with him, then the guns would fire. Sometimes when the artillery rounds came too close, we received orders to move back. Another helpful assistance for the ground troops was special detection teams. I saw one marine who had a dog with him that smelled out enemy locations, except for those in caves because of all the food and other things in them. He and his master had received training and knew how to locate these hidden enemy.

At times I was by myself, but most often I was located near the headquarters with another radio man. Dan Akee worked forward with different elements, and so I did not see him until the end of the fighting. Sometimes I wondered if he was the one talking to me on the other end of the radio, but I was not sure. This bothered me because I felt that I was just listening to the war rather than really participating. It seemed like I did not go anywhere but just sat on my butt and listened to all of the shooting. I do not know how many Japanese I killed with my words or how many marines I saved, but I did my job. I am very proud of all the marines who fought on Iwo Jima, but I felt like I was doing nothing. When you are in a war your fear of it goes away. That's how it was for me. When I went to Iwo Jima I felt a little cheated that I had not gotten a chance to fight the same way I had on Saipan and Tinian. I helped to win those islands by landing and fighting, but this one was different. It seemed like my job was incomplete, which I regretted but my assignment was not my choice. Years later when I saw pictures of how we had won at Iwo Jima I finally felt better, more complete, about it.

I remember the day the marines raised the flag on top of Mount Suribachi. Everybody everywhere started making happy noises. On the radio the code

Raising the flag on Mount Suribachi, Iwo Jima, February 23, 1945. Nothing symbolized triumph over the tenacious enemy on this small volcanic island like Old Glory waving on top of a mountain still inhabited by Japanese defenders. Navajo code talkers relayed the news and enjoyed the celebration, although there was still hard fighting ahead. (Photograph courtesy of the U.S. Marine Corps)

talkers were saying a wonderful thing had just happened and now this mountain belonged to us. Although I did not see the flag because we were closer to the ship and farther away from the mountain, I heard a lot of shouting everywhere and felt happy that we were winning the war. This was one of the few times as code talkers we held unofficial conversations like that. Otherwise, our communication had to be about serious matters to help win the battle.

One thing I was really afraid of was the big black lizards that seemed to be running around everywhere. They were black, about a foot long, and acted like they were going to chase after you. These lizards were very ugly and scary looking but harmless. They ran up trees very fast. Some were dead from shell explosions while others crawled around on everything. At times when I was in a foxhole I could see their eyes looking at me, hiding behind rocks. One time a big lizard on the wall in a small cave watched me and a white marine. The other man took out his combat knife, I thought to kill the lizard but he put his hand in his pocket and took out a hard twist of chewing tobacco, carved off a piece, and put it in his mouth. I was afraid that he would do something that would get lizard blood all over us then began to imagine the stink of the lizard blood. It affected me a little that way. Many of the white marines just kicked them around, stepped on them, and killed them out of frustration. We teased each other about it. "There's your friend," we would say to them, but I never touched one of those creatures, even though I heard the Japanese ate them.

Traditional Navajo teachings warn a person to respect lizards because they are like the children of the snake so are taboo.[5] I do not mind the ones we have around Utah and Arizona or the horned toad. A story from long ago is told about a giant who was going to kill and eat a young boy. The victim saw a horned toad, picked it up, moved closer to the giant, and then thrust it at him, scaring the giant away. That is why a person calls the horned toad grandfather. Some people rub the horned toad on themselves so that they will not be scared of things and be protected, just as its spikes on its back are for protection. Pollen shaken on one then taken off keeps a person safe if the creature is asked for protection. My mother told this to me, and so I treat lizards and horned toads with respect.[6]

At one point toward the end of the fighting, I thought I even heard the Japanese commander. Even though his transmission was in his native language, I could tell he was tired from the fatigue in his voice as he talked. An interpreter in the command post translated the message, saying the enemy had no more water and that they could not hold out any longer. "We have lost. We cannot regain our position unless you send battleships and bombers right away. That is the only way we have a chance to win. Otherwise, we have lost." That is what the message said that was sent to Tokyo.

Around this time I had a Navajo buddy named Jim Kelly from Teec Nos Pos.[7] We worked together in our communication post about 200 yards from the shore and never went far from it, operating the radio night and day. At one point Kelly went off a ways to relieve himself. He never came back, and later I was told marines found him shot between the eyes by a sniper who had probably remained hidden in a location near the landing beach for a long time. Kelly died while returning to the command post, but other marines killed the sniper.

Our forces moved across the island slowly, defeating the Japanese along the way. In the final days of fighting a group of desperate enemy soldiers sneaked around our flank just south of what was called Turkey Knob. I was told to join in the fight with other Navajo code talkers who were there. Everyone was shooting at very close range. Often when an enemy soldier was hit, he would jump right back up. There was a lot of shooting and hand grenades going off. Every now and then I got down or behind a rock when the Japanese opened fire. I could see the bullets bounce off the rocks and the dust pop up here and there. It was very rocky, with small cliffs, ravines, caves, and underground rooms scattered everywhere across this part of the island. Many marines were unlucky, being either killed or wounded then carried back to the first aid station. As I ran and crawled from rock to rock, I sneaked up on a Japanese soldier who was lying twisted between some rocks and a crevice, as if he were dead. My mind snapped when I saw him. "Jap!" I whispered to myself and started shooting at him along with some other marines. The firing stopped and he lay dead. Some men went down and turned him over; a hand grenade rolled out of his hand. The marines standing close by saw what had happened so we all jumped for cover, but it never detonated. After that I did not trust the Japanese, even when they were dead. I still wonder why the grenade did not explode—perhaps he had not pulled the pin out. I do know that I was lucky I did not get killed.

We continued advancing to the end of the island. At the tip close to the shore a marine charged in anger and was wounded. We could see the Japanese throwing hand grenades and shooting around him. The marine in charge of our group kept going back and forth checking on everybody then told me, "Go get him, Geronimo." I started forward with George Chavez. We ran to the wounded man, and the enemy really opened fire. As we dragged him back, sand flew up all around us. There were a lot of the code talkers involved in this last fighting. Somehow our leaders had made plans for us to do this because there were mostly Navajos in the group. Something was going on even though there were some white guys, too, but it was mostly code talkers who advanced and finished securing this part of the island. Maybe they wanted to see the Navajos fight the Japanese. The whole

This enemy position, like so many others on Iwo Jima, had to be taken with flamethrowers and bazookas, because the enemy refused to surrender. Minutes before this picture was taken, a Japanese soldier emerged from this cave, tossing grenades and wounding a number of marines before "dying for his emperor." (Photograph courtesy of the U.S. Marine Corps)

episode occurred during some of the last days of combat, when the enemy was desperate and the fighting short. Then it got quiet and we turned back to the staging area.

After we secured Iwo Jima on March 26, we returned to Hawaii. We knew then that the Japanese were losing the war, but we expected to head out again. Then the news announced that the war was over. Our country had used nuclear bombs on Japan.

COMMENTARY: OF BLACK SAND, EAGLES, AND WAR

The collective use of Navajo code talkers reached its height during the seizure of Iwo Jima, one of the landmark battles in the Pacific theater. This eight-square-mile island lies 750 nautical miles from Tokyo and is relatively flat and desolate, with the exception of the volcanic protrusion of Mount Suribachi. This dominating point of high ground was aptly named in Japanese "grinding bowl," a title that proved all too true during the battle. The island's name (lō tō) in Japanese means "sulfur," a mineral mined there. Its black volcanic sand mentioned by many who fought on it was often compared to walking in snow, making traction getting off the beaches difficult. For the marines fighting there this meant one step forward two steps back. The powdery sand sifted its way into everything—men and equipment—as Samuel points out, even blotting the sun. The shifting, boiling sands the Twins encountered on their journey to the Father could not have been better manifested than that found on this Pacific island during the invasion.

Like a sulfur match head struck against the marines' iron will, Iwo Jima erupted in continuous bombardment on December 8, 1944, seventy-two days before the actual invasion began. The island was well-prepared for this punishment. Lieutenant General Tadamichi Kuribayashi, commander of 23,000 troops on Iwo Jima, had built an impressive array of underground defensive positions to include the following:

> 150 concrete reinforced, bomb-proof pillboxes around the [two] airfields. In the northern sector, 16 miles of interconnecting tunnels with multiple entrances and exits had been excavated. This tunnel system would contain approximately 800 positions, including 120 75 mm guns, 90 large mortar and rocket launchers, 130 howitzers and 68 antitank guns. The beach defenses comprised 21 block houses, 92 concrete pillboxes, 32 camouflaged artillery emplacements and five freshwater distilleries, which supplied the entire island.[8]

The well-disciplined forces of his 109th Division, knowing that they would soon be attacked, prepared various beachheads for the expected onslaught with the anticipation of dying in their positions. The land battle started on February 19, 1944.

Facing this opponent were three marine divisions, one of which was the Fourth to which Samuel belonged. Its mission was to seize the Motoyama Airfield no. 1 while the Fifth Marine Division landed closest to Mount Suribachi, with its conquest as one of their objectives. The two divisions shared a 3,500-yard-long landing beach. The Third Marine Division remained on call in reserve. Hoping that three-to-one odds in the marines' favor would tilt the tide of battle, General Holland M. Smith, overall commander, ordered a day and a half bombardment of naval gunfire and carrier-based planes before sending the troops ashore. No doubt this bombing had its effect, knocking out some of the enemy emplacements along the beach, but the vast majority of the Japanese forces waited below ground for the firing to stop. Once the bombardment ceased they returned to their fighting positions and allowed the initial waves of Americans to get close to the landing site before springing their trap.[9] Prior to this, sporadic fire kept the first wave busy, but once the boats were well within range, all hell broke loose.

On board the transport ships anchored 4,000 yards from the island, the men made final preparation. "Around 4:30 A.M. some code talkers quietly made their way to the top decks to perform the ritual greeting to Father Sun. They reached into their pouches and retrieved small dabs of sacred corn pollen, placing it on their tongue then the top of their head and, finally, making an offering to the east. This would give them clear speech, clear thought, and a safe path to walk."[10] The prayers took effect. Thomas Begay and Johnny Manuelito stood on the deck of a battleship for their first look at the island while coordinating by radio the pre-landing fires. A sense of foreboding brought on by the ugliness of Iwo Jima was confirmed when a shell fired from onshore "bounced off just below where we were standing. It bounced off the next deck below and exploded on the third bounce. We would have been the first casualties of Iwo Jima if that shell had exploded on impact. Things like that made you glad you performed your ceremony."[11]

Praying continued as the first wave of marines made their way toward the beach about 9:00 that morning. Code talker Alfred Newman recalled: "You hear people praying, Catholics, I don't know what other religions. You could tell the Catholics praying because they go like this, mumble to themselves. And others, they just shut their eyes. . . . And when we hit the beach, all the equipment was just all bogged down in the sand, the trucks especially. And some of the boats were hit and were just useless. They were all just clutter on the beach. We're all trying to run ashore." [12] Kee Etsitty added, "Lots of these marines died there. . . . They are floating around. They need help. . . . They don't have no corpsmen. They don't have no doctor. . . . It was crowded, everything was shot up; it's like a junkyard, all the way down. A lot of these marines, you can see them out there, floating around. Try to ask for help . . . and these guys were drowning. That's where a lot of them died, I know."[13]

Paul H. Blatchford from Tuba City was a code talker with the First Reconnaissance Company for the Fifth Division. Because of his education and prior experience, he advanced to corporal but for the invasion served as a sergeant in charge of a platoon. As his element boarded the boats as part of the third wave, Paul noticed how preceding craft had approached the landing beaches in a straight line, making them easy targets for Japanese gunners. He spoke to the coxswain of his Higgins craft, suggesting that he take a zigzag course, but the coxswain had his orders and refused to comply. Captain Thomas, company commander, however, was in the same craft, discussed the situation with the two men, accepted the plan, then spread the word to the other landing craft to do the same. The plan worked, and although there was intense enemy fire at the approaching craft, the boats and men made it safely to shore, only to be pinned down for the rest of the day. Not until night fell did Blatchford's platoon get off the beach and start inland.[14]

In spite of the extremely accurate enemy fire on the beaches, the Fourth Division had its four assault battalions ashore in forty-five minutes. Thomas Begay said that during the first hour as he communicated back to the ships, "I was scared, very scared; mortars and artillery [shells] were landing everywhere, but I wasn't hit. The Iwo Jima sand was ashy and hard to walk on, but I had to carry my radio and other equipment across it."[15] Newman encountered a similar problem. Once out of the landing craft and onto the beach, he moved forward with others from his element.

> And while we were trying to climb this sandy beach, it was kind of steep. It was real sandy. You know how sand is: you try to climb it, you just slide back down. Edmund Henry and I were just trying our best to get up there, and there was—heard those shells coming. There was a great big ol' hole there in the sand. We all jumped in there, with about five or six guys right on top of us. Then about two or three minutes later we all started laughing and crawling out of there. So

> we were pinned down for about one day there; couldn't move, had to spend the night on the beach there just hoping that we don't get hit with a shell or something.[16]

Perhaps Dan Akee summarized not just the first few hours, days, or weeks on Iwo Jima but his entire war experience when he said, "The war was very sad. I saw dead Marines on the beach at Iwo Jima . . . we had to go through them."[17] The whole experience of being a code talker in combat was something they all "had to go through."

The Twenty-fifth Regiment to which Samuel belonged received the task of seizing the high ground to the right or northeast of Blue Beach Two. Heavily defended and capable of delivering raking fire on the beach, these enemy positions created havoc with those on shore. The Twenty-fifth now had to do a turning movement off of the beach and attack uphill to secure the area, which it accomplished that first day at the cost of 35 percent of the regiment's strength lost in casualties.[18] The next day was more of the same: slow-grinding combat that left the Fourth Division with 2,011 casualties.[19] As Lieutenant John C. Chapin, a participant, described it:

> There was no cover from enemy fire. Japs deep in reinforced concrete pillboxes laid down interlocking bands of fire that cut whole companies to ribbons. Camouflage hid all the enemy installations. The high ground on every side was honeycombed with layer after layer of Jap emplacements, blockhouses, dugouts, and observation posts. Their observation was perfect; whenever the marines made a move, the Japs watched every step, and when the moment came, their mortars, rockets, machine guns, and artillery—long ago zeroed-in—would smother the area in a murderous blanket of fire. The counterbattery fire and preparatory barrages of marine artillery and naval gunfire were often ineffective, for the Japs would merely retire to a lower level or inner cave and wait until the storm had passed. Then they would emerge and blast the advancing marines.[20]

This characterized the intense daily fighting that dragged on for twenty-four more days as the division pushed its way across the land in the most costly battle for a Pacific island the marines had faced up to that time.

As for the code talkers, they carried the brunt of the communications work, sending and receiving messages in support of the invasion. Each

This steel-reinforced concrete bunker was one of hundreds from which the Japanese provided interlocking fire that covered every square inch of Iwo Jima. Because the Japanese had months to prepare before the invasion, the island became one of the most hotly contested pieces of real estate in the Pacific. (Photograph courtesy of the U.S. Marine Corps)

division had approximately two dozen employed managing message traffic from ship to shore and amongst units locked in combat. Samuel Billison on board ship reported, "We were supposed to work in six-hour shifts with four hours off in between, but the first two days at Iwo there were no shifts. We were sending message after message for hours on end. Just about the time they told us to lay down or eat, they would come and get us to go back on the radios because more traffic was coming in."[21] Major Howard M. Connor, signal officer for the Fifth Marine Division, later stated,

> The entire operation was directed by Navajo code. Our corps command post was on a battleship from which orders went to the three division command posts on the beachhead, and on down to the lower echelons. I was signal officer of the Fifth Division. During the first

> forty-eight hours, while we were landing and consolidating our shore positions, I had six Navajo radio nets operating around the clock. In that period alone they sent and received over eight hundred messages without an error.
>
> A week later, when the flag was raised over Mount Suribachi, word of that event came in the Navajo code. The commanding general was amazed. How, he wanted to know, could a Japanese name be sent in the Navajo language?[22]

For twenty-six days the marines progressed in intense combat that often resulted in hand-to-hand fighting as well as in the use of hand grenades, tanks, and flamethrowers. Each of the divisions seized an airstrip while the Fifth Division sealed off and captured Mount Suribachi on February 23 followed by its famous flag-raising. This was the same day that the initial move to seize Airfield no. 2 with its elaborate defense system began by the Fourth Division. With the Japanese commander General Kuribayashi ordering each of his soldiers to kill ten Americans and to fight to the last man, there was no wavering in the resistance. Some of the most bitter fighting in the entire invasion centered around Hill 382, Turkey Knob, and what was called the Amphitheater, all of which were to the east-northeast of the Blue beachheads in the area of responsibility of the Fourth Division. For a week, every element in the division played a part in seizing this terrain, a task that was not accomplished until March 3. By the end of this tactical achievement, casualties for the Fourth Division had mounted to 6,591 men, or 50 percent of its fighting force.[23]

Yet it is through the individual experience of the code talker and the marine fighter that one understands most clearly what it meant to seize terrain. Acts of heroism were everywhere. Ralph D. Yazzie recalled that "At one point on the front line in Iwo Jima, during a huge barrage of guns and rockets, we received orders by radio to assist in the rescue of our platoon, which was under fire. We did, and got all of our men safely back to our regiment."[24] Bill Toledo had a similar experience as his element fought around the airfield. The assault had turned costly, and everyone was needed to bring in the wounded. Amidst mortar and small-arms fire, Bill went out with another man to retrieve on a stretcher an injured marine. "He got hit—the guy that was helping got hit. And the guy on the stretcher, he was screaming, you know because he was really hurting. And I was dragging him by myself into the back of the airfield, drag him in there and unload him there, just roll him off the stretcher; took the stretcher back over there where this guy was and rolled him on there; brought him in."[25] Uncommon valor was common that day.

Samuel Tso in Recon Company had a slightly different experience when his sergeant ordered him and another marine to cross the airfield and locate an enemy machinegun nest. On the way he encountered a number of dead and wounded marines, some of whom needed immediate attention. The two men stopped long enough to administer first aid until the sergeant roared from behind for them to complete their mission and leave the wounded for others to take care of. The two continued, spotted the enemy position, threw a grenade, and then ran back to a safe location. Other men in the unit did likewise, locating the enemy and returning to safety, where all of the information was plotted on a map and called in to friendly artillery. After a half-hour bombardment the airfield was secured with no return fire bothering those who moved forward to retrieve the wounded. In the meantime, Tso received a stiff reprimand from his sergeant. "'Goddamit Chief, don't you know how to take orders yet? That was not your duty to try to help those marines. Those are the guys that are going to go help them right now. They're specially trained for that.' Boy he was chewing me out."[26]

In some respects, Iwo Jima presented similar problems encountered on other islands—that of mistaken identity of code talkers for the enemy. Two incidents illustrate. Teddy Draper and a marine lieutenant set off to repair a break in a telephone land line. The two moved from a secure position, became somewhat disoriented, and ended crawling around in both friendly and enemy terrain until they got back on track, found the wire, made the repair, and returned to their fighting position. Draper said, "When we got back, a message came in saying, 'There is a Jap in marine clothes on the other side of the ridge.' Okay, who was just there? Me. I was the Jap in marine clothes. Boy that really killed me! The lieutenant explained what had happened and I never saw him again after that."[27]

Henry Hisey, Jr., a white marine, reported a second incident, again with Teddy Draper and another code talker, James Cohoe. The three had the responsibility to set out and repair a broken line. This time it was at night and so Hisey decided to talk loudly and use as many words with *L*'s and *R*'s that he could so that the marines in their foxholes would know that they were friendly troops on official business and not Japanese intruders. The Navajos, however, presented a problem. Hisey recounted events:

> Well things were going along just fine until Teddy and James started jabbering away in Navajo. I started hearing the click of safety latches come off weapons all around us. To Teddy and James, Navajo didn't sound anything like Japanese, but to anxious marines in their foxholes, it did! I yelled at them to keep quiet or we would all get shot for sure, but they just kept it up. Teddy said if he was going to die, he was going to die talking Navajo! Well that was fine for Teddy and James, but I wasn't Navajo and I wasn't ready to die. We made repairs and got back to our foxhole in one piece, but I'll never quite know how![28]

Each individual had his own experience that may or may not have been representative of what others encountered. Paul Blatchford shared a number of occurrences from this month of terrible combat, giving a glimpse of the variety of anguish and terror that filled the marines' lives. He told of some Navajo men coming to him to see if he would talk to the company commander, Captain Thomas, about not shaving on the battlefield. One of the lieutenants was insisting that the troops be clean shaven each morning. From the Navajo perspective, "once you touch your beard or pull your hair, you die." Captain Thomas considered the request but not before the lieutenant offered to shave the next day to prove that there was nothing to the belief and that it was not the reason for all of the men dying. By 9:00 the next morning, the officer was dead, shot through the forehead. Captain Thomas responded, "Okay, tell all the sergeants to come up and I'll tell them. If they want to shave, they can shave. If they don't want to shave, they don't have to." Paul concluded with, "After that, when they didn't shave any more, why none of our outfit got killed. And when it was all over you know, a lot of the men said, 'By golly, you guys have a good religion.' They noticed that everyone who shaved in the morning always got shot, you know."[29]

Blatchford shared other experiences, like the time he was moving across the battlefield and some single shots, interspersed with moments of peace, landed very close and seemed to be originating from another element nearby. After being reassured that the neighboring troops were not doing the shooting, he looked behind only to realize that the fire was coming from a stubby Joshua-tree-like plant. His men surrounded the tree and retrieved a Japanese soldier who had been underground firing between the roots. Another time a new nineteen-year-old replacement joined the platoon. Scared and untried in combat, he received orders from Paul to stay behind him, walk in his footsteps, and not pick up any souvenirs off the battlefield. Following a short engagement, the platoon moved forward only to hear a large explosion erupt to the rear. The young man had gotten away from Paul's trail, apparently picked up something that was booby-trapped, only to be blown fifty feet into the air turning him into "nothing but hamburger." Blatchford said, "You know, when I came back [from the war], it used to just hit my head all the time. I just couldn't get over it."[30]

Blatchford also told of two code talkers (names omitted) who received donations of alcohol provided to all marines in small doses each day. The pooled amount was too much, blurring their judgment to the point that they became careless and were killed. Another time, Blatchford's men had dug into a position during the dark, later to realize it was a graveyard. Before they became aware of their situation, they engaged a number of tombstones as enemy soldiers, because in the wavering light of the flares descending on parachutes they looked like the moving torsos of enemy soldiers. Neighboring elements feared that the firing would give away friendly troop locations. Not until daylight did the entrenched marines realize where they were and at what they had been shooting.[31]

One late evening and night was particularly memorable. It started off with a dispute between Blatchford and a sergeant as to where platoon defensive positions should be placed. The sergeant wanted to put them on the forward slope of a hill facing the enemy and Paul wanted to put them behind the hill for protective cover. Captain Thomas weighed in, agreeing that they should be on the back side to limit enemy observation. Later that night, the code talkers had some fun as they reported their status within the various divisions. The Japanese located the marines' radio frequency and began interfering with their broadcasts.

> One of the Japanese was saying "Could you call this guy, could you call him?" I said, "You know that sounds like 'Kujako' [kójigo] in Navajo. They must be saying 'this way.'" So we said "kujako, kujako, kujako," and then boy they started shelling. They were [hitting] just on that hill where we were supposed to dig in. They were shelling right

> there. Then they'd come back. They quit, you know, and then they came back and they said something I didn't understand and I told one of the boys, "go answer back, say 'haiee, haiee' [ha'át'íí abbreviated ha'íí]. That means yes [actually "what"]. So he said "haiee, haiee," and boy they were happy, you know, and then they started shooting that one spot all the time. Then we said back, "kujako haiee." We didn't know what noise we were saying. We just kept that up, and they just kept shelling that one spot all the time. And the funniest part was, it wasn't exploding. [The Japanese failed to arm the mortar shells they were firing.] Then, boy, they started talking and you could tell that they were excited the way they were talking to us. We got a United States Japanese interpreter and told him to listen. So we'd go back, "kujako haiee" and then they'd come back, and he said, "Oh they sound like they are excited. They sound like they are excited. Just go ahead, just keep them that way. They're excited; they think you're going crazy too." But he never did tell us what they were saying. All he told us was that they were getting excited, you know.[32]

Eventually the code talkers resumed their normal broadcasts, convinced that they had made it more difficult for their enemy, just as the Japanese were probably equally convinced they had done the same for their opponents.

The fighting on Iwo Jima wore on, even after the Fourth Division had completed capture of Hill 382, the Amphitheater, and Turkey Knob on March 3. Sporadic fighting with enemy entrenched in caves and tunnel systems required the marines to seal them in their positions, burn them out with flamethrowers, or force them to surrender, a generally unacceptable alternative for most Japanese soldiers. Samuel's Twenty-fifth Regiment cleaned out one of the last pockets of resistance between March 12 and 16, perhaps the combat he alluded to where a number of code talkers played a prominent role.

On the last day of this final push, the American commander declared the island secure, ending twenty-six days of hellish combat that cost both sides dearly. The Japanese lost approximately 22,000 men, with another 1,000 estimated sealed in caves and tunnel systems that would never again see the light of day. Only 1,083 Japanese soldiers and conscripted Korean laborers surrendered. American losses were 6,821 killed and another approximately 18,000 wounded.[33] To put it in different perspective: "Roughly

With the portable SCR-300 radio set, code talkers were able to move with infantry elements as they engaged the enemy on the front line. Most of the men preferred carrying the lighter 30-caliber M-1 carbine, pictured here, as opposed to the heavier M-1 rifle. Just as important for the traditional Navajo was prayer that protected him during battle. (Photograph courtesy of the U.S. Marine Corps)

one marine or corpsman became a casualty for every three who landed on Iwo Jima. . . . Nearly seven hundred Americans gave their lives for every square mile. For every plot of ground the size of a football field, an average of more than one American and five Japanese were killed and five Americans wounded."[34] In the future, however, this small island and its airstrips would save thousands of lives by offering refuge to damaged or mechanically failing aircraft on their way to or returning from bombing runs against Japan. A total of 2,251 B-29 bombers made forced emergency landings on the island by the end of the war, leaving one pilot to comment, "Whenever I land on this island I thank God for the men who fought for it."[35]

With the end of the most costly battle in the Pacific island-hopping campaign thus far, the marines had once again secured a part of the globe over which the eagle on their emblem perched. In Navajo thought, there could not be a better symbol of the United States' war-making ability than this bird. As the traditional teaching explains, the eagle represents the tie between Mother Earth and Father Sky as well as the "connective tissue" of prayer with the Holy People. For many of the code talkers this was an imperative link. On a less cosmic scale, however, there are other Navajo teachings that also apply.

One story tells of the origin of the Eagle, connecting it to war and violence. After the Twins received from their Father the weapons necessary to kill the monsters roaming the earth, Monster Slayer set off to slay these evil creatures. Two of these were the Tsé'náhalééh, large monster birds who carried off their victims as food for their young nested upon the volcanic crag now called Shiprock, New Mexico. Monster Slayer dispatched both of the adult birds with his lightning arrows then turned to the young who started to cry, asking if they too would be killed. Monster Slayer replied, "Had you grown up here you would have been things of evil; you would have lived only to destroy my people; but I shall now make of you something that will be used in the days to come when men increase in the land."[36] Swinging the older one around four times, he directed that it should furnish plumes for rituals and bones for whistles for the use of men. The bird soared away as an eagle. The Twin gave the younger one the same treatment, saying that men would listen to its voice to learn the future. The bird flew off as an owl.

Use of eagle plumes has already been discussed. This bird's larger feathers are considered powerful and fletch arrows for hunting and war. The dust from an eagle's wing, called a shake-off, holds so much power that if it is tossed in a person's face it will cause blindness.[37] Its feathers adorn the masks and hats of the Holy People while eagle-bone whistles are used to frighten evil and summon the power of good. The bald eagle is considered the leader of the birds; its sacred or ceremonial name is Yellow Beak Chief, while its non-honorific name "atsá" means "clenches its food."[38] Known for its bravery, keen eyesight, power, and protection, the eagle is an appropriate bird in Navajo teachings to represent the code talkers who fought on Iwo Jima.

It is also a fitting symbol for all of the marines involved there. On the U.S. Marine Corps emblem an eagle sits astride the globe of the world, its outstretched wings spread ready for flight. The bird, as a symbol of the United States, grasps in its beak a banner with the Latin words "Semper Fidelis," or "Always Faithful." In a pose somewhat similar to the national emblem, the bird represents power and protection. On the national symbol, however, it grasps thirteen arrows in its left talons and an olive branch in its right, very much in keeping with the Navajo traditional view that those things held by a Navajo in a ceremony with the left hand concern male power and protection and things that can harm, such as arrowheads or a knife. It is held there to keep away evil. That which is grasped in the right hand is peaceful and speaks to the female values of nurturing and tranquility, in keeping with the representative qualities of an olive branch. For Samuel, as a warrior, he was very much under the eagle as a bearer of prayers as well as the Marine Corps in combat. Through his words, he destroyed the enemy while remaining safe through the protection of the Holy People.

CHAPTER SEVEN

After the War

A Different Kind of Battle

ORIGIN OF ENEMY WAY

One of the Earth Surface People, a warrior, invited another man to go with him to kill enemies and gain wealth.[1] They agreed to meet five days later and enjoy a sweat bath together to prepare for their travels. Then on four successive days they entered the sweat lodge where they prayed, compared medicines and objects that provided power, and invoked the gods for assistance. After traveling for three days, they reached their foe, and "in view of the enemy [one of the men] held up his medicine and said a prayer, making a motion with it upon the enemy."[2] The man then killed a pregnant woman, claimed his trophies to use for future medicine, and returned home where the other man made "a pair of prayer sticks set within, in imitation of those which had been hanging at his entrance, copied from when Monster Slayer killed the monsters."[3]

Sometime later the two men again went to war, killing an unknown number of enemy, stealing at night a fine blue horse, then returning home. Five days later the horse disappeared. The next morning the two followed the tracks to Waters Flow Together, home of Monster Slayer, who admitted to having taken the horse for his father, Sun Bearer. Still, something should be exchanged and so the god gave the two men fifteen red yucca "unravelings" to be used in a ceremony to rid a person from the influences encountered through war. There was also information about blackening the patient with soot, another aspect of the ceremony. "Besides, the Enemy Way blackening, which is the ghost part of the Enemy Way, this shall include all enemies that travel about, for these blackenings shall be done."[4]

The men returned home to prepare for the ceremony. Animals and birds of all kinds—Bear, Snake, Chipmunk, Turkey—shared their medicines as did the Sun, Moon, and Changing Woman, providing in all thirteen sacred herbs to heal. Big Fly spoke up, saying, "As for myself, if an enemy's ghost ever takes possession of a person's interior, my medicine will be of use in such cases."[5] Other instructions followed, and many more materials were acquired in addition to the fifteen blades of yucca, which were to serve as bands on different parts of the body. After the medicine was mixed in a basket, the patient drank some as an emetic and applied more over his entire body then had the yucca bands tied upon him—all of this being accompanied with song. Lengthy songs and prayers continued, each removing the influence of evil and restoring good:

> Who time and again kills monsters, he of "Waters Flow Together" [Monster Slayer]!
> His feet have become my feet, thereby I shall go about,
> His legs have become my legs, thereby I shall go about,
> His body has become my body, thereby I shall go about,
> His mind has become my mind, thereby I shall go about,
> His voice has become my voice, thereby I shall go about,
> By which he is long life, by that I am long life,
> By which he is happiness, by that I am happiness,
> By which it is pleasant at his front, thereby it is pleasant at my front,
> By which it is pleasant behind him, thereby it is pleasant behind me,
> When the pollen which encircles Sun's mouth also encircles my mouth, and that enables me to speak and continue speaking,
> You shall take the death of the upright, of the extended bowstring out of me! You have taken it out of me, it has left me, it was returned upon him, it has settled far away!
> Therefore the dart of the Ute enemy's ghost, its filth, by which it bothered my interior, which had traveled in my interior, which had absorbed my interior, shall this day return out of me! This day it has returned out of me!
>
> . . . .
>
> The dart of the Ute enemy's ghost, its filth, has turned away from me, upon it has turned, far away it has returned.
> Right there it has changed into water, it has changed into dew [while] I shall go about in peace.

> Long life, happiness I shall be, pleasant again it has become, pleasant again it has become, pleasant again it has become, pleasant again it has become, pleasant again it has become.[6]

After four days and a variety of ceremonial activities, the patient was healed.

SAMUEL: BATTLING GHOSTS, FINDING A WAY

Following the announcement that the war was over and we were no longer needed to fight the Japanese, we sailed from Hawaii and reached San Diego in the middle of the day. We were there for about a week to receive physical examinations so we could get discharged. Corpsmen stood at the front of the line, checking the men and moving them to the next station. As we lined up some of the men grumbled, "I want to get out of here. To heck with the military," while the corpsmen were busy asking questions and examining us. Onboard the ship, my head and insides had not felt right. Now I was hearing bells and grinding metal, but I just wanted to get through the line, which I now regret. One of the corpsmen asked if I hurt anywhere; I never mentioned my loss of hearing and aching ear. I really regret that I did not tell him because it still hurts and gives me a hard time. Even though I have since had it examined and received a small hearing aid, I am still troubled by it. I thought then that I would soon get better and lose the funny feeling inside after things returned to normal. I just wanted to get out of there and go home, and so I said I was just fine and left.

I caught the bus from Los Angeles to Flagstaff, where I arrived at dark. I looked for a room in two hotels but nothing was available, so I went to the Mexican community on the south side of the city and slept there. In the morning I got up and went back into Flagstaff to find something to eat. As I passed a cafe a colored [African American] man approached me and said, "Hey buddy, let's eat in here." So we entered and a man, the cook I think, said, "No, no, no—white men only." We went back out, looked around, and spotted a Chinese cafe where we ate. The next night I tried again to find a place to sleep, but no hotel owners wanted Indians to stay in their place. I was wearing civilian clothes at the time and later wondered if I had been wearing my uniform if it would have been different. A year or two later I was told of a house in Flagstaff where Indians who were traveling could stay, so I went there, asked, and was told to go back to the reservation.

The people did not care about veterans, my going to war meant nothing to them; it seemed just like having a good horse, working it hard until the job was finished, then chasing it away. That is how I felt.

As I left to come home I thought about my mother and how things might be there. I also reminisced about my experiences in California before going overseas—my training, the museums, the aquarium, boxing arenas, and my children in the future and how I could take them on field trips so they, too, could experience the good things that I had. I wanted them to see the zoo, the aquarium, and the city of Los Angeles since these things had impressed me coming from the reservation. After the war it all seemed different and required so much money that a job to earn it became really important. That is what I found out.

Once I reached home my mother was very happy to see me. She immediately started looking around at the sheep, saying, "Now, which one is the fattest? That one, that one, or that one?" She had lots of fat sheep that were good to eat, the kind that many of the code talkers discussed while overseas, saying that when they got home they would have mutton. Some of them never made it while others just started living in cities, but I certainly was one who enjoyed a mutton feast. For a while I stayed around home and herded sheep.

At the same time, however, I also felt homesick for something even though I was home. I was very uncomfortable so went riding horses all day and at night began to have nightmares of the enemy standing over me smiling. When I slept it did not feel like I was sleeping but as if I was awake all the time. It seemed like I only slept for a few minutes or an hour, always on alert even while resting.

I was lonely and could never totally get away from the war. My mind sometimes went back to the time when I saw injured marines with blood everywhere, and in my dreams there were three Japanese, one of whom had a gold tooth, who were always attacking me. I would try to move, but I was fixed in place as they came at me; then I would wake up and could not go back to sleep because it seemed so real. I had a friend named Burnham of the Tódich'inii (Bitter Water) clan who had served on shore patrol. When he came home I told him about my nightmares, and he spoke to my father, who said I needed to have an Enemy Way ceremony performed for me. In order to do this we temporarily moved over between the mesas into an already established hogan near the canyon.[7]

Samuel in Monument Valley, 1946. His calm exterior, while posing on a movie set, hides the inner turmoil he felt, having recently returned from the horrors of war. (Photograph courtesy of Holiday family)

During the ceremony the patient's wife has to be blackened with ashes, but since I was not married, there was an assigned woman from the Haastiin Ké'tsoh (Mister Bigfoot) family who agreed to do it for me.[8] I had not been aware of this before, but she sat close by me and so I just went along with it because I was more concerned about myself and getting well. My father, who was the medicine man performing the ceremony, told me to take the decorated stick and with members of the group ride horses to Caine Valley.[9] The people familiar with the woman acting as my wife in the ceremony wanted me to marry her, but I refused because I did not know her. Days later my younger brother, Little John, saddled a horse for me and we went riding. When we got to the valley he pointed to the woman's house and said that her family was expecting me to visit them. There were several homes around so I intentionally went to the wrong one, visited for a short while, then left for my mother's place. I did not want to have anything to do with that woman; I did not know if she spoke English or what she knew, and my mind was not on marriage or anything to do with starting a family. So I visited my older sister and told her about these things and that I wanted a woman who spoke English as well as Navajo and was educated.

Months later my father performed a ceremony in Oljato. My older sister, Emma Nez, invited me to attend, and again I saw the woman but did not realize that my sister had brought her until they left together in her wagon the next morning. I returned home, and a few days later my father came to my mother's hogan to perform a ceremony. Again the same woman appeared, so this time I spoke to her and told her to go home. I explained that I did not know her, did not have a home or job, and had nothing to offer. I might want to settle down later but not now. My parents had asked me to haul wood for the ceremony, and so as I left I encountered three of her relatives who had been drinking. I took my time getting wood, not returning until it was nearly dark, only to learn that they made her get drunk then took her away. I was happy about that, she never came back, and I never said a word to my mother, although my sister was probably telling her what was happening.

Shortly after this my family tried again to get me married. I used to ride my horse, Red Ears (Jaa' łichíí'), a lot. One day when I came home there was a car parked in front of my mother's hogan. Inside were two ladies and a man who I did not know, my mother, and Grandmother Nez who was my mother's younger sister. Her husband's name was Coughing Man (Hastiin Dilkosí). These strangers had come to ask me to marry a woman that they knew. They must have discussed it with my mother before I came home because now I was told that I was to marry this person and the visitors had even brought a paper. Mother seemed pleased as she explained this woman had sheep, horses, and a good up-bringing—there was no questionable area of her life—and that my life would be strong if I married her. There was no choice given to say anything about it. They just told me this is what they wanted, that my life would be better if I settled down and got married, and that if I did not, my life would just go in meaningless directions, living here and there, jumping all over the place. "We don't want that for you. We want you to settle down and make a home." Finally they asked me what I thought about the proposal. I was shocked, stunned, and quickly replied I was not ready, I had just returned home, my thoughts were not yet normal and still painted with war, and that I was not prepared for marriage. I did not have a home or job and had nothing to offer. Furthermore I had not yet been cleansed from battle and was still a warrior.

They told me that all those issues are handled after marriage. My main concern was that I could not provide a home for a wife, which I knew was important. I needed time to think about this and would have to see how I felt later. That response shut everything down, and they did not look happy any more, saying that I had refused their plans. When my older sister heard this she scolded me severely, saying, "Why did you turn her down? She is the best one for you. She has everything!" My sister cried as she talked to me, "You could have walked in our ancestor's footsteps and been happy."

Life at home was becoming more difficult so I decided to earn money, landing a job at Belmont, an ammunition manufacturing factory, where I worked for three years. I was able to put about $300 in the bank before leaving for the West Coast. In Oregon I went to work on the railroad with other Navajo men as well as Mexicans, blacks, and whites. The Navajos were not well-educated and so I became a supervisor, recording their names and keeping track of their time. Later my boss promoted me to foreman for the whole gang. At that time they just used a bar to raise the rails, straighten them out, and put them in place. I had to walk along the side of the track and check the men's work. They spoke Navajo all the time. The blacks were always talking about cars and trucks, one bragging about how he was going to have a Cadillac, while the Mexicans were always talking about women, and the whites about how much money they were going to make. The Navajos constantly joked, nothing seemed to be serious, and they loved to tease each other. I worked on the railroad along the Columbia River for three years until it was time to depart. Ben Atene and his older brother begged me to be their interpreter because they had no education and I did. I did not want to leave at that time, but I told my supervisor I needed to go. He did not want me to go, offered a raise, and pleaded for me to stay but Ben got worse. [Ben was feeling lonesome and sick and wanted to return home but did not want to go without help in getting back to the reservation.] I helped him with his paperwork, arranged for transportation and lodging, traveled with him, and was there on the way home when he got better. I think Ben was just homesick.

I started to feel sick again so went home and visited some relatives in Tuba City. As long as I can remember, I wanted to marry a woman who was stable and educated like me. But I did not really pursue it because I was not ready, did not have a house, know how responsible some of them were, or the strength of their long-term plans. Maybe they just lived from day to day. So when I visited two of my classmates and clan brothers, Emerson and Teddy Goldtooth, marriage was far from my thoughts. When we met they were so happy to see me, gave me a big hug, then begged me to come to work with them as a policeman. They kept saying, "We need you, we need you!" They were then working at the police station, and I was on my way home and not looking for a job. They persisted and persuaded me to accept a position in Tuba City, and so I did for about five years.

Working with the Goldtooths, who were well-known in the area, was challenging because I did most of the work and all of the arresting, while they were always friendly with everybody. They had squaw dance [Enemy Way] patrol duties that got assigned to me. In the winter I provided police coverage at the Yé'ii Bicheii ceremonies, where one time a man attempted to cut me with a knife during a fight. At a summer squaw dance a man drew his gun ready to shoot me, but I reached him before he pulled the trigger. Another time I received a call to investigate a death at a Yé'ii Bicheii ceremony where a man had gotten drunk, fallen down, and been run over by a driver who never saw him. Once I was asked to find a lost man so went to the community to learn of his disappearance; no one knew anything about him, but everybody wanted to talk about their problems that I was supposed to solve because I was a policeman. I had always thought police work was easy, but in the five years I spent in that job I realized it was very hard and dangerous.

One time that it paid off, however, was when I visited the family of Harry Isaac, who had sheep that had gotten mixed in with their neighbor's livestock and needed help separating them. I had gone to school with Harry, and so when a pretty girl walked by us, he introduced me to his sister. I liked the way she smiled, her long curly hair, and pleasant personality. I learned that she worked at the Shonto boarding school as a dorm advisor close to where Teddy Goldtooth's girlfriend worked. When I went with him before, I used to wait in the car while they talked. Now he invited me to come in with him, so I began visiting Harry's sister, Lupita.

The first time we went to the school, we had a dead body that we retrieved from a winter Fire Dance ceremony and placed in the trunk of the police car.[10] I was anxious to get rid of it. As I moved the corpse about in the trunk by one of its frozen arms it appeared that the whole body sat upright, scaring Teddy to death. He later told the girls what had happened, and they became frightened and told us to get out of there immediately. We did not know where to take the body, so we brought it to a church and had the pastor help us bury it. Later Lupita said that she did not want me to be a policeman, partly because of this incident.

That was how I first got to know my future wife. Her voice was very pleasant, she spoke English well, and came to see me at work. Her mother, Mabel Isaac, was a medicine woman. I told her that I was very fond of her daughter and that we had gotten to know each other very well. Now I wanted to marry her, and she was anxious to have this happen. Mabel agreed but said that I must first build a house nearby, for only by doing so would our marriage be strong. She also told me that her family had a truck, a car, nice home, and lots of good things. They mined coal on their own land as part of their livelihood. But I had nothing to offer. "If you don't start taking care of yourself and your wife you will soon begin using our stuff and will ruin everything we have." Her relatives told me that I must find work and earn a living for my family. I told them that I was strong and willing to make my own home and go to work. She did not want me to depend on them or ask for anything, but rather I was to take care of my wife and soon have lots of children and grandchildren. I agreed and that is the reason I built our first house near Cow Springs. We had a small church wedding attended by friends from the Shonto school.

My wife's mother has not always been happy with me.[11] After I was married I went hunting on Comb Ridge, saw a large deer with big antlers, and shot it. I cleaned it and brought it home, ready to cut up. I was so proud of myself carrying it to the door and showing everyone it was ready to

Samuel and Lupita Holiday in later life. During interviews, Samuel mentioned often how much he loved his wife and missed her with her recent passing. She was highly supportive of the recognition he received as a code talker. (Photograph courtesy of Holiday family)

butcher. The family yelled, telling me to take it away because it was not supposed to be brought to the house that way but should be butchered in the spot where the animal had been killed. I had not understood how sacred it was to go hunting and how important it was to bring home the animal in a certain way.[12] We removed it from the vicinity of the hogan in a wagon and butchered it in the woods. At the time there was another family who had come to my mother-in-law's house for help with traditional medicine, and so my new family was embarrassed. I learned that day that hunting was done at a certain time of year with rituals from the beginning, when one prays to have the animals released by the Holy People, to the end, when one returned with the kill. For forty years now I have always kept hunting as a sacred event. Prayers and songs are very important in the things we do.

My wife encouraged me to quit my job as a policeman. Many times I went to ceremonies to keep the peace, during which there was social dancing with girls and women who wanted me to dance with them. I let them know I was on duty and could not do things like that, but I think my wife was getting jealous. She also did not like me hauling dead bodies around, and so I quit that job and started working odd jobs here and there. I first worked as a janitor then maintenance man operating three generators at the powerhouse in Kayenta. Two were on-line while the other rested, then the machines rotated in duty cycles. They were very loud, which brought back my headaches. I went to the doctor, who told me to get out of that noisy environment and work outdoors. He wrote a statement for me, so I quit but lost a good-paying job and returned to being a janitor. Next I spent three years working at the Monument Valley ranger station, built a house nearby, and held other jobs too. My wife worked at Gouldings, and I drove their company car for a while. One day my children were home with a babysitter who did not know how much wood to put in the stove. She overloaded it; the stove grew red hot and started the house on fire. By the time I received a call saying that my house was burning and arrived home, it was in ashes on the ground. We lost all our valuables; nothing was left.

Lupita and I went to Window Rock to ask for help with housing and were told to fill out an application. We went back twice to check on our assistance, which ended up in a small pile of lumber brought by some men early one morning. They eventually built us a new house. This was during the time that Raymond Nakai was running again for chairman of the

Navajo Tribe.[13] I visited with Nakai, who used to be a foreman at Belmont where I, along with many others, had encouraged him to run for chairman so that he could help Navajos—especially veterans—to obtain housing, electricity, and running water. Up to that point no one was aware of what we Navajo veterans had done during the war. Some of the veterans got together and held a meeting across from the old Warner trading post in a school building in Kayenta. Grandmother Russell, whose Navajo name was Asdzaan Nataani (Woman Leader) and clan was Tódich'inii (Bitter Water), was the leader in the area. I was there to campaign for Nakai, but some of the people had been drinking and were saying, "Give him some more whiskey." When it was my turn to talk, I introduced myself and started speaking on behalf of Raymond Nakai, saying that as a veteran I was there to promote him as chairman and that he would help us build houses with electricity and running water. As soon as I finished Grandmother Russell opposed what I said. She talked about beer that people drank for relaxation and accused me of advertising for a beer company. Then she said I was a womanizer and that I did not think of my people because I drank beer, even though I had nothing to do with this. Still, I did not defend myself and left. Nakai lost that year (1970) to Peter McDonald.

Next I went job-seeking at Peabody coal mine and put my application in for welding and bulldozer operator. The man hiring told me to report at 4:00 P.M. the next day, starting my career as a bulldozer operator, which I did for 10 years. When first reporting in I found that I knew some of the men employed there, but I was totally unfamiliar with the bulldozer—I did not even know how to start it and had to be taught since I had only worked with one a little bit before. I learned my job right away taking the coal out of the pit, making roads for the heavy equipment, and loading trucks. Soon I did not have to be told what to do and became a valuable worker. I said, "The company is mine too so that's why you can always depend on me." I became a foreman and advanced faster than some of the men with engineer degrees.

Another important part of my life has been my membership in the Native American Church.[14] I have worked with a medicine man, Wilford Redhouse from Table Mesa, for about twenty years and have seen some miraculous things take place. When he is going to hold a meeting he calls me and those who are sick to come, but it is the Holy People who heal. Wilford has given me the instruments to perform my own ceremonies, and

Photographer Joseph Muench's picture of Kayenta, 1950s. Since the turn of the century, this town evolved from a couple of trading posts to a significant reservation township. Coal extraction from Black Mesa on its outskirts gave a huge economic boost to the area and employment to skilled men like Samuel. (Josef Muench photograph, Northern Arizona University, Cline Library)

a lot of miracles have happened for all nationalities—blacks, Mexicans, whites, and natives. When I was visiting my son in Albuquerque, I held a ceremony for a black and a Mexican, also at powwows and in Kentucky.

When I perform a ceremony I put hot coals in the middle of the circle and hold the live eagle feather in my hand. One time I did a ceremony for a person whose sheep were restless while his dogs whimpered, indicating something was wrong. This man asked me to perform hand trembling so I told him to return home, build a fire for hot coals, and await my arrival in about forty minutes. When I entered everything was ready. I prayed for help in determining what was wrong and why the sheep were nervous. As I did I saw a man, actually his brother, using witchcraft on this family. I told the man I was doing this to help take the evil away, but he did not want me do anything and so I did not but just told his brother about it. What I saw was that they were envious of what each other had.

I also perform ceremonies for missing people. One evening a white lady and her son knocked on my door and asked if I was Samuel Holiday. She said, "We are from Salt Lake City and want you to do a hand trembling ceremony for us." I said I would do it in the morning at my son's house where we would put hot coals in the middle of the living room. The ceremony was for a teenage son who had not returned from an outing. The woman had contacted the police, but they had not found the boy—only the places where he and others had been drinking. Three months had passed since the search stopped near Delta, Utah. I saw in vision that there was a ditch running beside a dirt road that someone was walking on. As I watched that person I felt something literally hit me in my back then saw the walking person fall. There was blood all over, just as when the throat of a sheep is cut. That is what I saw so I told the lady that I thought someone killed her son and cut off his head. I saw this terrible thing happen. The police questioned some of the people who had been with him then went over the area as part of the investigation. They found nothing so the lady called me again and asked me to go to Delta, perform another ceremony, and then look around. I felt uneasy about it but soon learned that the police discovered his head, then the body, and determined what had happened to him.

Another time I heard there was going to be a peyote meeting and so hitchhiked, catching a ride on a truck only to learn that the men in the vehicle were going to the same meeting in Oljato. We arrived around 9:00 P.M. but nobody was there, so I went to sleep in the back of the truck. At midnight someone woke me up to let me know that the meeting was about to start. As I walked in everybody was waiting for the medicine man from Sweetwater, but he never showed up so they asked Francis Atene to conduct the meeting. The drum went around once, then a second time as the patient's mother started singing and a little boy, about two years old, came in and stood by the person next to the door. This boy was just a vision, but I saw him very clearly. He had light colored hair, approached and looked at me, then moved on. The time for the blowing of a whistle began and Francis said he would go outside and pray with it. I told him to wait because there was a little boy who was trying to contact the woman by sitting on her lap. She said that about seven years before she had been drinking homemade wine when everybody got drunk, departed, and left her alone. She was pregnant at this time when intense labor pains started. She walked to a sandy hill, where she gave birth to a baby boy that she buried alive in the sand because there was no help available and she did not know what to do. The next day she returned, took the baby to a different location, and buried it under some sagebrush. After she told her story, Francis sang the Beauty Way song then went on with the ceremony for a patient whose father had died. I thought to myself, there should be a different ceremony done for the woman, but I did not say anything. After many years I saw Francis and asked him how that lady was doing. He told me that everything involved with that ceremony went wrong. The lady had lost everything she owned, and the man for whom the ceremony was given died. I thought I should have said something back then, but because I did not, this happened. I could have helped by doing a different ceremony for them, but it was their business and I did not want to interfere.

These visions are miracles to me, blessings from the Holy People who work through the power of God because He made this earth. The prayers are to Him and his son Jesus. I plead to them in prayers that are carried by the cedar smoke from the burning coals. The prayers, which are sacred to the Navajo, are for protection against the evil of witchcraft. Through a special prayer and ceremony all the evils used against a person can be undone. The patient sits and concentrates on the prayer as the medicine man is told what is ailing the person by seeing the answer in the coals. That is his vision that comes through the spirit. If he does not see anything it is usually because the patient will already know the answer.

Medicine man Wilford Redhouse and Harry Dee, my son-in-law, came to me one evening three days before my son Gene went for an operation for gallstones. He arrived at the hospital in pain, the doctor insisting he have the stones removed, but Gene said no. So we built a fire, made the cedar offering, and prayed on his behalf, using peyote and water with it as I prayed. I put my faith in the power of the peyote that the stones would pass naturally then gave the patient a ball of peyote and told him that it would work on the gallstones if he would just swallow it, which he did. Three days later his daughter called and said he had the operation and almost died. My wife and I went to the Cortez hospital to visit and found him surrounded by his wife and children but in bad condition. His head had swollen beyond recognition and he had an IV with other tubes, draining pus out and putting medicine in. We prayed for him at his bedside and that was when I had a vision of a centipede beside him. I never learned what it represented. We stayed in a motel that night and received a call the next day saying that he was better and that the swelling had gone down. In four days he went home so we held an appreciation peyote meeting for him.

A year later he and his wife visited us, asking for another ceremony to win a lawsuit against the doctors at the hospital. I offered a second prayer after learning that their lawyer was not well known like the lawyer the doctors hired. This prayer was to give power to their lawyer and wisdom to the judge. In about three months they called again and asked for another prayer meeting for they had won the lawsuit and wished to express appreciation and settlement of the matter. My wife and I visited their home, where they had set up a tepee. The entire night we performed the peyote Beauty Way ceremony, after which they paid me. I am telling these stories because the people in them are witnesses to my medicine.

Even though I have had many of these different experiences, I never totally left my war ordeal behind. Because all of the code talkers had been sworn to secrecy about their war efforts, we never talked to anyone about them unless the government gave permission. We were men of integrity and kept our promise to never tell, but this silence bothered me. Once discharged from the marines I no longer had the pride I had while serving. I felt very empty now that my efforts were not recognized and thought no one will know anything about what the code talkers did. I felt worthless, was not a marine, and did not really care about anything anymore. I regretted going into the service and fighting on the Pacific islands. We were all forgotten. At one point I wanted to go back to school to learn a trade but was turned down. I just wandered around from town to town and job to job feeling lonely with something missing from my life.

I have already mentioned the first Enemy Way ceremony my mother and relatives arranged for me soon after my return because they knew things were wrong and wanted to help. With the first ceremony the spirit of sacredness, the holiness of healing, and the love of my mother and relatives overcame me so that I knew I was going to be helped and healed because they cared about me. Still, problems persisted. Eventually I had this ceremony performed for me three different times.[15] It can only be done in the summer so the next two times they had to find a spot for me to join in with another person. Every time I went to bed the three Japanese soldiers—one of them with a shiny, flashing gold tooth—came, pointing their fingers and laughing. Sometimes they poked me with a stick or something like it and laughed some more. I could not sleep at night. My relatives started telling me that I did not look well and wanted me to have another ceremony. During the Enemy Way the medicine man shoots an object called bich'į́į́díí (its ghost) to rid the patient of the evil influence by killing the ghost. Each time it was done in a holy way, although I did not know what kind of object was used for the bich'į́į́díí. After I had the first ceremony performed I felt better; the nightmares lessened in frequency but were still there. Another one was done, and I got even better. After the third ceremony I was healed, but then people used to come and ask me to have the decorated prayer stick brought to me. Several times I did that but sometimes I refused or just hid from the people because it is very expensive to have a squaw dance done for you.

Recently I had a reoccurrence of those evil thoughts while I was speaking in Los Angles. I could not talk but saw the wounded yelling and screaming with blood everywhere as my mind flooded with what had happened during the war. I could see code talkers struggling to carry their equipment and the Japanese pointing their guns at us. Sometimes my mind replays those things. When it happens and I cannot speak, I stop and try to think of where I am at the time, gather my thoughts, and continue with my talk. I have to bring myself back from those tragic times.

My son Herman later served in the U.S. Navy and had a protection ceremony performed for him in which I participated. It is called "Tóhee" (Of the Water) and provides safety and protection from unknown danger and enemies (Naayéé'ii). My mother-in-law, Mabel Isaac, performed the two prayers, each of which took about two hours as me and Herman participated. The prayer is given to recognize and honor the powers of water and plead for safety from it by mentioning both the rivers, Bits'íís Nineezí (long body), and the ocean, Bits'íís Niteelí (wide body), in the prayers. Water can harm or kill a person, and so the prayers talk to it through the Holy People and plead for the safety of those going overseas.

My wife accompanied me through the ceremony, repeating the prayer right after it was said. You have to concentrate and think only of the prayer and the Holy One. My son and I were given instructions on how to do it. At the beginning of the prayer my mother-in-law repeated the words when I fell behind, and soon I was able to say it right after her as she rapidly went on. Soon even the difficult words came out smoothly as I named Mother Earth, the sacred mountains, sacred stones, and colors as well as the different dangers of water. This prayer goes to the Creator since you are his child and asks that you return home unharmed. Today there is evil and danger everywhere, but through prayers one is protected. When in the marines, I could tell who had this protection ceremony performed for them. They showed respect for life by the way they talked and were not rowdy. I was baptized by water as a child when I got hurt in the water. It is called baptism when the water could have claimed your life but you survived. When you are baptized you are protected by the water. That's why I survived the stormy ocean when we had to swim ashore from the landing craft. I learned this more serious side, the medicine side, of prayers and thinking as an adult. The ceremony was a good thing for my son and me to do together.

Commentary: The Enemy Way and Healing

Samuel's account by now has made plain that the preparation for and fighting in war is waged on two levels according to Navajo beliefs—one physical the other spiritual. Although no Japanese enemy would ever be able to harm Samuel again in combat, the spiritual and mental conflict continued. Today more than ever there is concern about what Anglo medicine calls post traumatic stress disorder (PTSD) afflicting those who come from a war zone. The severity of an individual's problem varies according to previous life experience, the intensity of the combat, personal mental composition, and the post-combat experience. Navajo culture has recognized this affliction from the beginning of time, institutionalizing a ceremonial cure first encountered by the Twins in their war against the monsters.

The first enemy the Twins sought to kill was Yé'ii Tso (Big God), an offspring of Sun Bearer. As part of this war effort, they used a war language, similar to that discussed in a previous chapter. In many respects a word's power is greater than anything physical, since it was by words that physical things—ranging from the earth to everything on it—were created by the Holy People. When the Twins destroyed the monsters, they used a special language (saad bee ch'aa íídíidziih) to communicate and disguise their intent from those they fought. In ceremonies sacred language not only communicates with the Holy People but has protective powers that shield and cure a patient. After successfully killing Big God with Sun Bearer's help, the Twins took his scalp and hung it in a tree to prove to the Holy People that they indeed had the power to kill this giant. But shortly after they returned home and told their mother, Changing Woman, what they had done the Twins began to feel sick, overwhelmed with fainting spells and evil thoughts. She understood what needed to be performed and so prepared medicine made from lightning-struck plants and herbs, sprinkled the men with it, and then shot a spruce and pine arrow over them. The Twins recovered from the harmful effects of the dead.[16] The power to combat what is sometimes called ghost sickness through the Enemy Way (Anaa'jí or Anaa'jí Ndáá) ceremony has been passed on to the Earth Surface People from Monster Slayer. The story at the beginning of this chapter tells of the first time it was used for humans. What follows is an explanation of beliefs that arise from the very essence of a person's composition and ends with the killing of a ghost and the healing of affliction.

When the Holy People first created humans, they used four basic elements—two physical and two nonphysical—for the body. Earth and water comprised the physical, with five different types of water—sweat, tears, saliva, blood, and urine—found in the body. Sunlight and wind (níłch'i) came next, giving the body warmth and animation. There are a number of different explanations as to the derivation and function of this Holy Wind within a person, but all point to its importance as the essence of life. As the Holy People worked to create man, they encountered a problem. The wind could be forced in but did not come back out naturally; thus, breathing was impossible. Coyote the trickster, with his many powers and abilities, at times blesses man but can also create problems. He knew that he could solve the issue, but as with most of what he touches, there would also be a negative consequence. Coyote went to work, pushing his breath into the form. The human came alive, drawing in and expelling the air, now awake to life. But inside, there was also a part of Coyote, a streak of evil or hostile instinct that remains to this day. With this aggressive force present, people could now protect themselves but were also capable of being both good and evil. Each is a necessary part of the human experience and part of survival.

When a person dies, the elements of composition return from whence they came—the water and earth to the soil, the spirit to Níłch'i, and the sunlight to the sun, which explains why a corpse turns cold. The evil part left by Coyote remains with the body and is now uncontrolled by the spirit, anxious to attack and attach itself to someone living.[17] Frank Mitchell, Blessing Way singer, said it this way: "We all have something living in us that is taken out of us when we die. And in the case of each one of us, that spirit has a superior that it goes back to. If we have not been treating someone's spirit right during our lives, after it goes back to its superior, it can come back and punish us."[18] Thus the Navajos' fear of the dead is based on ghost affliction; those who have been in combat like Samuel and other code talkers were surrounded by the dead and the possibility of contamination by spiritual forces seeking to punish those who treated them poorly.

There are two types of ceremonies to help a Navajo person affected by ghost sickness. Both belong to a general category of Navajo practices known as Evil Way (Hóchxǫ'íjí), which differs from two other broad categories of Life Way (Iináájí) and Holy Way (Hózhǫ́ǫ́jí). The former is for healing injuries from specific accidents whereas the latter is for the restoration of a patient needing the assistance of the Holy People to return to a state of peace (hózhǫ́), harmony, and blessings. The Evil Way chants (sometimes glossed as Ghost Way but literally translated as Ugly Way) have the purpose of removing evil influences to include ghosts and the effects of witchcraft. There is a specific ceremony called Evil Way within this broad category of the same name as well as the Enemy Way, Shooting Way, Big Star Way, and Upward Reaching Way. All of these ceremonies address physical problems associated with evil to include "bad dreams, insomnia, fainting, nervousness, mental disturbances, feelings of suffocation, loss of appetite, loss of weight, or other alarming disturbances."[19] The Franciscan Fathers also noted that the ceremony can be used in cases of "swooning, or weakness and indisposition attributed to the sight of blood, or of a violent death of man or beast, especially if this has occurred to a pregnant woman or even to a husband or father during the period of her pregnancy."[20]

If the spirit of the deceased is Navajo, then the Evil Way ceremony is used to pray away the influence to the North, the place of the dead. On the other hand, if the bothering spirits are non-Navajo, as in Samuel's case involving the Japanese he encountered during the war, then the Enemy Way ceremony is used. This ceremony is a serious undertaking because the purpose of this rite is not to chase away the enemy but to rid the patient of this spirit by killing it.[21] To ensure total healing, the ceremony may be repeated in longer or shorter forms a total of four times, which can be done over a number of years. Samuel had three that were spread over thirty-eight years, assuming his reconstruction of dates is correct.

The expense and time entailed in holding an Enemy Way ceremony is significant, indicating its importance to the Navajo. Anthropologist Gary Witherspoon provided some calculations, based on his views in 1975, that show how meaningful this practice is. He suggested that for the ritual activities more than thirty people are involved; for the logistical side, including construction of the cooking area, the hauling of firewood, and general camp and guest maintenance, another hundred people may be added; when guests and spectators join the list, more than five hundred people may be counted. Next, he calculated the time required:

> From initial planning to completion, the ritual requires around two weeks, with the last three days containing the major aspects of the ritual. By assuming that the ritual is performed an average of five times each summer in each community, and with approximately one

Navajo encampment prepared for an Enemy Way ceremony, Monument Valley. Hundreds of participants attend this ceremonial to add strength in group solidarity while curing the patient by removing the influence of enemy spirits. As many as four ceremonies may be held for the same individual to complete the healing process. (Photograph courtesy of Utah State Historical Society)

> hundred Navajo communities, it is likely that the ritual occurs five hundred times each summer. An average of two thousand dollars is spent or exchanged in the performance of each ritual, and so it is likely that a million dollars is spent yearly by Navajo in the performance of Enemyway.[22]

This ceremony has evolved over time as older forms of Navajo warfare have changed. In the 1800s, warriors returning from a successful raid that netted scalps would stand before the hogan of one of the victors and hold a "swaying singing," or yik'áh, which is literally translated as "grinding something to a fine point" because of the men "grinding" and singing with their voices.[23] In one version, an enemy scalp was placed on the ground in front of the structure then shot and sung over using the non-ceremonial name of the enemy in these impromptu melodies. The men sang and swayed back and forth to the accompaniment of a pottery drum until the occupant tossed out goods such as meat, plunder from the raid, or other desirable objects and the men went away to the next warrior's home. After a number of hogans had been visited, the men took the scalps and hid them among rocks and in crevices where they would not be found and rain would not touch them. These trophies were not retrieved until an Enemy Way ceremony and dance were held.

Cleansing from the problem of ghost sickness was available for both men and women. The use of the sweat lodge was the first line of defense, but if ill effects appeared, then a ceremony became necessary. In the past the Enemy Way was most frequently used for men returning from war, but women who came in contact with a scalp or blood from the enemy by mistake could also be affected. If a man went to war when his wife was pregnant, the unborn child later in life could be bothered by the enemy that the father killed. Also, if a man or woman had sexual intercourse with an enemy who later died, they could be afflicted by its ghost. Anyone who is not Navajo can be categorized as an enemy and so even though there may not be combat involved, there is still potential for contamination. Each nationality—Mexican, Anglo, Ute, Comanche, Hopi, and so forth—has a sacred name that is used in the ceremony to sing against them. If a Navajo comes in contact with an object that has the blood of an enemy on it, sickness can result. In the past, if a woman was washing a white man's clothes and inhaled the steam from the water, she could become contaminated and require a ceremony.[24] Marriage to a non-Navajo as well as involvement with a white prostitute can also give rise to this necessity.

Even the procuring of the enemy object—scalp, bone, clothing—for the ceremony must be done with caution. Although some of these things may be taken in war and then sent home for use in a ritual later, they may also be obtained through purchase from a pawn shop or from an individual. When a person travels to get an object of this nature for a ceremony, it is said "he goes on the warpath." Once it is obtained, it must be treated carefully by limiting exposure and contact with the person who has it. In the old days, it might be tied to a horse's tail or carried on a stick away from the procurer's body. It is then hurried to the place of the ceremony and hidden in a spot away from people until needed. To prevent contamination with the enemy's spirit, blackening (jint'eesh) of an individual is done to keep the evil away.

Preparation for and conduct of the Enemy Way ceremony is filled with symbolic complexity that is only touched upon here.[25] A brief overview of the activities gives a sense of its meaning to participants. As already mentioned, the main performance of this ritual is only three nights, four days. Among the first tasks is the patient's family selecting another family to receive the rattle stick; the sponsoring group then sets the date for the ceremony, chooses a medicine man to make the drums and decorate the rattle stick, picks an unmarried girl to carry the stick, and hires an old, infertile man to obtain and prepare a "scalp." On the first day the rattle stick is put together and in the afternoon is brought to the receiver's camp. The object is carried on a horse whose hoofs "make medicine" as it travels. A dance is held that night that "stomps the enemies' spirits into the ground," rejoicing at their defeat. The girl who received the stick dances with all of the patient's relatives while other women select their own dance partners, thus giving the activity its common name of "squaw dance." The next day after a gift exchange the camp of the rattle stick's receiver moves halfway toward where the final ceremony will take place. The third day, the final move is made to where the ceremony will be held, gifts are handed out from the patient's family to that of the receiver's, and the blackening and other activities described below take place.

The rich symbolism embedded in this ceremony expresses deep cultural values concerning the dead. A preliminary blackening of a patient to prevent the enemy ghost from recognizing him and that may exorcise the offending evil spirit is performed to see if it has a positive effect. If it does, then preparation for a full Enemy Way ceremony begins. A "scalper," often an old man who has been involved in war, "goes on the warpath and brings home the scalp" using Bear and Snake songs (two powerful protectors) for his defense.[26] At the same time two medicine men, one to prepare the rattle stick and another to receive it, select a date for the stick's preparation and the start of the ceremony. Each also makes a pot drum that when played beats the enemy ghosts into the ground. Blessing Way singer Frank Mitchell says that decorating the stick is a remaking of the damaged spirit of the patient as a type of payment for the harm it has sustained. At the conclusion of the ceremony, this object is retired to a place it will not be disturbed but can peacefully return to its elements.[27] After the rattle stick is prepared, the patient or his representative takes it, mounts a horse, and rides with companions to the camp of the receiver, usually ten to twelve miles away. After the second medicine man in the receiver's camp has inspected it, he chooses an unmarried, reliable girl, who then conducts a dance at which the men perform sway-singing. The next morning, friends and relatives of the stick receiver bring small presents such as money, candy, food items, and so forth, which represent gifts given when enemies make peace; they then distribute the presents by tossing them out of the hogan's smoke hole. The patient with his group now returns to the original camp.

Other activities include more sway-singing, the patient washing his hair in a Navajo basket containing yucca soap suds, and the patient taking an emetic that promotes vomiting of the offending enemy ghost within the patient. When the receiver's people reach the patient's camp, both groups greet and discharge their firearms, riding in a wide circle around the camp four times. Gifts are exchanged, another tossing of presents out of the smoke hole takes place, and the patient prepares for a blackening with ashes made from desert plants and an application of a pungent herbal mixture.

Intensity of activity escalates. Dancing and exchanges continue, and at one point preparations to "attack the enemy" become central. Just as Monster Slayer did following his return from war, the blackening of a patient and his wife (or surrogate) is performed to make them invisible to the ghost. The patient also receives a sacred name used only in the ceremonies, if he has not already received one. This sacred name is kept secret.[28] He next puts on his left shoulder a yucca sash with a pouch attached containing an object from the enemy and an arrowhead, proof of his ability to vanquish the foe.[29] There are also yucca fiber bands tied with slip knots on his soles, ankles, knees, hips, back of each shoulder, palms, ears, and top of head. A specially commissioned man called the "scalp shooter" and "strewer of ashes" selects a place distant from camp to place the enemy scalp or object. He then approaches it with the group observing and fires a rifle or arrows at the enemy. Next the patient and his wife symbolically, without touching the ash-covered object, act out thrusting a crow bill into the ashes. The scalp shooter intones, "It is dead. It is dead" having sprinkled the enemy object with ashes. As the group leaves the "attack" site and returns to the hogan for concluding ceremonial activities, the participants must be careful never to look back at the scalp.

By now the sash has been moved to the right shoulder; one of the concluding activities in the hogan is the removal of the different strands of yucca as part of an "unraveling." Here the fear, frustration, and stress of the situation are removed for a final time, placing the patient on the road to recovery. Just before sunset, there is a final exchange of goods and preparation for the last night's dance. More sway-singing follows, which continues through the evening. Before dawn, members of the receiver's camp depart for home. In the morning light, final prayers are said, the patient makes small offerings with corn pollen, and the patient inhales dawn's breath four times, which ends the ceremony.

Returning to the use of the Enemy Way ceremony for World War II code talkers, one finds that some participated and others did not. W. Dean Wilson, for instance, waited eleven years before having one because he came from a less traditional background, whereas John Benally never had one.[30] Compare that with Sidney Bedoni from Navajo Mountain whose father sent him off with a medicine pouch for protection and held an Enemy Way upon his return. "Since I had it done over me, I never thought of it [the war]."[31] Paul Blatchford suffered from nightmares upon his return but could not afford the large expense incurred by holding his own Enemy Way ceremony. He attended a large ceremony given for another person and "just paid for the medicine," which cured him.[32] Carl Gorman, on the other hand, had lost belief in the traditional ways and did not have the money for it anyway. An older medicine man and friend offered to perform a one-night chant for him, so Carl accepted. "I participated in the sing and felt a great weight leave my mind and body. I felt very rested afterwards. I realized then that I needed to make peace with what I had experienced during the war."[33] Dan Akee, Samuel's companion on Saipan, told of how he had frequent nightmares with images of Japanese soldiers pursuing him as he screamed. After a year he went deaf, and there was nothing the doctors could do. His father had a Gourd Dance held for him. "It was just unbelievable what happened to me. The first night I heard a drum and my ear popped and I could hear again. . . . After the Gourd Dance, I gained back my weight and the nightmares slowly faded."[34]

Those people familiar with N. Scott Momaday's *House Made of Dawn* or Leslie M. Silko's *Ceremony*—works by two Native American authors who created fictional characters suffering from the effects of combat in the Pacific during World War II—will find the haunting experience of Chester Nez comparable. In his book, Nez shares an account of his PTSD experience that takes the reader through a number of thoughts similar to those encountered by Samuel: "The days stretched out as long as a highway and nightmares invaded both my waking and sleeping hours. I felt lost. Sometimes I actually thought I'd been killed. And the dreams—horrifying dreams of unearthly battles, with Japanese faces leering at me—refused to end. . . . Months dragged by, filled with the grinding repetition of nightmares, of Japanese enemies appearing even during the day."[35]

All code talkers had been sworn to silence because of the secret nature of their assignment in combat. While most marines could share their experience with others, there was no emotional catharsis for the Navajos sworn to secrecy; everything had to remain bottled up inside. Six months home with his frightening mental condition made Chester realize he needed help, which he sought through a traditional ceremony. His father and grandparents understood his problem and hired a hand trembler who also used a crystal to diagnose specifically what Chester was experiencing and the necessary cure. Enemy Way was the answer. The "scalp" needed for the ceremony was easily obtained. "We were lucky that some of the Navajo soldiers . . . had cut hair and clothing from the dead Japanese and sent the items home to be used in ceremonies. The items were purchased by medicine men who utilized them as 'scalps' in the Enemy Way ceremonies."[36] Participants played the pot drum with its two holes for "eyes" and one for a "mouth," striking the hide and symbolically beating the enemy ghosts into the ground. When it came time to attack the scalp, the shooter used a sling made of rubber and buckskin. The final result: "The sing was a success. Hózhǫ́'jí [Beauty Way] was exhibited toward all who attended the ceremony, just as tradition mandated. I reentered the trail of beauty. For a long time afterward, my dreams and visions of the Japanese subsided."[37]

Thus the Enemy Way ceremony, from start to finish, follows the prescribed pattern outlined by Monster Slayer for the Earth Surface people. Even this holy being's name figures into the practice. Naayéé is generally glossed as "monster" but is more accurately defined as "enemy" or "things that torture a person," whereas neezghání means "he has gotten rid of it," translated as "slayer"; ana'í, the root word for the ceremony, translates as "an enemy gotten rid of."[38] That is exactly what happened during the Anaa'jí held for Samuel and many of the other code talkers. They were redeemed through the ceremony with power provided by the Holy People.

CHAPTER EIGHT

Recognition and Reconciliation

Samuel and the Code Talkers Association

THE TWINS: RECOGNITION AND PEACE

When Monster Slayer and Born for Water had killed all of the creatures bothering mankind, they returned home. The Holy Wind no longer spoke to them about fighting and protection. The conflict was over—time for peace. Off came their battle moccasins, leggings, war shirt, headdress, and weapons, which they laid in a pile. Next the two set off to see how the world was, only to return to their mother in four days. Monster Slayer reported, "I find that this is now a peaceful world. . . . I have been everywhere, and everywhere I find it the same. I have been to the edge of the waters. I have been to the boundaries of the sky. I have been among the highest peaks. I have been deep in the lowest crags and canyons. And wherever I went I found no one who was not my friend and a friend to all people."[1]

Soon Sun Bearer visited his sons to see how they had faired against their enemies. Monster Slayer again reported that he had killed the monsters and now all who remained were friends. He showed the trophies taken from his opponents and gave them—along with the weapons and armor initially received from their father—back to Sun Bearer, who then departed. Shortly after, Changing Woman also left to take up new residence with Sun Bearer in the West on a floating island in the ocean some distance from the shore. But before leaving, she reminded her sons, "You are grown men now and you have done much for your people and for the five-fingered Earth Surface People who will soon occupy this world. You need parents no longer, so I am no longer necessary here."[2] With their parents now gone, the Twins moved to the San Juan River, where the two built a home. "To this very day the Navajo people go there to pray. But they do not pray for rain at that place, and they do not pray for good crops. . . . They pray only for victory over their enemies at that place. They go there to pray only when they recognize the need to restore order and harmony in the world, it is said."[3]

SAMUEL: FROM THE SHADOWS INTO THE LIGHT

In the late 1960s, I was looking through my old marine memorabilia packed away in a metal trunk left at my mother's hogan when I found the address of my buddy Nick Stanley. I wrote a letter to see how he was doing. We started writing back and forth when about the third time he said that the Fourth Marine Division was having a reunion in Chicago and he wanted me and Dan Akee to attend so that we could be honored as code talkers. I did not feel right about just the two of us going since we were not the only ones so I wrote back to Nick reminding him that there were others. Soon I received a letter saying that the Fourth Marine Association was going to try to get all the code talkers together, which made me feel better.

There were these missionaries named [Philip] Johnston, a man and his wife, who came to this code talkers' reunion in Chicago. They spoke Navajo and attended all kinds of ceremonies so they knew a lot about the culture. He had lived in the Shonto and Navajo Mountain area, where he learned the language and ceremonies when he was a little boy. He and his wife came to the reunion, and the code talkers were teasing him and telling him that he still looked very young but called him our cheii (grandfather). He answered them in perfect Navajo, "T'ahnidi yee' tahn áshnah" (I still bathe in cold water). He told us we were getting old because we were not doing it or rolling in the snow.

There was another meeting, this time in New York. Raymond Nakai was the chairman of the Navajo Nation at the time, and so Dan Akee and I went in our marine uniforms, showed him a letter I received, and asked him to fund our airfare to New York for recognition as Navajo code talkers. He said that he would get it approved. I then thought that there were others who needed to be there, too, but did not realize that not only would the tribe provide funds for us but it also advertised in the newspaper for all Navajo veteran code talkers. When Dan and I arrived at the Albuquerque airport, I was surprised and shocked to see so many other men, many unfamiliar, who

The first official recognition of Fourth Marine Division code talkers who served in World War II occurred in Chicago, 1968. Samuel (*second from left*), with fellow veterans, could now share his war experiences with the public. (Photograph courtesy of Marriott Library, University of Utah)

had served in this capacity. I thought there was just going to be a few of us. These others were younger, highly educated men who had entered the service later than I did. I regretted answering that letter because those younger ones treated me like I was not a part of them, ignoring and pushing me away. Their names became known, and my efforts in getting them there were forgotten. This is how the Navajo Code Talker Organization started. If I had not answered that letter there would not have been an organization.

Now I get a once-a-year visit from its president to ask for money to renew my membership. Every so often they contact me for a code talker reunion, but I usually don't have any money for gas to travel there. All I want is to be recognized for my efforts as a code talker because all of these years I felt like I was nothing, not even a marine. I felt this same nothingness when I was mistaken as a Japanese soldier several times by my fellow soldiers. They treated me like an animal and made me feel worthless, so I know how the Japanese felt when they were captured. I saw it and experienced it. That is how those younger code talkers made me feel. Now, I just leave it alone, but I wish deep in my heart that they would treat me with more respect. I do not know if I will ever overcome feeling like nothing after my discharge.

One thing that I enjoy doing now is sharing my experiences with others. My granddaughter used to look at a book about the fighting in the Pacific, stare at the pictures, and ask "Which one are you?" but I always told her I knew nothing about it. When she was older she told her teacher that her grandfather was a code talker and showed her the book, saying that he was in there somewhere. One day her teacher asked me to speak at school and tell the children about my experience as a code talker. It was very difficult to talk to them at their level of understanding. There were things they wanted to know, but it was hard to tell young children about such experiences. The teacher asked questions, and sometimes I did not hear or understand so I did not know if I ever answered them. Since I still do not hear very well, I do not like being in a crowd with all of the noise. But those children were so excited to hear about it that I tried to tell them in words they could understand. Following that I received requests from other schools and organizations, but it seemed to get harder and harder for me to understand. With some people I could hear clearly, with others not as well. Even though I was hard of hearing and became increasingly uncomfortable with this, especially when teachers asked questions that confused me, I still accepted appointments.

Helena, my daughter, became my interpreter, and I started traveling to other places. Now I have told my story in Kentucky, Washington, Idaho, and New York about three times in each state as well as in many other places. Although I have gone on speaking engagements all over the United States, the one I remember best was in Yakima, Washington. The people there were so kind and we ate a lot of salmon, which tasted so good that it really surprised me. They held a feast for us and killed a lot of deer but used every bit of it like we do sheep. Nothing was wasted.

One time my wife, who was not used to flying, and I visited Honolulu, Hawaii. We were coming back on the plane when about 150 or 200 miles from Los Angeles we felt some shaking and heard noises. An announcement over the intercom said that the landing gear would not come down. There were a lot of people on board—old and young, different nationalities, some drinking, others just looking around. It had been quite noisy, but when the announcement came everyone quieted down. I saw an old lady start praying, and later we received instructions to get all the safety things ready and the floating device from under our seat in case the plane dropped into the water. I was not worried about myself but I was for my wife because she was kind of heavy. The plane started to jerk around as the pilot tried to get the landing gear down again about a hundred miles out while people were crying aloud. Then the landing gear descended, the captain announced everything was all right, everybody quieted down, and things went back to normal. People prayed their thanks, and we landed safely. Since that time I have traveled many places in airplanes with my family, but that was the last plane trip my wife would take.

I have traveled with my daughter Helena and my grandson and granddaughter to Tokyo. The Japanese people were very respectful of our visit, and I wore my uniform. When I first saw the Japanese in their homeland it brought tears to my eyes; everything I saw touched my heart. The experience was so powerful that it almost paralyzed me. The people were very kind and polite. When I saw the little children it reminded me of my own grandchildren and more tears came. I thought of the many fathers who were killed during the war. It was not these humble people who made war but the big leaders who ran the government. I am so thankful that my grandchildren do not have to experience such tragedy. Before leaving the people presented a beautiful gold trimmed Samurai sword to me, which I still keep in a nice case by my living room window.

Another time I encountered Japanese people in New York at the site where the Twin Towers once stood. All I saw was the yellow fence with signs on it and beyond that was the railing where the reporters were. I was dressed in my uniform when I saw some Japanese in a tour group. They spotted me and one older man stepped over to where I was, shook my hand, and thanked me. As he took my hand I could not hold back my tears, which flowed like a river. It was just like being in Japan again. Those people are so polite they overpower you. There have also been Japanese visiting here in Monument Valley. I gave some a tour so they could take pictures. There were more women than men so my grandchildren teased me about them being my girlfriends. A young Japanese man was with them. I could not help but embrace him as my tears started to flow. They took pictures of me with cute little Japanese boys who looked like Navajo children. It made me love them no matter what.

Now the world is changing, just as it did at the time of the Anasazi who lived around here before the Navajos came from the north. My mother

Samuel and Lupita in 1975 during one of their many speaking engagements, this time in Hawaii. After this trip, Lupita had little desire to travel. (Photograph courtesy of Holiday family)

told me that the Anasazi were a peaceful people who started doing evil that destroyed them. They ate and drank things that caused intoxication, no longer honored sacred traditional ways, and destroyed themselves. Those who were good separated from those who were evil and moved away, burning their homes as they left before going to Hopi land. There they continued to live as they had as Anasazi, keeping to themselves and farming their lands.[4]

In the early days there were Navajos who told stories of how in the future they would experience fast travel and many marvelous things. This referred to our day. We travel quickly in the air and on the ground, and we have electricity, cell phones, and medicine to cure many ailments. Objects are being designed for everything that we do. I know we are now living at that time spoken of earlier. It is also the time when our people do not honor their traditions anymore. To me, the Navajos are now destroying themselves. I see many evil things going on—we no longer respect our sacred ceremonies but have turned them into competition events like Song and Dance. Enemy Way songs and dances are sacred and should never be used to compete against each other. The old medicine men who performed these ceremonies correctly are dying off, with only a few left. The people who sing at these events now are just drunks. Some of the dances are not even Navajo dances but are made up or come from somewhere else. Our language is changing; we do not speak it or teach our children traditional knowledge.

Things like this are slowly destroying who we are, and that is why there is no rain and the land is dry. We depend on the Sun because it is a main element of life as is Mother Earth, who was made by the Holy People and is big, moving all the time. One day it will reach a point when there will be no more time for Mother Earth or the moon, and the heavenly bodies will change because of the incorrect behavior of people. All of these things are holy and sacred; everything is in operation under the direction of deity; humans' work is very small. Thinking about all of this is very complicated, but through the Holy Wind one can understand it. God said to the wise people on the earth, if you obey me you will be able to do seemingly impossible things today. Those are God's words. Mother Earth is trying to warn us that we are doing wrong, but we are not listening. My mother said that is what happened to the Anasazi.

Life is full of change. I heard in a meeting at Window Rock that Dan Akee had a car accident that almost killed him because of serious head injuries. He now says that after the accident he no longer remembers very much about the past. Now it is up to this book to speak of what happened. Time has also taken its toll with my wife of fifty-eight years. One day she suddenly fell and could not move or talk as she suffered through a stroke. Slowly she regained her strength and ability to speak but later was diagnosed with pancreatic cancer. I was by her bedside when she told me that she was not going to recover from the cancer and that I was to take care of our children and grandchildren. She was very happy to have them and asked me to be strong for them. Soon after this she died; I miss her.

Three days ago I saw her as I bent over to pick up a towel. She was wearing a light green skirt, and I saw her shoes. She told me that she was glad that I was taking good care of our children. Then as I stood up to take a look at her, she faded. At first I thought it was Helena, but her shoes were not Helena's and I knew it was my wife. I feel that she is around sometimes and maybe even helps me. Eventually I will join her and my story will be finished.

Commentary: Hózhǫ́

Samuel now lives in his twilight years, surrounded by loving family while busy with public recognition. As with the Twins who rid themselves of the implements of war, were cleansed with an Enemy Way ceremony, and finally established themselves in a home of peace, Samuel has reached his own state of well-being. In Navajo it is called hózhǫ́, a highly complex concept whose meaning has been the topic of significant discussions.[5] This word is really a shortening of the more complete phrase of "są'a naghái bik'e hózhǫ́," which is literally translated as "Long Life Happiness." Often glossed as "harmony" or "peace," the words actually carry far stronger connotations, moving toward an ideal existence comparable, in a sense, to that of a holy being. Maintaining that state as an imperfect person in an imperfect world is next to impossible. Still, the ideal goal is to attain harmony and happiness derived either from life choices or by the restoration of good through ceremonial practices if a person has done something wrong. "The goal of Navajo life in this world is to live to maturity in the condition described as hózhǫ́, and to die of old age, the end result of which incorporates one into the universal beauty, harmony, and happiness described as są'a naghái bik'e hózhǫ́."[6] Samuel's protection and Enemy Way ceremonies were helps and corrections along life's path in assisting him to arrive at old age and hózhǫ́. Still, it is obvious that there are challenges now just as there were in the past. In life this state of being is a continuing goal as opposed to a recognized achievement.

For Samuel, there have been both external and internal forces and events important in his achieving happiness and peace. The external ones that helped bring his war-time experience to a satisfying resolution include the declassification of the code talker project in 1968 and the subsequent recognition that accompanied it. The government removed the Navajo code from its secret status twenty-six years after its inception, opening the door for the code talkers to tell their story. Having agreed to remain silent about their activity during the war, they now could share with family, friends, and the public what they had experienced. The next year for the twenty-second reunion of the Fourth Marine Division, Lee Cannon, a member of the Honors Committee, suggested that the Navajo code talkers be officially recognized. Planners received the idea enthusiastically, Cannon traveled a number of times to the reservation and Washington, D.C., to coordinate

Samuel (*second from right*) and other code talkers received further recognition in 1971 at Window Rock on the Navajo Reservation. During this celebration, the veterans formed the Navajo Code Talkers Association. (Photograph courtesy of Marriott Library, University of Utah)

the event to be held in Chicago, and the committee agreed on a design for a medallion. In June 1969 fifteen code talkers from the Fourth Marine Division, with Samuel among them, attended the event along with a code talker from each of the First, Second, Third, Fifth, and Sixth Divisions. Each man received a medallion and public recognition that had been a long time in coming. They also decided to gather again and form some type of an organization.[7]

In July 1971 sixty-nine code talkers met in Window Rock at a reunion sponsored by the Navajo Tribal Museum. The two-day activity proved formative. The Navajo Code Talkers Association grew out of this event, creating an organization with an elected president, vice president, secretary, treasurer, and a representative from each of the six marine divisions. Also at the meeting, the University of Utah, as part of the Doris Duke Oral History Project, conducted eight oral history interviews between code talkers and Frank M. Bemis representing the U.S. Marine Corps History and Museum Division. Twenty hours of transcribed interviews resulted.[8] Two years later, the association had designed its official uniform, flag, and logo, while civilian Doris A. Paul published the first substantive book on the subject, *The Navajo Code Talkers*.

Teddy Draper, Sr., provided another contribution, done very much in the traditional Navajo way. Song and prayer, so prominent an expression within the culture, found its way into a song he wrote and performed about his experience on Iwo Jima. Chanted in characteristic Navajo style, he sang,

> Iwo-Iwo, Iwo-Iwo, at a place called Iwo Jima.
> Our soldiers, it happened, were almost killed,
> Heye, yana.
> Iwo-Iwo, Iwo-Iwo, at a place called Iwo Jima.
> Our soldiers, it happened, were almost killed,
> Heye, yana.
> Suribachi, Suribachi, Suribachi, on top of it
> Up there flying, it happened, up there was the flag,
> hiyi, yana.
> Suribachi, Suribachi, Suribachi
> On the third day, our soldiers, it happened,
> Up there,
> Flying, it happened, up there, the flag,
> hiyi, yana.
> Suribachi, Suribachi, Suribachi, on top of it,
> Up there flying, it happened, up there flying,
> hiyi, yana.
> Red white and blue striped, up there flying
> heye, yana.
> Iwo-Iwo, Iwo-Iwo, at a place called Iwo Jima,
> Ours, on top, flying, it happened on top, flying,
> heye, yana.

Iwo-Iwo, Iwo-Iwo, at the place called Iwo Jima,
Ours, on top, flying, it happened on top, flying,
heye, yana.[9]

Further national recognition blossomed when President Ronald Reagan declared August 14, 1982, National Navajo Code Talkers Day. Twelve years later the Navajo Nation proclaimed August 14 "as the official day to honor and give special accolade annually to all members of the Navajo Code Talkers. The Navajo Nation Council further authorizes the president of the Navajo Nation to issue a proclamation designating August 14 as an official day to observe and call upon all tribal, federal, state and local governmental agencies and the people of the Navajo Nation to observe the day with appropriate programs, ceremonies, and activities."[10] During this time span, a number of these veterans became nationally famous for their achievements in civilian life: Peter MacDonald, who had worked in space engineering, served four terms as Navajo tribal chairman/president; Carl Gorman was employed as director of Native American Studies at University of California–Davis; Perry Allen worked as tribal prosecutor; Wilson Skeet was vice chairman of the tribe; and W. Dean Wilson served as a tribal judge.[11]

President Bill Clinton also capitalized on recognizing this group when he signed into law the Honoring the Navajo Code Talkers Act in 2000, which authorized a Congressional Gold Medal to the first Twenty-nine who devised the code and a silver medal for all other code talkers. "The Congressional Gold Medal is not a military decoration but is the highest civilian award, determined by the majority of the U.S. Congress, that Congress can bestow to honor a particular individual who or institution that performs an outstanding deed or act of service, and it requires congressional legislation."[12] The Twenty-nine received their Congressional Gold Medals on July 26, 2001, in Washington, D.C., while those awarded the silver medal, including Samuel, obtained theirs in Window Rock on November 24, 2001. Approximately 3,000 people attended the latter to watch the remaining code talkers and families of the deceased receive their awards.[13] President George W. Bush broadened the scope of recognition by including over twenty other small groups of Native Americans who used their language to transmit important tactical information during combat. He signed the Code Talkers Recognition Act of 2008 on October 15 as a way of thanking all American Indians for their contribution during World Wars I and II.

There were other, less formal ways of recognizing the code talkers. In 2000 Hasbro toys initiated a G.I. Joe Navajo Code Talker doll that spoke authentic Navajo, using the voice of a veteran code talker: Samuel Billison. Dressed in an authentically styled World War II marine uniform and equipped with a camouflaged helmet, web belt, hand phone set, backpack radio, M-1 rifle, and dog tags, the twelve-inch-high doll spoke seven different phrases followed by an English translation. Billison, who at the time was the president of the Navajo Code Talkers Association, had all proceeds from his part in the project go to the organization.[14] Two years later the movie *Windtalkers* opened for public viewing. The film starred Nicholas Cage and a handful of Native American actors, the main one being Adam Beach, a Salteaux (Ojibwe/Anishinaabe) from Canada. Roger Willie and Natalie Yahzee were beginning Navajo actors who also received parts. Based on events on Saipan, the movie was criticized for historical inaccuracies and use of stereotypes; it did not do well at the box office.

But the reaction from those code talkers who had fought in the war was different. When the film opened in Kayenta, the theater was packed. A dozen code talkers and family members of deceased code talkers attended. Their reaction to the film is instructive, because they were involved in either Saipan or similar actions. Paul Blatchford, wiping tears from his eyes while recalling Iwo Jima, said that he did not want to see the movie again while repeating, "I never got hit. Everybody around me splattered like hamburger. I never got hit. I was just lucky. Well, actually I prayed. I was a Christian. I guess that's why I didn't get hit."[15] Dan Akee liked the movie, saying that he was there and when they showed the men praying in the Navajo way with corn pollen, that was true and a real blessing to the code talkers. The movie's portrayal of white marines being assigned as bodyguards for the code talkers was also true, but like so many others, Dan did not find out about it until after the war. He closed by saying, "I'm not a hero. Something I had to do. Volunteered twice. Being a good American. Fight for our country. I'm proud of it. One thing I'll say is that every Navajo should be proud that our language has made history."[16] Bill Toledo commented on the savagery of war and how the Enemy Way ceremony cured him of the startling memories. Samuel agreed, recounted his capture twice by his own men, and concluded by reminiscing about calling in artillery fire and the destruction it caused. For everyone in attendance that night, it was a sobering recollection of what had occurred in the past. The movie provided more public exposure regarding the existence of code talkers and their experience in the war.

Closer to home, over the years, Samuel has given dozens of talks, marched in parades, and been honored by various organizations across the United States. Among the places he has spoken are New York; Chicago; Vancouver, British Columbia; Blount, Tennessee; Montgomery, Maryland; Camp Pendleton, California; Lebanon, Montana; and many cities throughout the Southwest. A few of these experiences give an idea of the popularity of today's code talkers. In 2004 the marines at Camp Pendleton invited Samuel as a guest speaker to help boost morale. Dressed in his distinctive code talker uniform, traditional moccasins, and silver jewelry, he eventually shook hands with many in attendance, later saying that the experience almost made him want to cry. While visiting sixty-two years after he had been there as a recruit, he had an opportunity to transmit a message to another Navajo marine who was almost sixty years his junior. Some of the men in attendance were being promoted that day, reminding Samuel about his promotion under very different circumstances. With this ceremony, he felt it was "much better, more respectful" than when he had just been handed his stripes and told to sew them on. Later, after eating, it was his turn to share some of his war experiences. He concluded by recalling how he felt when he saw all of the ships steaming toward an objective during the war and how it made him feel safe. "I look out at you marines here [and] I feel the same way today."[17]

The year 2005 was particularly busy for Samuel. In April he visited his granddaughter's school class to share his experiences.[18] Two weeks later he and two dozen other code talkers were saluting the American flag in Monument Valley at the visitors center, a mile from where he was born. They were assembled with several hundred other people to participate in the dedication of "Our Fathers, Our Grandfathers, Our Heroes . . . The Navajo Code Talkers of World War II" exhibit. Created by a group of students in the Circle of Light Navajo Education Project, the materials now would be permanently located here.[19] Six months later he was in Lebanon, Missouri, addressing members of the Community of Christ Church for Veteran's Day. During this presentation he told of being at Ground Zero in New York City, dressed in his code talker uniform, when a group of Japanese tourists approached him. Among others, a young boy from the group approached him. "'Thank you very much for stopping the war,' Holiday recalled. 'When this boy hugged me, I couldn't help it. I started crying. I remember that.'"[20] This was not the first nor the last time that he felt these emotions. Even during the interviews done for this book, he held the Japanese in high regard, never referring to them as "Japs" and always being respectful.

This quality should be emphasized. Samuel is a sensitive man; unlike some veterans who faced a tenacious, crafty, and at times merciless foe, he felt compassion for his enemy. Quoting from a talk cited in Montgomery, Maryland, newspaper:

> When asked if he would go back in time and be a code talker again, Holiday said, "No." He is deeply saddened by wars going on around the world as well as the United States' pending war with Iraq. . . . "Watching the Japanese suffer at the hands of the Americans was heart-wrenching," Holiday explained. "These Japanese were just young guys and they looked like Navajos," he told the audience.[21]

As the years pass, recognition of the code talkers has become more formalized. The association receives a full-time assist from the Navajo Nation Museum, which serves as a repository for information, handles requests for speakers, manages a website, and is helping with plans for a multimillion-dollar National Navajo Code Talkers Museum and Veterans Center. Each August 14 the tribe sponsors a celebration of Navajo Code Talker Day with activities such as the ones held in 2009. That day in 2009 started with a motorcycle cavalcade from Shiprock to Window Rock; followed by a parade from the Navajo Nation Museum to Veterans Memorial Park, where the colors were posted; a wreath laying at the base of the veterans monument accompanied by a twenty-one gun salute and "Taps"; then speeches by keynote speakers. Prayer opened and closed the ceremony. Twenty code talkers attended, a normal number for most occasions.[22]

Fewer and fewer Navajo code talkers are available now, as some have died and others are incapacitated so they can no longer greet the public. The Navajo Tribe tries to maintain a list of those who are still alive, but there are some code talkers who never came forward to be identified and others do not have an interest in reliving the past. When I contacted employees at the Navajo Nation Museum who work for the Code Talker Association, they were hard-pressed to give specific figures on the current number of living code talkers, how many in the past were from Utah, and how many had actually been in combat. This lack of exact figures is not their fault

In 2008 Samuel and family members traveled to Japan, where this young girl requested their picture be taken. Unlike many veterans who have faced an enemy and thus harbor hatred and emotional wounds long after the conflict is over, Samuel holds a deep respect for the Japanese people. (Photograph courtesy of Holiday family)

because to obtain this type of information requires extensive research in many repositories plus wide-ranging oral history interviews. Perhaps the estimates given by code talker Samuel Sandoval in a recent presentation are close. He believes that of the 420 Navajo men who received code talker training, somewhere between 135 and 145 of them were in actual combat. Twelve were killed in the line of duty. Not more than forty are now still alive, although the usual number given today is closer to thirty.[23]

Samuel stands among that dwindling number. When not traveling to an engagement, he spends his time at home with near and extended family. Eighty-eight years old, slightly stooped with age, and hard of hearing, he remains jovial and attentive, living as a patriarch among his loving children. While no one may achieve a perfect state of hózhǫ́ in this life, Samuel is getting close. Certainly the "long life" is there, he being remarkably nimble given the years he has lived and circumstances encountered. "Happiness" is always relative. If feeling that he has lived a good life, having served his country faithfully in time of need, having found spiritual well-being in following traditional Navajo teachings, and being a loving family man to wife and children is a part of that happiness, then Samuel qualifies. He also has not forgotten how to laugh along the way. Many times during his interviews, he would start with a chortle and progress into full laughter as he waved his arms and pointed with animation, recalling those early days in Monument Valley and how unaware he was of the outside world. Samuel was just as serious when discussing the war. Although the topic of war was anything but happy, in traditional Navajo beliefs, one is taught that without evil there can be no good, without fear there can be no joy, without sadness there can be no happiness. His life has had its fill of each. Now, as he waits to join his wife, Lupita, on the other side, he can reflect that what he has accomplished is good. If nothing else, that should bring him the "long life happiness" embodied in hózhǫ́. As for the younger generations he leaves behind, as long as they remain under the eagle, they will be safe.

Notes

INTRODUCTION

1. Mark Bahti, *A Guide to Navajo Sandpainting* (Tucson, Ariz.: Rio Nuevo Press, 2000), 22.

2. See John Holiday and Robert S. McPherson, *A Navajo Legacy: The Life and Teachings of John Holiday* (Norman: University of Oklahoma Press, 2005).

3. Christopher Chabris and Daniel Simons, *The Invisible Gorilla: And Other Ways Our Intuition Deceives Us* (New York: Crown Publishers, 2010).

4. Ibid., 49.

5. Ibid., 78.

6. Doris A. Paul, *The Navajo Code Talkers* (Bryn Mawr, Pa.: Dorrance and Company, 1973).

7. Sally McClain, *Navajo Weapon: The Navajo Code Talkers* (Tucson, Ariz.: Rio Nuevo Publishers, 2001).

8. Chester Nez, *Code Talker: The First and Only Memoir by One of the Original Navajo Code Talkers of WWII*, with Judith Schiess Avila (New York: Berkley Caliber Publishing, 2011).

9. Ibid., 23.

10. Maureen Trudelle Schwarz, *Blood and Voice: Navajo Women Ceremonial Practitioners* (Tucson: University of Arizona Press, 2003), 144.

11. Clyde Kluckhohn and Dorothea Leighton, *The Navaho* (Rev. ed.; Cambridge, Mass.: Harvard University Press, 1974), 182.

12. Rebecca Jacobs, "Heroes in Word and Deed," *Indian Country Today*, 10 August 2011, 21; and William C. Meadows, "Honoring Native American Code Talkers: The Road to the Code Talkers Recognition Act of 2008 (Public Law 110-420)," *American Indian Culture and Research Journal* 35, no. 3 (Fall 2011): 4.

13. Jacobs, "Heroes in Word," 21.

14. Meadows, "Honoring Native American Code Talkers," 10.

15. Ibid., 6, 8.

16. Jacobs, "Heroes in Word," 21.

17. L. T. C. Wethered Woodworth to Director Division of Recruiting, 26 March 1942, Navajo Code Talkers, Special Collections, Cline Library, Northern Arizona University, Flagstaff, Ariz. (hereafter cited as Navajo Code Talkers Collections, Cline Library). These figures concerning males seem somewhat skewed. No doubt the census-taking ability at this time was not what it is today, with some isolated communities not having accurate reports. Also, by this time there was an increasing number of males leaving the reservation for wartime employment in the cities, on the railroads, and in government facilities. Perhaps this figure reflects only who was on the reservation at that time.

18. Samuel Moon, *Tall Sheep: Harry Goulding, Monument Valley Trader* (Norman: University of Oklahoma Press, 1992), 167, 170.

19. Philip Johnston, "Indian Jargon Won Our Battles!" n.d., Special Collections, Cline Library, Northern Arizona University, Flagstaff, Ariz.

20. Ibid., 3.

21. Ibid., 4.

22. See McClain, *Navajo Weapon*, for additional details of the U.S. Marine Corps' scrutiny in the early stages of the project.

23. Philip Johnston, interview by John Sylvester, Doris Duke #954, pp. 46 and 56, Doris Duke Oral History Project, Special Collections, J. Willard Marriott Library, University of Utah, Salt Lake City, Utah (hereafter cited as Doris Duke Oral History Project).

24. Johnston, "Indian Jargon," 5, Special Collections, Cline Library.

25. Major Frank L. Shannon to Colonel Roscoe Arnett, 3 July 1945, Navajo Code Talkers Collections, Cline Library.

26. "Navajo Talkers Course—Methods of Instruction," n.d., Navajo Code Talkers Collections, Cline Library.

27. Ed Gilbert, *Native American Code Talkers in World War II* (New York: Osprey Publishing, 2008), 25–26.

28. Paul, *Navajo Code Talkers*, 53.

29. Gilbert, *Native American Code Talkers*, 26; and Mark Flowers, "World War II Marine Equipment—SCR 300 Field Radio," World War II Gyrene, http://www.ww2gyrene.org/equipment_SCR_300.htm (accessed 30 April 2012).

30. Mark Flowers, "World War II Marine Equipment—SCR 536 Field Radio," World War II Gyrene, http://www.ww2gyrene.org/equipment_SCR_536.htm (accessed 30 April 2012).

31. Alex Williams, interview by Frank Bemis, 9–10 July 1971, Manuscript 0504, p. 34, Navajo Code Talker Collection, Special Collections, Marriott Library, University of Utah, Salt Lake City, Utah (hereafter cited as Navajo Code Talker Collection, Marriott Library).

32. "The Use of Navajo Indians for Radio Transmission Security Purposes," 15 April 1944, Navajo Code Talkers Collections, Cline Library.

CHAPTER 1

1. Navajo mythology, based in oral tradition, is not always clear as to the difference between and roles of Changing Woman and White Shell Woman. For instance, Berard Haile and the Franciscan Fathers believe that there is only one person who has two names (Franciscan Fathers, *An Ethnologic Dictionary of the Navajo Language* [Saint Michaels, Ariz.: Saint Michaels Press, 1910, 1968], 355). In most versions of the myth of the Twins' visit to the father, there is only one mother: Changing Woman. However, Matthews's account is used throughout this book (Washington Matthews, *Navaho Legends* [Salt Lake City: University of Utah, 1897, 1994]) as the basis of this story because it is one of the earliest and more complete versions. Where I have used other material, a citation follows. The two women are distinct individuals, each giving birth to one of the boys. One of the best general discussions of these differing views is given by Gladys A. Reichard in *Navaho Religion: A Study of Symbolism* (Princeton, N.J.: Princeton University Press, 1963), 494–95. Reichard points out that in some versions the two are sisters, in others White Shell Woman and Turquoise Woman are sisters and are both daughters of Changing Woman. Whether one or two individuals, there is no doubt that soon after the birth of the Twins, White Shell Woman fades in importance and Changing Woman becomes an extremely prominent Navajo deity because of her powers and her relationship with the Twins.

2. River Junction Curly, "Blessingway—Version III," in Leland C. Wyman, *Blessingway* (Tucson: University of Arizona Press, 1975), 529.

3. Ibid., 535.

4. The Navajo people often have more than one name for a landmark, Eagle Rock and Eagle Mesa being no exception. Samuel Holiday referred to it as Tsé Łichii Dahazkani (Elevated Red Rock Sitting Up).

Marilyn Holiday, raised near this site, suggests that the mesa received its title Where the Eagles Roost because in the past it seemed to attract these birds during the nesting season (telephone conversation with the author, 12 September 2011). Stephen C. Jett, a noted scholar of Navajo geography, provides other names for Eagle Mesa that include Wide Rock and Trees Hanging from Surrounding Belt because there used to be a lot of trees around the mesa. Standing beside the main formation is a slender pinnacle that looks like an eagle, perched on a stand, giving Eagle Mesa its name. Navajo names for this rock include Eagle Alongside Mesa, Standing Slim Rock Alongside, and Big Finger Is Pointed (Stephen Jett, "Navajo Place Names," unpublished manuscript in possession of author).

John Holiday, also raised in the area, said, "Eagle Mesa is called Water Basket Sits. People say there is a male hogan on top of it. A while back, when I used to live within view, we used to see moving lights on top. I do not know which direction the lights went down the mesa, and I do not know who it was. The rock standing by itself beside Eagle Mesa is the Key, and the one behind it that looks like a sitting bird is called Turkey [Setting Hen]" (interview with author, 25 August 2000).

5. When the Holy People created the first humans, they took four materials: two physical, earth and water, and two spiritual, wind and sunshine. The wind (Níł'chi) gives a person life (the spirit), sunshine the warmth, while soil and water the physical tabernacle. When death occurs, the spirit goes back to the wind from which it came, the sunshine departs and so the body becomes cold, and the water and soil go back to Mother Earth (Harry Walters, phone conversation with author, 16 January 2012).

6. This ceremony belongs to the general Holy Way category in the Shooting Chant subgroup. It was almost extinct at the turn of the twentieth century but was used to cure a person from the ill effects of water, frost, snow, or hail, which could include such things as drowning, frostbite, lameness, or sore muscles. Leland C. Wyman, "Navajo Ceremonial System," *Handbook of North American Indians—Southwest*, vol. 10 (Washington, D. C.: Smithsonian Institution, 1983), 544.

7. The Oljato Trading Post, built in 1921 by Joseph Heffernan, should not be confused with one built earlier (in 1906) by John Wetherill a few miles south of the store Samuel is referring to.

8. Hand trembling and crystal gazing are two forms of divination used to diagnose an illness afflicting a patient. In the first, songs, prayers, and pollen are used to prepare the singer and patient. The person performing the ceremony receives signals in his or her hand as it passes over but does not touch the patient. The hand suggests possible causes of the sickness as it stops, points, or trembles to give a signal. In crystal gazing, an individual sees pictured in the crystal the event that is causing the patient the problem but must also be sensitive to spiritual impressions in order to interpret the illness. What Samuel's mother is performing here is not just a diagnosis but a healing: the hand passes lightly over the injured area and draws out the pain and sickness. This simple act, when combined with songs and prayer, is curative in nature.

9. Harry and Leone (Mike) Goulding came to Monument Valley in 1925 and for three years lived in and ran a trading post from tents they erected close to where today's post, motel, and restaurant are now located. A complete history of their experience in the Valley is found in Samuel Moon, *Tall Sheep: Harry Goulding, Monument Valley Trader* (Norman: University of Oklahoma Press, 1992).

10. For a history of the early movie-making in this area, see the chapter "Indians Playing Indians: Navajos and the Film Industry in Monument Valley, 1938–1964" in Robert S. McPherson, *Navajo Land, Navajo Culture: The Utah Experience in the Twentieth Century* (Norman: University of Oklahoma Press), 2001, 142–57.

11. Today those two roads are state highways 160 and 163.

12. The Warren Trading Post was operated by H. K. Warren, who had a third interest as a partner with David and William Babbitt, who owned the remaining two-thirds. In 1923, the Babbitt Brothers incorporated it with four other posts. Frank McNitt, *The Indian Traders* (Norman: University of Oklahoma Press, 1989), 266.

13. John and Louisa Wetherill moved south twenty miles from Oljato to Kayenta in 1910 to establish a trading post that became nationally famous for its exploration and tourist expeditions and for Louisa's work with Navajo culture. The second individual that Samuel is describing is most likely Clyde Colville, John Wetherill's partner, rather than one of his brothers, all of whom were involved to some degree in the trading business.

14. Range riders were men—most Anglo, some Navajo—who worked for the Soil Conservation Service during the 1930s when livestock reduction was in full force. Among other duties, these men had the responsibility to locate herds of livestock and determine how many animals were to be destroyed in order to align flocks and herds with the carrying capacity of the land. Many Navajos feared and hated these men for their slaughter of sheep, goats, horses, and cattle, which were all viewed as part of their wealth and prosperity. An additional duty was to locate children to be sent to boarding school, another task that many Navajos did not appreciate.

15. A brief outline of Hashké Neiniih's life during this time is in Robert S. McPherson, *The Northern Navajo Frontier, 1860–1900: Expansion through Adversity* (Logan: Utah State University Press, 2001), 9–10; J. Lee Correll, "Navajo Frontiers in Utah and Troublous Times in Monument Valley," *Utah Historical Quarterly* 39 (Spring 1971): 145–61; Charles Kelly, "Chief Hoskaninni," *Utah Historical Quarterly* 21 (July 1953): 219–26; and Charles Kelly, "Hoskaninni," *The Desert Magazine* (July 1941): 6–9.

16. Navajo teachings about hair include that one should keep it tied in a traditional bun in order to keep one's thoughts good and protected, that it is a symbol of rain brought by the Holy People, and that it is a means by which they recognize a person as being Navajo. How one takes care of his or her hair is an indicator of the type of person he or she is. It is taken out of its bun only to wash, for ceremonies, and at death.

17. For information of what life was like for the Navajo people in and around Monument Valley at this time, see Frances Gillmor and Louisa Wade Wetherill, *Traders to the Navajos* (Albuquerque: University of New Mexico Press, 1953); Holiday and McPherson, *Navajo Legacy*; and Moon, *Tall Sheep*. For a more general picture of Navajo history, see Peter Iverson, *Diné: A History of the Navajos* (Albuquerque: University of New Mexico Press, 2002).

18. Gary Witherspoon, *Navajo Marriage and Kinship* (Chicago: University of Chicago Press, 1975), 15.

19. Ibid., 20.

20. Maureen Trudelle Schwarz, *Molded in the Image of Changing Woman: Navajo Views on the Human Body and Personhood* (Tucson: University of Arizona Press, 1997).

21. See Charlotte Johnson Frisbie, *Kinaaldá: A Study of the Navaho Girl's Puberty Ceremony* (Salt Lake City: University of Utah Press, 1993); and Ruth Roessel, *Women in Navajo Society* (Rough Rock, Ariz.: Navajo Resource Center, Rough Rock Demonstration School, 1981).

22. Kluckhohn and Leighton, *Navaho*, 102.

23. Schwarz, *Molded in the Image of Changing Woman*, 156–73.

24. Fred Yazzie interview with author, 6 August 1991.

25. For a detailed discussion of these and other monsters killed by the Twins, see Paul G. Zolbrod, *Diné bahane': The Navajo Creation Story* (Albuquerque: University of New Mexico Press, 1984), 219–56.

26. The classic work that is most often cited with this view is by Clifford E. Trafzer, *The Kit Carson Campaign: The Last Great Navajo War* (Norman: University of Oklahoma Press, 1982). Others that follow this school of thought to a lesser extent include Lynn R. Bailey, *The Long Walk: A History of the Navajo Wars, 1848–1868* (Pasadena, Calif.: Westernlore Publications, 1978); and parts of Broderick H. Johnson, ed., *Navajo Stories of the Long Walk Period* (Tsaile, Ariz.: Navajo Community College Press, 1973).

27. Based primarily on the written records of the time, scholars have attacked the works just cited. For instance, R. C. Gordon-McCutchan, ed., *Kit Carson: Indian Fighter or Indian Killer?* (Niwot: University Press of Colorado, 1996), argues that Carson, as a frontiersman, was humane in his approach, trying to save lives while still waging a campaign that would cause the Navajos to surrender. The author attacks Trafzer's position on almost a page-by-page basis, showing how from his perspective, historical documents have been misused or information falsified. A more sympathetic rendering of the entire situation is also found in Gerald Thompson, *The Army and the Navajo: The Bosque Redondo Reservation Experiment, 1863–1868* (Tucson: University of Arizona Press, 1982); Tom Dunlay, *Kit Carson and the Indians* (Lincoln: University of Nebraska Press, 2000); and parts of Johnson, *Navajo Stories.* For the best collection of original contemporary documents for this period of history, see J. Lee Correll, *Through White Men's Eyes: A Contribution to Navajo History,* vols. III–VI (Window Rock, Ariz.: Navajo Heritage Center, 1979).

28. See Louisa Wade Wetherill and Harvey Leake, *Wolf Killer: Wisdom from a Nineteenth Century Navajo* (Salt Lake City, Utah: Gibbs Smith, 2007); McPherson, *Northern Navajo Frontier*; and McPherson, "'Enemies Like a Road Covered with Ice': The Utah Navajos' Experience during the Long Walk Period, 1858–1868," *American Indian Culture and Research Journal* 33, no. 2 (Spring 2009): 1–22.

29. See McPherson, "History Repeats Itself: Navajo Livestock Reduction in Southeastern Utah, 1933–1946," *American Indian Quarterly* 22, nos. 1 and 2 (Spring 1998): 1–18.

CHAPTER 2

1. "The gods, and such men as they favor, are represented in the tales as making rapid and easy journeys on rainbows, sunbeams, and streaks of lightning. Such miraculous paths are called etin digini, or holy trails. They are also represented as using sunbeams like rafts to float through the air" (Matthews, *Navaho Legends,* 230n93).

2. The following account of the origin of the Navajo language comes from James Kale McNeley, *Holy Wind in Navajo Philosophy* (Tucson: University of Arizona Press, 1981), 10–11.

3. The Tuba City Agency began in 1901 and was called the Western Navajo School and Agency, later shortened in 1923 to simply the Western Navajo Agency. The Tuba City Boarding School at first enrolled small numbers and offered primarily elementary school education. By the early 1940s the school began offering a high school education, and by 1960 it had 600 students enrolled. See Peter Iverson, *The Navajo Nation* (Albuquerque: University of New Mexico Press, 1981), 60.

4. According to Wyman, the Navajo have

> two major song ceremonial complexes, the Blessing Way (Hozhǫ́ójí) and the Enemy Way (Anaa'jí) rites. . . . Blessing Way is concerned with peace, harmony, and good things exclusively, while Enemy Way, a rite designed to exorcise the ghosts of aliens, makes much of war, violence, and ugliness. . . . The Blessing Way rites, of which there are some five kinds that differ only slightly from each other, are used for a multitude of reasons; in general they are not for curing but "for good hope," for good luck, to avert misfortune, to invoke positive blessings that man needs for a long and happy life and for protection and increase of his possessions. Thus they are used to protect livestock, aid childbirth, bless a new hogan, consecrate ceremonial paraphernalia, install a tribal officer, protect a departing or returning soldier, strengthen a neophyte singer, and consecrate a marriage. . . . Every chant, and even the Enemy Way rite, includes a Blessing Way song near the end to correct possible errors and insure the effectiveness of the performance." (Wyman, "Navajo Ceremonial System," 539–40)

5. When humans were first created by the Holy People they were made of four elements: earth, water, wind, and sunlight. When a person dies, the earth and water go back to Mother Earth, the sunlight joins other sunlight, and the wind or spirit (níłch'í) returns to the Holy Person Níłch'í, which is comparable to the Holy

Ghost in Christian theology (Harry Walters, personal communication with author, 16 January 2012).

6. Samuel makes an important point concerning Navajo beliefs when he says the stories have a spirit. A fundamental concept in Navajo thought is that teachings and words hold a tremendous power that can either help and bless or curse and destroy, depending on how they are told then used. There may be certain times of year, specific places, required conditions, and so forth when something may or may not be discussed. If respect is not shown and the condition is ignored, the Holy People will be offended and bad things will happen; conversely, a blessing may be received if done appropriately.

7. The Native American Church that Samuel is referring to as the peyote religion entered Utah around 1915 and by 1930 had become well established. This belief uses peyote buttons, taken from cactus, as a sacrament, providing visions that connect this world with that of the spirit. It has no specific dogma but incorporates many important teachings from general American Indian culture, specific Navajo principles, as well as Christian teachings. Among those teachings are beliefs in strong families, sharing, inner peace, brotherhood and sisterhood, environmental stewardship, abstinence from alcohol, and respect. See David F. Aberle, *The Peyote Religion among the Navaho* (Norman: University of Oklahoma Press, 1982).

8. There are four types of Navajo divination or diagnosing—listening, stargazing, crystal gazing, and hand trembling—all of which are related and serve similar functions. They are used to examine the unknown, find lost people or objects, identify a thief or witch, locate water or other desirable resources, prevent danger or evil, and, most frequently, determine the cause of an illness in order to remedy it. With crystal gazing, a person who holds the power can look into a clear stone and see or sense the answer being sought; it is as much an intuitive response as a visual signal.

9. The National Youth Administration (NYA) was a New Deal agency that focused on providing work and education for Americans between the ages of sixteen and twenty-four. It operated from 1935 to 1939 as part of the Works Progress Administration (WPA) but was then transferred to the Federal Security Agency. In 1942, the NYA was transferred to the War Manpower Commission (WMC) but officially ended in 1943. By 1938, it served 327,000 high school and college youths, who were paid from $6 to $40 a month for "work study" projects at their schools. Another 155,000 boys and girls from relief families were paid $10 to $25 a month for part-time work that included job training. The youths normally lived at home and worked on construction or repair projects. The NYA annual budget was approximately $58,000,000, providing numerous programs for out-of-school youths (Wikipedia, s.v. "National Youth Administration," http://en.wikipedia.org/wiki/Nationall_Youth_Admnistration, accessed 2 February, 2012).

10. Robert W. Young, "Apachean Languages," in *Handbook of North American Indians—Southwest,* vol. 10, ed. Alfonso Ortiz (Washington, D.C.: Smithsonian Institution, 1983), 393.

11. Ibid.

12. See William B. Carter, *Indian Alliances and the Spanish in the Southwest, 750–1750* (Norman: University of Oklahoma Press, 2009), 24–44.

13. Kluckhohn and Leighton, *Navaho,* 273–74.

14. Gary Witherspoon, "Language and Reality in Navajo World View," in *Handbook of North American Indians—Southwest,* vol. 10, ed. Alfonso Ortiz (Washington, D.C.: Smithsonian Institution, 1983), 571.

15. Ibid., 578.

16. For different versions of this creative process, see Pliny Earle Goddard, *Anthropological Papers of the American Museum of Natural History,* vol. 34, pt. I, *Navajo Texts* (New York: American Museum of Natural History, 1933), 127–79; Berard Haile, *The Upward Moving and Emergence Way: The Gishin Biyé Version* (Lincoln: University of Nebraska Press, 1981); Aileen O'Bryan, *Navaho Indian Myths* (New York: Dover Publications, 1956, 1993); and Zolbrod, *Diné bahane'.*

17. Gladys A. Reichard, "Human Nature as Conceived by the Navajo Indians," *Review of Religion* 7 (May 1943): 360.

18. Witherspoon, "Language and Reality," 574.

19. Ibid., 575.

20. Harry Walters, personal communication with author, 28 January 2012.

21. Reichard, "Human Nature," 354.

22. Witherspoon, "Language and Reality," 577–78.

23. See McPherson, "Indians Playing Indians: Navajos and the Film Industry in Monument Valley, 1938–1964," in *Navajo Land, Navajo Culture,* 142–57.

24. Gary Witherspoon, *Language and Art in the Navajo Universe* (Ann Arbor: University of Michigan Press, 1977), 71.

25. Gary Witherspoon, "Language in Culture and Culture in Language," *International Journal of American Linguistics* 46, no.1 (January 1980): 12.

CHAPTER 3

1. Don Mose, *The Legend of the Navajo Hero Twins* (Blanding, Utah: San Juan School District Media Center, 2009), 10–11.

2. "By life-feather or breath-feather (hyiná biltsós) is meant a feather taken from a live bird, especially one taken from a live eagle. Such feathers are supposed to preserve life and possess other magic powers. They are used in all the rites. In order to secure a supply of these feathers, the Pueblo Indians catch eaglets and rear them in captivity; but the Navahoes, like the wild tribes of the north, catch full-grown eagles in traps and pluck them while alive" (Matthews, *Navaho Legends,* 232n107).

3. "Pollen being an emblem of peace, this is equivalent to saying, 'Put your feet down in peace'" (Ibid., 232n108).

4. Ibid., 109; passage is from Mose, *Legend of Navajo Hero Twins*, 11.

5. Mose, *Legend of Navajo Hero Twins*, 11.

6. Curly, "Blessingway—Version III," in Wyman, *Blessingway,* 619.

7. Ibid.

8. Ibid., 621.

9. Story provided by Don Mose, in conversation with the author, 7 June 2011.

10. To belong to the "Twenty-nine," or first group of Navajo code talkers who devised the initial code, became a point of honor and prestige. Originally, thirty men had been selected to create a system of communication to be field-tested in training then combat. One man was injured and so never joined this first group, thus the Twenty-nine. With only a few small glitches, the system that was developed at Camp Elliot outside of San Diego was used in training exercises during June of 1942 then in combat three months later in September on Guadalcanal. For an organizational approach to the process of creating the code, see McClain, *Navajo Weapon*, 49–62; for a view from a participant, see Nez, *Code Talker*, 101–15.

11. As discussed in the introduction, Philip Johnston (1892–1978) is credited with approaching the Marine Corps shortly after the attack on Pearl Harbor (7 December 1941) with the idea of using Navajos as code talkers to transmit unbreakable messages. With the advent of World War II, he joined the marines as a staff sergeant, serving as adviser and liaison between the corps and the Navajo code talker program. In June 1943, the military accused him of leaking information about this top secret program to *Arizona Highways* magazine, creating a security breech that the Marine Corps would not tolerate. Other people could have also been responsible and so after a thorough investigation, letters of warning went to those involved. In 1944, Johnston approached the army about establishing a similar program. The marines were irate, felt this was another breach of security, and had no desire to share their "secret weapon" with another branch of service. The marines soon replaced him, ending his active involvement in the program. See McClain, *Navajo Weapon*, for further information.

12. The initial code had a number of revisions and a lot of vocabulary additions during the war. The final edition released on 15 June 1945 had 625 words representing everything from rank to types of ships and ammunition. There were also sixty-three different words for letters in the alphabet. For instance there were three interchangeable words that could be used to transmit the letter *A*, three more for the letter *B*, and so forth. When Samuel comments that there were a lot of words for him to write, there were also a lot to memorize.

13. "Unraveling is a complicated procedure, felt to be of great importance as a releasing process. The rite consists of pressing specific unraveler bundles to the patient. The pressing with bundle equipment was more forceful each night than on the preceding night" (Reichard, *Navaho Religion*, 729). These bundles have different types of sacred herbs and objects that are fastened to the patient with a slip knot on the feet, knees, chest, back, and top of head. The ceremony can take up to eight nights during which the application of soot, the ingestion of an emetic, the brushing

away of evil, and the unraveling (removal) of applied bundles is accomplished to free the patient of his problem. The overall purpose is to remove the evil afflicting a person by returning him to the condition that existed before the issue started.

"Unraveling in the Holy Shooting chants and in the Big Star Chant represents the delivery of the Twins from danger; they were able to walk on the talking prayersticks because of the life feathers given them by Spider Woman, symbolized by the feathers of the unraveling strings. In the War Ceremony unraveling songs are the same as those sung by Changing Woman when her sons returned safely with Big Monster's trophy; they are called 'the songs-with-which-the-he-customarily-returned'" (Reichard, *Navaho Religion,* 732–33).

14. Don Mose, in discussion with the author, 20 October 2011.

15. For a description of this process and the accompanying myth, see Franc J. Newcomb, "Origin Legend of the Navajo Eagle Chant," *Journal of American Folklore* 53, no. 207 (January–March, 1940): 50–77; and W. W. Hill and Dorothy W. Hill, "The Legend of the Navajo Eagle-Catching-Way," *New Mexico Anthropologist* 6–7, no. 2 (April–June, 1943): 31–36.

16. Reichard, *Navaho Religion*, 533.

17. Newcomb, "Origin Legend of the Navajo Eagle Chant," 64, 73.

18. Matthews, *Navaho Legends*, 129.

19. Witherspoon, *Language and Art*, 61.

20. Gladys A. Reichard, *Prayer: The Compulsive Word,* American Ethnological Society Monograph 7 (Seattle: University of Washington Press, 1944).

21. Kluckhohn and Leighton, *Navaho*, 223.

22. Franciscan Fathers, *Ethnologic Dictionary of Navaho Language*, 119–21.

23. Reichard, *Navaho Religion*, 272.

24. Washington Matthews, *The Night Chant: A Navaho Ceremony*, 1902, Reprinted in American Museum of Natural History Memoirs, vol. 6, Anthropology Series 5 (Salt Lake City: University of Utah Press, 1995), 42.

25. See James K. McNeley, *Holy Wind in Navajo Philosophy* (Tucson: University of Arizona Press, 1981), for a complete evaluation of the functions of níłch'i.

26. Mary C. Wheelwright, *Myth of Willa-Chee-Ji Degínnh-Keygo Hatrál* (Santa Fe, N.Mex.: Museum of Navajo Ceremonial Art, 1958), 1–2.

27. McNeley, *Holy Wind in Navajo Philosophy*, 34–35; Ada Black, interview by author, 11 October 1991; and Shone Holiday, interview by Samuel Moon, 21 July 1975, Southeastern Utah Project, Utah State Historical Society and California State University Oral History Program, Fullerton, Calif.

28. Karl Luckert, *A Navajo Bringing-Home Ceremony: The Claus Chee Sonny Version* (Flagstaff: Museum of Northern Arizona Press, 1978), 198.

29. Mary C. Wheelwright, *Myth of Natóhe Bakáji Hatrál* (Santa Fe, N.Mex.: Museum of Navajo Ceremonial Art, 1958), 15.

30. Witherspoon, *Language and Art,* 76.

CHAPTER 4

1. Mose, *Legend of Navajo Hero Twins*, 10–11.
2. Ibid., 15.
3. The two stories presented here come from Franc Johnson Newcomb, *Navaho Folk Tales* (Albuquerque: University of New Mexico Press, 1967, 1990), 57–77.
4. Ibid., 60.
5. Ibid.
6. Ibid., 64.
7. Ibid.
8. Ibid., 72.
9. Ibid., 76.
10. Ibid., 77.
11. A fundamental concept in Navajo culture is that everything in the universe is paired in a male and female dichotomy. Based on mythological teachings, mountains, rivers, moon and sun, and many other inanimate bodies are designated with gender. The human body is divided longitudinally so that those elements that are on the right side—eye, ear, nostril, lung, and so forth—is female while its counterpart on the left side is male. When Samuel says that his father prayed first to the female side and then the male side of the ocean, he is referring to a number of things. First, many ceremonies have both a female and male or gentle versus strong side in its teachings and performance, such as the male or female Mountain Top Way chant. Second, there are male and female creatures being petitioned for assistance that live in the ocean. And finally, the wind, waves, and weather also have either male or female designation. In his prayers, Samuel's father is asking both sides of the equation to bless, protect, and assist his son as he crosses over the sea and fights on its islands.
12. W. W. Hill, *Navaho Warfare*, Yale University Publications in Anthropology 5 (New Haven, Conn.: Yale University Press, 1936), 3–19.
13. Ibid., 6.
14. Jim Dandy, in discussion with author, 29 November 2011.
15. Seth Bigman, quoted in Moon, *Tall Sheep*, 173.
16. Ibid.
17. Hill, *Navaho Warfare*, 7.
18. Ibid., 8.
19. Ibid., 9.
20. Ibid., 11.
21. Berard Haile, *Legend of the Navaho Enemy Way*, Yale University Publications in Anthropology 17 (New Haven, Conn.: Yale University Press, 1938), 282.
22. Clyde Kluckhohn, *Navajo Witchcraft* (Boston: Beacon Press, 1970), 94, quoted in Ruth M. Underhill, *The Navajos* (Norman: University of Oklahoma Press, 1956), 76.
23. Hill, *Navaho Warfare*, 12.

24. Reichard, *Navaho Religion*, 269.

25. Haile, *Legend of Navaho Enemy Way,* 153–54, as quoted in Reichard, *Navaho Religion*, 269.

26. Hill, *Navaho Warfare*, 13.

27. Ibid., 14.

28. Ibid.

29. "Master Schedule Navajo Talkers Course," 1 February 1945, Navajo Code Talker Collections, Cline Library.

30. Nez, *Code Talker*, 101–103.

31. Eugene Crawford, quoted in McClain, *Navajo Weapon*, 54

32. Nez, *Code Talker*, 109.

33. McClain, *Navajo Weapon*, 251–87.

34. "Navajo Talkers Course: Methods of Instruction," n.d., Navajo Code Talker Collections, Cline Library.

35. Nez, *Code Talker*, 112.

36. Joe Kieyoomia interview, Doris Duke #664, Special Collections, Marriott Library, University of Utah, Salt Lake City, as quoted in McClain, *Navajo Weapon*, 119–20.

37. Ibid., 121.

38. Kenji Kawano, *Warriors: Navajo Code Talkers* (Flagstaff, Ariz.: Northland), 58.

39. "Extract: Action Report of the 5th Marine Division on Iwo Jima, 19 February 1945 to 26 March 1945," Navajo Code Talkers Collections, Cline Library.

40. Carl W. Proehl, *The Fourth Marine Division in World War II* (Washington, D.C.: Infantry Journal Press, 1946), 27.

41. Ibid., 33.

42. Keith M. Little, as quoted by Kawano, *Warriors*, 64.

43. Proehl, *Fourth Marine Division*, 35.

44. David Patterson, as quoted by Kawano, *Warriors*, 75.

CHAPTER 5

1. Mose, *Legend of Navajo Hero Twins*, 18.

2. Ibid., 19.

3. Samuel is referring to the Navajo code names given for each of the ships. For instance, a battleship was called a "whale," aircraft carrier a "bird carrier," submarine an "iron fish," mine sweeper a "beaver," and a cruiser a "small whale."

4. Proehl, *Fourth Marine Division in World War II*, 58.

5. Ibid.

6. Ibid., 59.

7. Ibid., 60.

8. Ibid., 63.
9. Ibid., 69.
10. Ibid.
11. Ibid., 101.
12. Ibid., 106.
13. Nez, *Code Talker.*
14. A. F. Howard to Commandant, U. S. Marine Corps, 22 June 1943, "Recruitment in Action and Investigation of Leaking Information about Navajo Code Talkers Project 1943," Navajo Code Talkers Collections, Cline Library.
15. Nez, *Code Talker*, 139–40.
16. Stephen Mack, *It Had to Be Done: The Navajo Code Talkers Remember World War II* (Marana, Ariz.: Whispering Dove Design, 2008), 38.
17. Jimmy King, Sr., interview with Frank Bemis, 9–10 July 1971, Manuscript 0504, p. 52, Navajo Code Talker Collection, Marriott Library.
18. Paul, *Navajo Code Talkers,* 66.
19. Ibid., 56–57.
20. Bill Toledo, quoted in Mack, *It Had to Be Done,* 34, 45.
21. Nez, *Code Talker*, 141, 186.
22. Ibid., 202–203.
23. Ibid., 199–200; and Mack, *It Had to Be Done*, 44–45.
24. King, interview with Frank Bemis, 56–57.
25. Nez, *Code Talker*, 209.
26. Etsitty, quoted in Mack, *It Had to Be Done*, 45.
27. Nez, *Code Talker*, 129–30.
28. W. Dean Wilson, interview with Frank Bemis, 9–10 July 1971, Manuscript 0504, p. 155, Navajo Code Talker Collection, Marriott Library.
29. Sidney Bedoni, interview with Frank Bemis, 9–10 July 1971, Manuscript 0504, pp. 11–12, Navajo Code Talker Collection, Marriott Library.
30. Nez, *Code Talker*, 144.
31. Ibid., 142, 171.
32. See Kluckhohn, *Navaho Witchcraft*.
33. Nez, *Code Talker*, 162.
34. Alex Williams, interview with Frank Bemis, 11–12, Navajo Code Talker Collection, Marriott Library.
35. Ibid., 29–30.
36. Samuel Tso, quoted in Mack, *It Had to Be Done*, 56.

CHAPTER 6

1. This narrative is from Zolbrod, *Diné bahane'*, 204.
2. Dził na'oodiłii is Huerfano Peak in New Mexico.

3. Haile, *Upward Moving and Emergence Way*, 182.

4. Mose, *Legend of Navajo Hero Twins*, 23.

5. Samuel is referring to Big Snake, a powerful creature during the time of myths who served as a guardian and supernaturally potent individual. He left his marks around Navajo land, and his representatives, today's snakes, live in the desert. There are a lot of Navajo teachings about snakes, but the underlying belief is that they should be respected and generally left alone.

6. Jim Dandy adds further information about the importance of the horned toad in Navajo traditional teachings. After sharing a detailed account of the boy and the giant, he offered that all of this creature's clothing is considered protective and that its power is like a shield. Its clothing represents arrowheads and the powers used by the Twins to destroy the monsters on the earth. A horned toad can be used to remove leg pain by singing a song that calls upon its protective clothing to shield a person from discomfort, giving another reason that this creature should not be bothered. His power can also protect a cornfield from harmful influences, ensuring a good harvest. Every field should have at least one. And when a person finds a horned toad, "It is good to pick him up and hold him to your heart and say, 'I am going to be healthy and strong in beauty just as horny toad is,' before putting him down. On both sides of a horny toad is a yellow stripe that shows his relationship to corn pollen, which is used to bless." (Robert S. McPherson, Jim Dandy, and Sarah Burak, *Navajo Tradition, Mormon Life: The Autobiography and Teachings of Jim Dandy* [Salt Lake City: University of Utah Press, 2012]), 189–92.

7. There is some confusion as to who Samuel is talking about. During his interview he said that the man he was working with was Jim Kelly. On the roster of code talkers provided by the Marine Corps and located in Window Rock, Arizona, there is no Jim Kelly. There was a Jimmy King, Sr., who was listed as killed in action (no place specified) who is on the list. King, however, was still alive in 1971 and interviewed by Frank Bemis from the Marine Corps' History and Museum Division. Obviously, somewhere the records are incomplete; most likely the man named Jimmy Kelly King, Sr., on the list is a combination of two names, with Jimmy Kelly being the one who Samuel is referring to having been killed on Iwo Jima. In Appendix 7 of McClain's *Navajo Weapon*, this same list is reproduced with a disclaimer: "The following list of Navajo code talkers was compiled through documents found in the 'Navajo Code Talker' file, Marine Corps Historical Center, Philip Johnston Collection and the Navajo Code Talkers' Association. Because the Navajo Communication School records have not been made available, the following list is considered incomplete and in some sense unverified" (288).

8. McClain, *Navajo Weapon*, 157.

9. Proehl, *Fourth Marine Division in World War II*, 147–48.

10. McClain, *Navajo Weapon*, 165.

11. Ibid., 166.

12. Alfred Newman, quoted in Mack, *It Had to Be Done*, 53.

13. Kee Etsitty, quoted in Mack, *It Had to Be Done*, 53.

14. Paul H. Blatchford, interview by Frank Bemis, 9–10 July 1971, Manuscript 0504, pp. 103–105, Navajo Code Talker Collection, Marriott Library.

15. Thomas Begay, quoted in Kawano, *Warriors*, 28.

16. Newman, quoted in Mack, *It Had to Be Done*, 53.

17. Dan Akee, quoted in Kawano, *Warriors*, 17.

18. Proehl, *Fourth Marine Division in World War II*, 152.

19. Ibid., 153.

20. John C. Chapin, quoted in ibid.

21. Samuel Billison, quoted in McClain, *Navajo Weapon*, 168–69.

22. Howard M. Connor, quoted in Paul, *Navajo Code Talkers*, 73.

23. Proehl, *Fourth Marine Division in World War II*, 154–57.

24. Ralph D. Yazzie, quoted in Kawano, *Warriors*, 99.

25. Bill Toledo, quoted in Mack, *It Had to Be Done*, 55.

26. Samuel Tso, quoted in Mack, *It Had to Be Done*, 55.

27. Teddy Draper, quoted in McClain, *Navajo Weapon*, 192–93.

28. Henry Hisey, Jr., quoted in McClain, *Navajo Weapon*, 176–77.

29. Blatchford interview, 108–109, Navajo Code Talkers Collection, Marriot Library.

30. Ibid., 110–12.

31. Ibid., 110, 112, 115.

32. Ibid., 113–14.

33. McClain, *Navajo Weapon*, 201; and Joseph H. Alexander, *Closing In: Marines in the Seizure of Iwo Jima* (Washington, D.C.: Marine Corps Historical Center, 1994), 47.

34. Alexander, *Closing In*, 47.

35. Ibid., 49.

36. Matthews, *Navaho Legends*, 120.

37. Hausman, *Gift of the Gila Monster*, 161.

38. Franciscan Fathers, *Ethnologic Dictionary of Navajo Language*, 158, 172.

CHAPTER 7

1. This version of the origin of the Enemy Way ceremony is by Berard Haile, *Origin Legend of the Navaho Enemy Way*, Yale University Press Publications in Anthropology, no. 17 (New Haven, Conn.: Yale University Press, 1938).

2. Ibid., 205.

3. Ibid.

4. Ibid.

5. Ibid, 207.

6. Ibid., 208–209.

7. In 1971, Ernest Bulow interviewed Samuel Holiday as part of the Doris Duke Indian Oral History Project (Duke #1167, Special Collections, Marriott Library). During the interview Samuel was asked if he had ever had an Enemy Way ceremony, and he replied that he had not. When asked during a clarification interview with the author why he had said that, he and family members thought that it was because he had not heard the question correctly.

8. The practice of the Enemy Way will be discussed later, but according to its origin story:

> After the first ceremony was held over the young man and his wife they recovered. The young man went out again and killed more enemies. After a time again they both sickened. Dotso [Big Fly] came and told the young man that when he went out and killed the enemy, the blood of the enemy was upon him when he returned to his wife. That accounted for her illness as well as his. Therefore the ceremony was held a second time. . . .
>
> Today a wife goes through the same ceremony with her husband. The sick man remains in the hogan. Then they throw over her shoulders the robes, buckskins, belts, long strips of velvet, calico, red flannel, ancient squaw dresses, etc. These are the gifts of the friends and family of her husband. She takes them and gives them to her relatives one by one. She keeps nothing; everything is given to her relatives. (Sandoval, quoted in O'Bryan, *Navaho Indian Myths*, 142–43)

9. The decorated, or "rattle," stick is an important part of the Enemy Way ceremony and is imbued with healing symbolism. At sunrise a man is selected to find a juniper limb, measure it for a certain length (approximately a yard), score its bark with an arrowhead (symbol of protection), and cut it with a knife, making sure that the east side of the branch is noted. He returns to the ceremonial hogan and places it in a circle of pollen. Next the medicine man, with song and prayers, marks on the north side of the stick a symbol of an extended bowstring as first prescribed by Monster Slayer. Other symbols of the Twins are added along with deer or mutton tallow, burnt herbs, red ochre, unwounded buckskin, turkey tail feathers, strands of red bayeta yarn to represent blood, and deer hoofs. Each of these materials represents and calls forth the power of physical, mental, and spiritual healing. From Berard Haile, *The Navaho War Dance* (Saint Michaels, Ariz.: Saint Michaels Press, 1946), 12–19.

Gary Witherspoon in *Navajo Kinship and Marriage* adds further detail: "The first design put on the stick is that of the extended bowstring. It symbolizes Monster Slayer and the power he had over his enemies the monsters. Its source is the Sun, the father of the Twins and all Navajo. The second design put on the stick is that of the outline of Changing Woman's hair bun at the time she gave birth to the Twins. This design symbolizes Born for Water. Its source is Changing Woman or Earth Woman, the mother of the Twins and all Navajo. One is thus a symbol of power, and the other is a symbol of life, especially its sustenance and reproduction" (61).

10. The Fire Dance is held the last night of a nine-night Mountain Way ceremony during the late fall and winter months. The event takes its name from dancers who have juniper bark torches and, amid a shower of sparks, move about a circular dance corral. The purpose of the dance is to work against the ill effects associated with bears, arthritis, and mental illness. For a complete explanation of this ceremony, see Leland C. Wyman, *The Mountainway of the Navajo* (Tucson: University of Arizona Press, 1975).

11. According to Navajo custom, a new husband is a servant to his in-laws, never sleeps in their home, and immediately responds to their requests. He is in charge of supplying them with chopped wood and water. For up to ten years he may be in this subservient position, but eventually they will start asking his advice; then he will know that he has won their respect. If he receives a grazing permit from his wife's family, he understands that he is now accepted. The new in-law must be strong while showing humility and a cooperative spirit in his new setting. Depending on the family he has joined, they may cautiously accept his ideas and incorporate him into their planning or they may keep him at a distance, fearing that he does not know their way of dealing with issues and will do things wrong. On the other hand, there is a more positive side. Jim Dandy shares an additional view of the son-in-law relationship:

> Sometimes sons-in-law are not very well accepted because they are strangers to the family and might be a little trouble. Anglos also joke about their in-laws and how they are different. To Navajos, an in-law can be helpful by keeping the wind away and may protect a family. By saying "naa daaní" their power helps push wind aside. An early winter storm is called an "in-law chaser" . . . as the little hailstones encourage the in-law to carry the water, chop wood, and get the livestock fed. A person might come into the house and say, "The in-law chaser storm chased me all over." When you talk about this, everyone laughs at the situation it describes, bringing families together. (From McPherson, Dandy, and Burak, *Navajo Tradition, Mormon Life*, 166–67).

12. There are a number of traditional principles violated here by bringing a deer home. Among these principles are that one should leave the deer's remains in the place it was killed so that it can reproduce; one should not bring home antlers, which hold power and attract lightning; one should not bring home any deer hair because it can affect domesticated livestock, making them wild; and one should cleanse oneself before and after the butchering.

13. Raymond Nakai held office two terms as Navajo tribal chairman (an office now termed "president") from 1963 to 1970. Having served in the U.S. Navy during World War II and been involved in the battles for Guadalcanal, Attu, Makin, and Tarawa, he would obviously have sympathy for Samuel and other veterans to improve their lives. Known as the first "modern" chairman, he stressed economic

development, improved education, and compatibility with white values. For a good summary of his years in office see Iverson, *Diné*, 227–45.

14. There is extensive literature on the Native American Church and its acceptance across the Navajo Reservation. Two standard works are Omer C. Stewart, *Peyote Religion: A History* (Norman: University of Oklahoma Press, 1987), and Aberle, *Peyote Religion among the Navajo*. Part of a Pan-Indian movement, the Native American Church is based primarily on Plains Indian material culture (tepee, feather fans, crescent-shaped altar, and so forth) and the ingestion of peyote (a cactus button) as a sacrament for a visual and auditory religious experience. Infused within its teachings are Navajo values and practices that emphasize the importance of family, good health practices to include forsaking alcohol, the fostering of native pride, and the pursuit of community responsibility.

15. There was a great deal of discussion with Samuel and family members as to when these three ceremonies occurred. The generally agreed upon dates were 1945–1946 (shortly after he returned from the war), 1978, and 1983. The point to consider is that this problem of enemy visitations persisted over a fairly long time—if these dates are correct, for thirty-eight years.

16. Franciscan Fathers, *Ethnologic Dictionary of Navajo Language*, 366.

17. Harry Walters, in discussion with the author, 16 January 2012.

18. Charlotte J. Frisbie and David P. McAllester, eds., *Navajo Blessingway Singer: The Autobiography of Frank Mitchell, 1881–1967* (Tucson: University of Arizona Press, 1980), 294.

19. Wyman, "Navajo Ceremonial System," 542.

20. Franciscan Fathers, *Ethnologic Dictionary of Navajo Language*, 366.

21. Harry Walters, in discussion with the author, 16 January 2012.

22. Witherspoon, *Navajo Marriage and Kinship*, 57–58.

23. Hill, *Navaho Warfare*, 17.

24. Ibid., 18.

25. For two excellent, detailed accounts see Haile, *Origin Legend of Navaho Enemy Way*, and Franciscan Fathers, *The Navajo War Dance* (Saint Michaels, Ariz.: Saint Michaels Press, 1946).

26. Franciscan Fathers, *Navajo War Dance,* 8–9. The following information about the Enemy Way comes from this source, 9–49.

27. Frisbie and McAllester, *Navajo Blessingway Singer,* 294.

28. Ibid., 295.

29. Barton and Salabye, "Anaa'jí Jish Stories," 20.

30. W. Dean Wilson, interview by Frank Bemis, 9–10 July 1971, Manuscript 0504, p. 163, Navajo Code Talker Collection, Marriott Library; John Benally, interview by Frank Bemis, 9–10 July 1971, Manuscript 0504, p. 123, Navajo Code Talker Collection, Marriott Library.

31. Sidney Bedonie, interview by Frank Bemis, 9–10 July 1971, Manuscript 0504, p. 11, Navajo Code Talker Collection, Marriott Library.

32. Paul Blatchford, quoted in McClain, *Navajo Weapon*, 227.
33. Carl Gorman, quoted in ibid.
34. Dan Akee, quoted in ibid.
35. Nez, *Code Talker*, 216.
36. Ibid., 224.
37. Ibid., 227.
38. Frisbie and McAllester, *Navajo Blessingway Singer*, 294.

CHAPTER 8

1. Zolbrod, *Diné bahane'*, 269.
2. Ibid., 276.
3. Ibid., 278.
4. Navajo teachings about the Anasazi (Ancestral Puebloans) are extensive. Briefly, they were a gifted people blessed by the Holy People. As they prospered and were able to do unbelievable things like controlling the weather, moving over terrain at superhuman speed, managing lightning, and so forth, they forgot to pay respect to the beings who gave them that power. Their behavior became abominable in the sight of the Holy People, who destroyed them in a number of ways—depending on the account. Wind, water, fire, absence of oxygen, and other means ended much of their existence.

According to some versions, today's pueblo cultures are the remnants of this once proud and haughty people. More important, what happened to the Anasazi is predicted to happen to Navajos if they continue to follow Anglo culture. Tied in with other beliefs concerning the end of the world as we know it, the teachings about the Anasazi warn the Navajo to stay true to their culture and language. See Robert S. McPherson, *Sacred Land, Sacred View* (Provo, Utah: Brigham Young University Press, 1992), 77–127.

5. See John R. Farella, *The Main Stalk: A Synthesis of Navajo Philosophy* (Tucson: University of Arizona Press, 1984); Witherspoon, *Language and Art*; Reichard, "Human Nature"; and Wyman, *Blessingway*.
6. Witherspoon, *Language and Art,* 25.
7. McClain, *Navajo Weapon,* 230–33.
8. Ibid., 234.
9. Teddy Draper, Sr., quoted in McClain, *Navajo Weapon*, 228.
10. Nathan J. Tohtsoni, "A Matter of Respect: Code Talker Concerned over Lack of Respect," *Navajo Times*, 7 September 2000.
11. Edwin McDowell, "When the Navajos Baffled the Enemy," *Wall Street Journal*, 31 December 1974.
12. Meadows, "Honoring Native American Code Talkers," 18.

13. Christine Benally, Harrison Lapahie, Jr., and Jean Whitehorse, "Comments Concerning the Silver Congressional Medal of Honors Ceremony for the Navajo Code Talkers," 5 December 2001, http://www.lapahie.com/NCT_Silver_Awards.cfm (accessed on 5 May 2011).

14. Marley Shebala, "G.I. Joe Navajo Code Talker Speaks Authentic Navajo," *Navajo Times*, 2 March 2000.

15. Marley Shebala, "Movie Emotional for Code Talkers," *Navajo Times*, 20 June 2002.

16. Ibid.

17. Jim Heuston, "Word Warrior, 80, Accepts Another Mission," *The Camp Pendleton Scout*, 12 August 2004.

18. Elaine D. Briseno, "America's Secret Weapon," *Rio Rancho (N.Mex.) Journal*, 22 April 2005.

19. Darrel Beehner, "A Salute to Heroes," *Gallup (N.Mex.) Independent*, 9 May 2005.

20. Julie Turner, "The Unbreakable Code," *The Lebanon (Ky.) Daily Record*, 11–12 November 2003.

21. "Navajo Code Aided U.S. Victory during World War II," *Montgomery (Md.) Gazette Regional News*, 27 November 2002.

22. Karen Francis, "Code Talkers Day 2009: Heroes," *Gallup (N.Mex.) Independent*, 15–16 August 2009.

23. Samuel Sandoval, presentation on 13 April 2012, Eighteenth Annual Language Heritage Conference, Monument Valley, Utah; and Nathan J. Tohtsoni, "A Matter of Respect: Code Talker Concerned over Lack of Respect," *Navajo Times*, 7 September 2000.

BIBLIOGRAPHY

BOOKS AND ARTICLES

Aberle, David F. *The Peyote Religion among the Navaho*. Norman: University of Oklahoma Press, 1982.

Alexander, Joseph H. *Closing In: Marines in the Seizure of Iwo Jima*. Washington, D.C.: Marine Corps Historical Center, 1994.

Bahti, Mark. *A Guide to Navajo Sandpainting*. Tucson, Ariz.: Rio Nuevo Press, 2000.

Bailey, Lynn R. *The Long Walk: A History of the Navajo Wars, 1848–1868*. Pasadena, Calif.: Westernlore Publications, 1978.

Benally, Christine, Harrison Lapahie, Jr., and Jean Whitehorse. "Comments Concerning the Silver Congressional Medal of Honors Ceremony for the Navajo Code Talkers." December 5, 2001. http://www.lapahie.com/NCT_Silver_Awards.cfm (accessed May 5, 2011).

Carter, William B. *Indian Alliances and the Spanish in the Southwest, 750–1750*. Norman: University of Oklahoma Press, 2009.

Chabris, Christopher, and Daniel Simons. *The Invisible Gorilla: And Other Ways Our Intuition Deceives Us*. New York: Crown, 2010.

Correll, J. Lee. "Navajo Frontiers in Utah and Troublous Times in Monument Valley." *Utah Historical Quarterly* 39 (Spring 1971): 145–61.

———. *Through White Men's Eyes: A Contribution to Navajo History*. Vols. III–VI. Window Rock, Ariz.: Navajo Heritage Center, 1979.

Curly, River Junction. "Blessingway—Version III." In Wyman, *Blessingway*, 495–634.

Dunlay, Tom. *Kit Carson and the Indians*. Lincoln: University of Nebraska Press, 2000.

Farella, John R. *The Main Stalk: A Synthesis of Navajo Philosophy*. Tucson: University of Arizona Press, 1984.

Flowers, Mark. "World War II Marine Equipment—SCR 300 Field Radio." World War II Gyrene. http://www.ww2gyrene.org/equipment_SCR_300.htm (accessed on April 30, 2012).

———. "World War II Marine Equipment—SCR 536 Field Radio." World War II Gyrene. http://www.ww2gyrene.org/equipment_SCR_536.htm (accessed on April 30, 2012).

Franciscan Fathers. *An Ethnologic Dictionary of the Navajo Language*. Saint Michaels, Ariz.: Saint Michaels Press, 1910, 1968. Page references are to the 1968 edition.

———. *The Navajo War Dance*. Saint Michaels, Ariz.: Saint Michaels Press, 1946.

Frisbie, Charlotte Johnson. *Kinaaldá: A Study of the Navaho Girl's Puberty Ceremony*. Salt Lake City: University of Utah Press, 1993.

Frisbie, Charlotte Johnson, and David P. McAllester, eds. *Navajo Blessingway Singer: The Autobiography of Frank Mitchell, 1881–1967*. Tucson: University of Arizona Press, 1980.

Gilbert, Ed. *Native American Code Talkers in World War II*. New York: Osprey, 2008.

Gillmor, Frances, and Louisa Wade Wetherill. *Traders to the Navajos*. Albuquerque: University of New Mexico Press, 1953.

Goddard, Pliny Earle. *Anthropological Papers of the American Museum of Natural History.* Vol. 34, pt. I, *Navajo Texts*. New York: American Museum of Natural History, 1933.

Gordon-McCutchan, R. C., ed. *Kit Carson: Indian Fighter or Indian Killer?* Niwot: University Press of Colorado, 1996.

Haile, Berard. *Legend of the Navaho Enemy Way*. Yale University Publications in Anthropology 17. New Haven, Conn.: Yale University Press, 1938.

———. *The Navaho War Dance*. Saint Michaels, Ariz.: Saint Michaels Press, 1946.

———. *Origin Legend of the Navaho Enemy Way*. Yale University Press Publications in Anthropology 17. New Haven, Conn.: Yale University Press, 1938.

———. *The Upward Moving and Emergence Way: The Gishin Biyé Version*. Lincoln: University of Nebraska Press, 1981.

Hausman, Gerald. *The Gift of the Gila Monster: Navajo Ceremonial Tales*. New York: Simon and Schuster, 1993.

Hill, W. W. *Navaho Warfare*. Yale University Publications in Anthropology 5. New Haven: Yale University Press, 1936.

Hill, W. W., and Dorothy W. Hill. "The Legend of the Navajo Eagle-Catching-Way." *New Mexico Anthropologist* 6–7, no. 2 (April–June, 1943): 31–36.

Holiday, John, and Robert S. McPherson. *A Navajo Legacy: The Life and Teachings of John Holiday*. Norman: University of Oklahoma Press, 2005.

Iverson, Peter. *Diné: A History of the Navajos*. Albuquerque: University of New Mexico Press, 2002.

———. *The Navajo Nation*. Albuquerque: University of New Mexico Press, 1981.

Jacobs, Rebecca. "Heroes in Word and Deed." *Indian Country Today*, August 10, 2011, 20–25.

Johnson, Broderick H., ed. *Navajo Stories of the Long Walk Period*. Tsaile, Ariz.: Navajo Community College, 1973.

Kawano, Kenji. *Warriors: Navajo Code Talkers*. Flagstaff, Ariz.: Northland, 1990.

Kelly, Charles. "Chief Hoskaninni." *Utah Historical Quarterly* 21 (July 1953): 219–26.

———. "Hoskaninni." *The Desert Magazine*, July 1941, 6–9.

Kluckhohn, Clyde. *Navajo Witchcraft*. Boston: Beacon Press, 1970.

Kluckhohn, Clyde, and Dorothea Leighton. *The Navaho*, rev. ed. Cambridge, Mass.: Harvard University Press, 1974.

Luckert, Karl. *A Navajo Bringing-Home Ceremony: The Claus Chee Sonny Version*. Flagstaff: Museum of Northern Arizona Press, 1978.

Mack, Stephen. *It Had to Be Done: The Navajo Code Talkers Remember World War II*. Marana, Ariz.: Whispering Dove Design, 2008.

Matthews, Washington. *Navaho Legends*. 1897. Reprint, Salt Lake City: University of Utah Press, 1994. Page references are to the 1994 edition.

———. *The Night Chant: A Navaho Ceremony*. 1902. Reprinted in *American Museum of Natural History Memoirs*. Vol. 6. Anthropology Series 5. Salt Lake City: University of Utah Press, 1995.

McClain, Sally. *Navajo Weapon: The Navajo Code Talkers*. Tucson, Ariz.: Rio Nuevo, 2001.

McNeley, James K. *Holy Wind in Navajo Philosophy*. Tucson: University of Arizona Press, 1981.

McNitt, Frank. *The Indian Traders*. Norman: University of Oklahoma Press, 1989.

McPherson, Robert S. "'Enemies Like a Road Covered with Ice': The Utah Navajos' Experience during the Long Walk Period, 1858–1868." *American Indian Culture and Research Journal* 33, no. 2 (Spring 2009): 1–22.

———. "History Repeats Itself: Navajo Livestock Reduction in Southeastern Utah, 1933–1946." *American Indian Quarterly* 22, nos. 1 and 2 (Spring 1998): 1–18.

———. *Navajo Land, Navajo Culture: The Utah Experience in the Twentieth Century*. Norman: University of Oklahoma Press, 2001.

———. *The Northern Navajo Frontier, 1860–1900: Expansion through Adversity*. Logan: Utah State University Press, 2001.

———. *Sacred Land, Sacred View*. Provo, Utah: Brigham Young University Press, 1992.

McPherson, Robert S., Jim Dandy, and Sarah Burak. *Navajo Tradition, Mormon Life: The Autobiography and Teachings of Jim Dandy*. Salt Lake City: University of Utah Press, 2012.

Meadows, William C. "Honoring Native American Code Talkers: The Road to the Code Talkers Recognition Act of 2008 (Public Law 110-420)." *American Indian Culture and Research Journal* 35, no.3 (Fall 2011): 3–36.

Moon, Samuel. *Tall Sheep: Harry Goulding, Monument Valley Trader*. Norman: University of Oklahoma Press, 1992.

Mose, Don. *The Legend of the Navajo Hero Twins.* Blanding, Utah: San Juan School District Media Center, 2009.

Newcomb, Franc Johnson. *Navaho Folk Tales*. Albuquerque: University of New Mexico Press, 1967, 1990. Page references are to the 1990 edition.

———. "Origin Legend of the Navajo Eagle Chant." *Journal of American Folklore* 53, no. 207 (January–March 1940): 50–77.

Nez, Chester. *Code Talker: The First and Only Memoir by One of the Original Navajo Code Talkers of WW II.* With Judith Schiess Avila. New York: Berkley Caliber Publishing, 2011.

O'Bryan, Aileen. *Navaho Indian Myths*. New York: Dover Publications, 1956, 1993.

Paul, Doris A. *The Navajo Code Talkers*. Bryn Mawr, Pa.: Dorrance, 1973.

Proehl, Carl W. *The Fourth Marine Division in World War II*. Washington, D.C.: Infantry Journal Press, 1946.

Reichard, Gladys A. "Human Nature as Conceived by the Navajo Indians." *Review of Religion* 7 (May 1943): 353–60.

———. *Navaho Religion: A Study of Symbolism*. Princeton, N.J.: Princeton University Press, 1963.

———. *Prayer: The Compulsive Word.* American Ethnological Society Monograph 7. Seattle: University of Washington Press, 1944.

Roessel, Ruth. *Women in Navajo Society*. Rough Rock, Ariz.: Navajo Resource Center, Rough Rock Demonstration School, 1981.

Schwarz, Maureen Trudelle. *Blood and Voice: Navajo Women Ceremonial Practitioners*. Tucson: University of Arizona Press, 2003.

———. *Molded in the Image of Changing Woman: Navajo Views on the Human Body and Personhood.* Tucson: University of Arizona Press, 1997.

Stewart, Omer C. *Peyote Religion: A History*. Norman: University of Oklahoma Press, 1987.

Thompson, Gerald. *The Army and the Navajo: The Bosque Redondo Reservation Experiment, 1863–1868*. Tucson: University of Arizona Press, 1982.

Trafzer, Clifford E. *The Kit Carson Campaign: The Last Great Navajo War*. Norman: University of Oklahoma Press, 1982.

Underhill, Ruth M. *The Navajos*. Norman: University of Oklahoma Press, 1956.

Wetherill, Louisa Wade, and Harvey Leake. *Wolf Killer: Wisdom from a Nineteenth Century Navajo*. Salt Lake City, Utah: Gibbs Smith, 2007.

Wheelwright, Mary C. *Myth of Natóhe Bakáji Hatrál*. Santa Fe, N.Mex.: Museum of Navajo Ceremonial Art, 1958.

———. *Myth of Willa-Chee-Ji Degínnh-Keygo Hatrál.* Santa Fe, N. Mex.: Museum of Navajo Ceremonial Art, 1958.

Witherspoon, Gary. *Language and Art in the Navajo Universe*. Ann Arbor: University of Michigan Press, 1977.

———. "Language and Reality in Navajo World View." In *Handbook of North American Indians—Southwest,* vol.10, edited by Alfonso Ortiz, 570–78. Washington, D.C.: Smithsonian Institution, 1983.

———. "Language in Culture and Culture in Language." *International Journal of American Linguistics* 46, no.1 (January 1980): 1–13.

———. *Navajo Marriage and Kinship*. Chicago: University of Chicago Press, 1975.

Wyman, Leland C. *Blessingway*. Tucson: University of Arizona Press, 1970.

———. *The Mountainway of the Navajo.* Tucson: University of Arizona Press, 1975.

———. "Navajo Ceremonial System." In *Handbook of North American Indians—Southwest,* vol. 10, edited by Alfonso Ortiz, 536–57. Washington, D.C.: Smithsonian Institution, 1983.

Young, Robert W. "Apachean Languages." In *Handbook of North American Indians—Southwest,* vol. 10, edited by Alfonso Ortiz, 393–400. Washington, D.C.: Smithsonian Institution, 1983.

Zolbrod, Paul G. *Diné bahane': The Navajo Creation Story*. Albuquerque: University of New Mexico Press, 1984.

INTERVIEWS

Bedoni, Sidney. Interview by Frank Bemis, July 9–10, 1971, Manuscript 0504. Navajo Code Talker Collection, Special Collections, Marriott Library, University of Utah, Salt Lake City.

Benally, John. Interview by Frank Bemis, July 9–10, 1971, Manuscript 0504. Navajo Code Talker Collection, Special Collections, Marriott Library, University of Utah, Salt Lake City.

Black, Ada. Interview by author, October 11, 1991, Monument Valley, Ariz.

Blatchford, Paul H. Interview by Frank Bemis, July 9–10, 1971, Manuscript 0504. Navajo Code Talker Collection, Special Collections, Marriott Library, University of Utah, Salt Lake City.

Dandy, Jim. Conversation with author, November 29, 2011, Blanding, Utah.

Holiday, John. Interview by author, August 25, 2000, Monument Valley, Utah.

Holiday, Marilyn. Conversation by author, September 12, 2010, Blanding, Utah.

Holiday, Samuel Tom. Interview by author and Priscilla Holiday, May 9 and 11, 2011, Kayenta, Ariz.

———. Interview by author and Lucille Hunt, September 2, 2011, Kayenta, Ariz.

———. Interview by Ernest Bulow, Doris Duke #1167. Doris Duke Oral History Project, Special Collections, Marriott Library, University of Utah, Salt Lake City.

Holiday, Shone. Interview by Samuel Moon, July 21, 1975. Southeastern Utah Project, Utah State Historical Society and California State University Oral History Program, Fullerton, Calif.

Johnston, Philip. Interview by John Sylvester, Doris Duke #954. Doris Duke Oral History Project, Special Collections, Marriott Library, University of Utah, Salt Lake City.

King, Jimmy, Sr. Interview by Frank Bemis, July 9–10, 1971, Manuscript 0504. Navajo Code Talker Collection, Special Collections, Marriott Library, University of Utah, Salt Lake City.

Mose, Don. Conversation with author, June 7 and October 20, 2011, Blanding, Utah.

Walters, Harry. Phone conversation and personal communication with author, January 16, 26, and 28, 2012.

Williams, Alex. Interview by Frank Bemis, July 9–10, 1971, Manuscript 0504. Navajo Code Talker Collection, Special Collections, Marriott Library, University of Utah, Salt Lake City, Utah.

Wilson, W. Dean. Interview by Frank Bemis, July 9–10, 1971, Manuscript 0504. Navajo Code Talker Collection, Special Collections, Marriott Library, University of Utah, Salt Lake City, Utah.

Yazzie, Fred. Interview by author, August 6, 1991. Monument Valley, Utah.

MANUSCRIPTS AND ARCHIVES

Doris Duke Oral History Project. Special Collections. J. Willard Marriott Library, University of Utah, Salt Lake City.

Holiday, Herman H. "Samuel Tom Holiday: Navajo Code Talker." January 1993. In the author's possession and Holiday family's possession.

Jett, Stephen C. "Navajo Place Names." Unpublished manuscript in author's possession, used with permission.

Johnston, Philip. "Indian Jargon Won our Battles!" n.d., Special Collections, Cline Library, Northern Arizona University, Flagstaff, Ariz.

Navajo Code Talker Collection. Special Collections. Marriott Library, University of Utah, Salt Lake City.

Navajo Code Talkers Collection. Special Collections, Cline Library, Northern Arizona University, Flagstaff, Ariz.

Index

References to illustrations are in *italics*